Praise for Maude Barlow

D1110301

"Canada's best-known voice of dissent." — CBC

"It's time we listened to the Maude Barlows of the world on this." — CNN

"Her work will inspire equal parts outrage and encouragement in anyone who is concerned about this most vital natural resource." — *Publishers Weekly* on *Blue Future*

"Probably the most eloquent call to arms we're likely to hear about the politics of water." — *The Globe and Mail* on *Blue Gold*

"Those concerned about the environment and about the costs of economic globalization will find much to get riled up about in this book." — *Publishers Weekly* on *Blue Gold*

"This well-researched book provides a sobering, in-depth look at the growing scarcity of fresh water and the increasing privatization and corporate control of this nonrenewable resource." — *Library Journal* on *Blue Gold*

"Every Canadian should read it. . . . [A] wake-up call . . . informative and timely." — *The Globe and Mail* on *Too Close for Comfort*

"This smart book provides passionate arguments as to why this social program needs to be saved, without sounding preachy or sanctimonious." — *The Globe and Mail* on *Profit Is Not the Cure*

"Maude Barlow first establishes water as a human right, and then takes us through the titanic struggle, country by country, to make that right come alive. It's jolting, compelling, astonishingly comprehensive and beautifully organized. No one but Maude could have written this tour de force." — Stephen Lewis, author of *Race Against Time*, on *Blue Future*

For Molly
In friendship
Maude Barlow

BOILING POINT

MAUDE BARLOW

BOIL

P

ING

OINT

GOVERNMENT NEGLECT, CORPORATE ABUSE AND CANADA'S WATER CRISIS

EG
W

To our grandchildren,
Madelaine, Eleanor, Angus and Max,
with love.

"We are going to forget all about the economy when we run out of water."

— David Schindler, Canadian water scientist

~

"Water is speaking to us but are we listening?
We are all treaty people — a piece of us is dying.
Complacency and ignorance are no longer acceptable.
We have to be the voice for generations to come.
Our grandchildren will look back and ask, Why did
they not act to save our precious water? I want to
be able to look in the mirror and know that I
did my best."

— Randall Kahgee, former chief, Saugeen First Nation

Contents

Introduction

For over three decades, I have travelled the world, learning about water, learning that abundance is not a given, and that the future of the human race and the species with whom we share this planet is literally dependent upon it. I have stood in solidarity with those fighting for water justice in their communities or trying to save endangered lakes and rivers from contamination, overextraction and corporate malfeasance, and I am always amazed at how far away these struggles appear to be to most Canadians when I return home.

For make no mistake, the world is running out of accessible water. On World Water Day 2015, the UN reported that demand for water will increase by 55% over the next 15 years. By that time global water resources will meet only 60% of the world's demand. A 2016 report from leading scientists warned that two-thirds of the global population currently lives with severe water scarcity for at least one month of every year and almost 2 billion suffer severe water scarcity for at least half of every year. The water crisis could affect as many as 7 billion people by 2075. UN secretary-general Ban Ki-moon gathered 500 scientists together who concluded that our global abuse of water has caused the planet to enter a "new geologic age" akin to the retreat of the glaciers over 11,000 years ago.

It is no surprise that some parts of the world, such as Australia, many countries in Africa and all of the Middle East, are in water crisis as they had few water resources to begin with. But the crisis has suddenly moved well beyond the expected. Canadians would be wise to look at other traditionally water-rich countries for insight into what could happen to us if we do not plan, if we do not hold our governments accountable to build a coherent water strategy for the future. Brazil, listed by the UN as being the most water-rich country in the world, is experiencing such devastating drought in its southern region that 20 million people are at risk, and the city of São Paulo almost ran its reservoir dry last year. Muddy sludge clogged municipal pipes as residents turned on their taps. In China, over half the rivers have disappeared in just 25 years. The United States, listed as the eighth water-richest country in the world, has been experiencing a multi-year drought rivalling the Dust Bowl of the 1930s throughout large swaths of its south and west. In 2015, California had to impose strict water rationing in many communities, and neighbour turned against neighbour as people battled over compliance. While it is true that El Niño–driven rains have provided some relief to the most drought-stricken parts of the U.S., scientists believe that it is short-lived and that droughts in the arid parts of the U.S. will become both more frequent and longer lasting.

A perfect storm of declining water supplies, rising poverty levels and climbing water rates has brought what we have always thought of as third-world issues to our own doorstep.

Despite our shared mythology of limitless water, Canada is not immune to this, the world's most pressing problem. We face serious issues of water contamination, eutrophication, overextraction, glacial melt and climate change. Extractive energy and mining projects endanger our waterways. Corporations are eyeing Canada's water, setting up bottled water operations and bidding to run water services on a for-profit basis. There are even renewed calls to allow bulk commercial water exports to drought-stricken states.

Water protection regulations across the country are uneven and generally inadequate, and federal rules are almost non-existent. They are a patchwork of outdated, vague and even conflicting regulations with no coherent overarching principles or rational planning. Many of our laws were originally enacted well over a century ago for a country that was still largely rural and agrarian and whose population mostly extracted water for their own use. As our economy grew and industrialized, our governments updated laws, enacted new ones and set regulations piecemeal as situations and need arose. There was little understanding, among either the general population or elected officials, of the consequences of pollution, overuse or overextraction. Our forebears genuinely believed that clean water would always be available and that there was more than enough for every purpose.

We have only recently begun to realize how mistaken that belief was.

This book is a cry from the heart. It is time to abandon our erroneous beliefs that Canada has unlimited supplies of

water, that Canadians have taken care of this water heritage or that we still have lots of time to do so. We need a
strong, national plan of action based on a new water ethic
that puts water protection and water justice at the heart of
all our policies and laws. The path forward is clear, if not
simple.

one

A History of Neglect and Abuse

The 306-kilometre-long system of manmade locks, canals and channels of the St. Lawrence Seaway is recognized as one of the most challenging engineering feats in history and boasts the world's most spectacular lift system. The 15 locks along the journey lift ocean-going ships twice as long and half as wide as a football field, the height of a 60-storey building, allowing them to move across a vast expanse of water from the Atlantic Ocean to Lake Superior.

Opened in 1959 to allow international shipping and trading in the Great Lakes, the seaway created one of the most prosperous economic regions on Earth. For the first time, deep draft ocean-going vessels were able to come right into the heartland of North America, and this created huge new opportunities for industrial growth. Major manufacturing operations in steel, paper, chemicals and automobiles set up shop or expanded, all attracted by plentiful water and ships to carry their goods to market. Large-scale farms grew up around the Lakes, now more easily able to use the seaway to export their commodities to foreign markets.

The seaway was considered an industrial miracle in its time. But like the massive dams built in the U.S. during the "New Deal" era between the 1920s and the 1940s to create employment and wealth, there are now concerns about the environmental impacts of this project. It changed water-courses and hardened shorelines. It required much dredging and blasting as well as the building of the Moses-Saunders Power Dam at Cornwall and Massena. With prosperity came unforeseen consequences — more effluent dumping from industrial agriculture; more blue-green algae; more sewage from growing urban centres; more pollution from factories; more destruction of wetlands, forests and healthy shorelines; large-scale bird die-offs and invasive species that would come to plague the Great Lakes Basin.

It is largely forgotten now that for the seaway to be built, a number of villages and inhabited shorelines along the route were submerged and their people displaced, particularly on the Canadian side. Most of the lands and villages destroyed belonged to the Mohawk First Nation of Akwesasne, which also witnessed the destruction of its fishing grounds, wet-lands, arable farming land and access to the river.

Like many industrialized countries, Canada has used its water resources to promote economic development with-out questioning the impact on the natural world. In the post-war era, progress was seen as an unmitigated good, and millions were lifted out of poverty. Water, land, for-ests and minerals were so abundant it was hard to imagine any serious threat to them. Canada built its economic and development policies on the myth of abundance, assuming that nature would always provide. It is only in hindsight that we can begin to see the impact of industrial development on our water heritage.

As a consequence, generations have dumped whatever waste we wanted into water, overextracted it for chemical-laden commercial food production and diverted it from where it was needed to sustain a healthy ecosystem to where it was convenient for industry and urban populations. We dredged wetlands and canals, built mighty dams, hardened shorelines, moderated watershed levels and modified waterways, once in the name of survival, later in the name of economic prosperity.

Our understanding of the implications of such wholesale intervention in freshwater sources is slowly catching up to the damage we have caused, both planned and inadvertent, but the time for complacency is over. While it is true that compared to many parts of the world Canada is blessed with plentiful clean water, there are serious limits and threats to it, and too little is known for us to be complacent. Centuries of abuse and neglect are catching up.

The First Threat: Water Loss

Lakes and Rivers ~
We have all grown up with the statistic that claims that 20% of the world's water is found in Canada. This estimate is correct only if we calculate all the water in our rivers and lakes, but not all of that water is usable or accessible. Canada's total annual *renewable* freshwater supply — the rain and snow that replenish water stocks and that we can sustainably harvest — is about 3,472 cubic kilometres, roughly the equivalent to the volume of Lake Huron. This represents about 6.5% of the world's renewable water.

But 60% of that flows northward in mighty rivers, leaving about 2.6% of the world's total to the 90% of Canadians who live along the Canada-U.S. border.

With the growth in population and industry, demands on this surface water are relentless, and water supplies within Canada are in serious decline. Statistics Canada reported that, between 1971 and 2004, water yield — the net income of water received in precipitation over water lost by various methods — fell each year by 3.5 cubic kilometres in southern Canada, almost as much water as is supplied annually to the residential population of the country. This represents a loss of 8.5% in just over three decades.[1] In May 2016, Statistics Canada released a preliminary update to this study, covering up to 2013. While the detailed analysis will not be available until the spring of 2017, the basic linear trend line makes it clear that the decline in water yield in southern Canada continues.

Climate change will speed up this process. Lakes around the world are warming up far more quickly than anticipated, say researchers from a number of collaborating international post-secondary institutions, including Toronto's York University. In their December 2015 report, "Rapid and Highly Variable Warming of Lake Surface Waters around the Globe," the experts found that lakes are warming at a rate faster than either the oceans or the air.

But they were surprised to find that lakes in Canada are warming faster than most, twice as fast as air temperatures and twice as fast as the majority of other lakes in the study. Lake Superior has one of the fastest rates of warming in the world because its ice is now either incomplete in most years or melting earlier in the spring. The National Oceanic and Atmospheric Administration (NOAA) reports that ice coverage on the Great Lakes declined by 71% between 1973 and 2010. Warmer lakes evaporate more quickly and in greater volume.[2]

The Great Lakes are particularly vulnerable both to climate change and the growing demand from industry and populations. The bulk of the Great Lakes water is actually ancient fossil water, in place since the Great Melt after the last ice age. Less than 1% is renewed annually by precipitation. And if lake levels fall below 80% of their historic volume, that water will never return.

In a 2014 study for the Council of the Great Lakes Region, the University of Toronto's Mowat Centre chronicled the decline in water levels of the Great Lakes between 1997 and 2013. In those years, water levels in Lakes Superior, Michigan and Huron were substantially below historic averages, reaching in 2013 the lowest levels since the measuring and tracking of water levels began in 1918. Water levels in the St. Lawrence River were below historic averages for 78% of those years.[3]

While levels have risen with the heavy winter precipitation of 2014–2015, many scientists believe that these years are anomalies on the long-term trend lines and that water levels in the Great Lakes will again drop. The Great Lakes Integrated Science + Assessment Center confirms that most climate models project that evaporation from the Great Lakes will outpace precipitation. The Union of Concerned Scientists further warns that Great Lakes water levels could drop by another two feet (0.61 metres) within decades.[4]

It is not just the Great Lakes. Canada's major rivers are also at risk. World Wildlife Fund Canada cites dams and diversions, overextraction for city use and food production, and climate change in its risk assessment of Canadian rivers. As an example, *Canadian Geographic* has called the South Saskatchewan the most threatened river in Canada and reports that it has lost 12% of its flow in the last century due to overextraction. Many of the country's large free-flowing rivers such as the Skeena, the Athabasca and the Mackenzie will soon follow if we do not take immediate action, says WWF.[5]

The Peace-Athabasca Delta in northern Alberta is one of North America's most vibrant ecosystems, home to as many as a million birds and the world's largest free-roaming bison herd. In 2013, environmental journalist Ed Struzik reported that the delta is "drying out" from alpine and boreal forest warming and from diversion for tar sands mining, an industry that currently withdraws about 170 million cubic metres of freshwater annually from the Athabasca River to drive operations. There are also plans to build more hydroelectric dams on the Peace River.

The controversial Site C dam would flood as much as 100 square kilometres of boreal forest and restrict river flows downstream and has been the target of passionate protests.[6] Site C would submerge 78 First Nations heritage sites, including burial grounds and places of cultural and spiritual significance. Treaty 8 member Helen Knott said she is not a typical protester, but a visible reminder of her people's right to the land: "I am the great-great-granddaughter of Chief Bigfoot, who was the last to sign Treaty 8 in 1911. I am of his blood, of the original intent of his signing for what were a proud and fierce people, the tribe they were waiting to die off so they wouldn't have to sign. We are still here. This land is sacred."[7]

Glaciers ~
Glaciers in Canada hold as much water as all that is contained in the country's lakes and rivers and are a major source of replenishment for many watersheds. There are

17,000 glaciers in British Columbia and research by the University of Northern British Columbia shows they are all melting.

There is perhaps no more breathtaking iconic Canadian scene than the Bow glacier that lies just beyond Lake Louise in Banff National Park. When I first visited, I was, like everyone, both in awe of its majesty and disturbed by the markers that showed its decline from a once-mighty ice field to the receding ice pack it is today. Running along the Bow River in Calgary days later, I was again startled by the exquisite turquoise-emerald colour of the water caused by "rock flour" carried from the glacier into Lake Louise and on into the Bow. What will happen to the Bow and so many other rivers at least partially dependent on these remnants of another age, I wondered.

Glacial coverage on the Alberta side of the Canadian Rockies has declined by as much as 25%, and at least 300 glaciers have already been lost in the last three decades. John Pomeroy is the director of the Centre for Hydrology at the University of Saskatchewan. A fit man with an open, friendly face, Pomeroy has been studying hydrology across the globe since the late 1980s and is one of the world's foremost scholars in the field. The data he has been collecting on regional hydrology points to dramatically reduced river flows across B.C., Alberta and Saskatchewan as a result of glacier loss. He says this shortage of runoff water could lead to drought across much of western Canada and affect weather patterns across an even larger area.[8]

University of California geography professor Laurence Smith is one of a growing number of scientists who have been tracking the disappearance of Arctic lakes around the world as warmer global climates dry out the northern landscape. He compared satellite images of Siberian rivers from the early 1970s to 2004 and noticed that many were carrying far more freshwater than usual. He believed that it was because the permafrost beneath the lakes was melting, causing flow surges. He predicted that when the permafrost melt was finished, the lakes would dry up. Sadly, he was proven right and in a 2005 *Science* article, he reported that 1,170 lakes had become smaller and that 125 had disappeared altogether.[9]

The same is happening in Canada. In July 2015, scientists in the Northwest Territories warned of "catastrophic drainage" due to thawing permafrost at a remote lake just south of the treeline. CBC reported that the Northwest Territories Geological Survey warned that a flash flood could happen anytime on the lake, which lies 20 kilometres west of Fort McPherson and is home to about 800 people.[10] Scientists are building models to try to understand the impact of permafrost thaws across the Canadian Arctic for both humans and the natural world. We are entering uncharted territory.

A team of researchers from the University of Laval has documented the dramatic decline in water levels of 70 lakes around Old Crow, Yukon, and Churchill, Manitoba. The team cites the lack of snowfall in recent years and says the drying of these and other lakes is actually visible to the naked eye. They say there has not been desiccation this significant in hundreds of years.[11]

Canada is in just as much danger of massive water loss, drought and forest fires as other parts of the world. The distinguished Canadian aquatic scientist David Schindler said the ash-laden air and sepia skies of summer 2015 in British Columbia will become the norm in a hotter and drier western Canada and that drought is here to stay. He told a B.C. audience to get used to forest fires that make

Vancouver look like Beijing and that this is the quality of life they are facing if Canadians continue to operate as if it is business as usual.[12]

The Second Threat: Endangered Drinking Water

Most municipal water systems in Canada deliver safe, clean, frequently tested drinking water that Canadians can trust. But we lack adequate and up-to-date regulation to protect source water, and we are falling behind in pollution prevention, making it harder for municipalities to do their job. I have stood at both the Atlantic in St. John's and the Pacific in Victoria, where local environmentalists pointed to raw sewage being released into the sea. How could this still be in the 21st century in our country? I asked myself. Thankfully in 2015, St. John's completed its treatment plant and stopped the practice, and Victoria has pledged to follow suit.

Environment Canada (now Environment and Climate Change Canada) reported that over 150 billion litres of untreated or undertreated sewage is dumped into our waterways every year. This is the largest source of pollution for all Canadian bodies of water, about four times the average flow of the Ottawa River.

Roughly 185 million litres of raw sewage have been dumped into Winnipeg's rivers since 2004 due to the city's antiquated sewer system. While Halifax (only recently) no longer dumps its sewage raw into the harbour, many coastal communities still do. Victoria and Esquimalt dump about 130 million litres of raw sewage every day into the Juan de Fuca Strait, much of which lands on Washington State's shores and has caused the state to file more than one formal complaint with B.C.'s provincial government.[13]

The NAFTA Commission for Environmental Cooperation wrote that untreated waste contains detergents, surfactants, disinfectants, pharmaceuticals, food additives, pesticides, herbicides, industrial chemicals, heavy metals and other synthetic materials. The ability for even conventional treatment processes, never mind substandard systems, to break these down is limited, said the commission.[14]

And it's not just sewage and flushed chemicals. The pharmaceuticals we consume are finding their way into our water supplies. The CBC reported that researchers have detected traces of acetaminophen, codeine, antibiotics, hormones, steroids and anti-epileptic compounds in the Great Lakes at levels high enough to be "of environmental concern." And Environment Canada officials told a Senate committee hearing that more than 165 individual pharmaceuticals and personal care products have been identified in water samples.[15]

The amount of chemicals that our bodies can safely process is a hotly debated subject. How much is too much? Which chemicals are the most toxic to us and other species? How well are our regulatory agencies keeping up with the tsunami of new chemicals entering Canada in new products? What decisions should we ask our governments to take when the long-term effects of many chemicals are still unknown?

In their highly informative 2013 book, *Down the Drain: How We Are Failing to Protect Our Water Resources*, Ralph Pentland and Chris Wood note that the number of distinct chemical compounds in commercial use in North America may run to as many as 100,000, and they estimate that Canada produces or imports at least 1 trillion kilograms of chemicals every year. They note that in 2012, the Council of Canadian Academies called together a panel of experts to review how federal scientists reach their determinations for assessing and regulating potentially dangerous chemicals. The panel reported that toxicity data are missing for 87% of chemicals on the Canadian market.

The authors warn that the level of exotic, persistent bioaccumulative or endocrine-disrupting compounds appear to be rising. Some, but not all, will be caught by more advanced treatment systems now coming online, but those that pass through untreated or undertreated systems are being released into the wild with possible serious repercussions.[16]

Even with state-of-the-art disposal systems, municipalities must sometimes release raw sewage when there is an overflow problem. Rather than let this sewage back up into basements, the City of Toronto, for example, sends the excess into Lake Ontario, according to Lake Ontario Waterkeeper. The group reported that in July 2013, the city infrastructure was so overwhelmed by rain, it released more than 1 billion litres of raw sewage into the lake in one day.[17] While the City of Toronto has recognized these problems and is in the process of upgrading the Ashbridge's Bay facility and building a network of underground retention tanks to hold storm runoff, other communities still lack the resources or the will to improve their waste treatment, and sewage continues to be a serious pollution threat.

The Third Threat: Endangered Source Water

Source water protection is as crucial for safe, clean water as waste treatment. It is important for the watersheds themselves, but also because keeping contaminants out of source water means you don't have to remove them from drinking water sources later. As well, clean source water is the only protection for the nearly 25% of Canadians dependent on individual or small community wells. Yet there are many stressors acting on our source waters.

Toxins and Carcinogens ~

Every year, more than 35 million kilograms of herbicides and pesticides are applied on agricultural land, 84% of it on the prairies,[18] and the chemicals have been found in water sources all over North America. Many are linked to problems with animal and human health. Glyphosate is the active ingredient in Monsanto's herbicide Roundup, widely used to control weeds. It is the top pesticide ingredient sold in Canada: its use tripled between 2005 and 2011. In April 2015, the World Health Organization announced that it now deems the chemical as "probably carcinogenic to humans."[19]

Health Canada was court ordered in 2011 to review its support for the herbicide in a case brought by West Coast Environmental Law and it released its decision in late 2015, finding that glyphosate was not harmful in the concentrations that most Canadians are exposed to. Many disagree, and the case stands as a seminal example of the battle to define how much exposure is too much. Other examples of chemicals once thought benign, most famously DDT, have since been found to be toxic.

The David Suzuki Foundation, Équiterre and their lawyers at Ecojustice also took the federal government to court in 2012 to review 383 already approved pesticides containing 23 active ingredients with links to cancer and water contamination. They argued the pesticides pose a risk to the environment and health. One is the well-known hormone disrupter atrazine, widely used in Canada on corn, but banned in the European Union since 2004 due to widespread groundwater contamination.[20] In December 2015, Health Canada reapproved atrazine, again confirming that Canada has much lower standards for such products than does Europe. In May 2016, the U.S. Environmental Protection Agency released its first risk assessment of the pesticide and found that it is "likely harming most species of plants and animals in the U.S."[21]

Industrial Pollution ~
Fracking, tar sands and the consequent oil spills and leakage are very damaging to source water. David Schindler, one of North America's most respected environmental scientists, has spent years tracking the effects of the tar sand mines in northern Alberta. He reported that the 170 square kilometres of tailings ponds leach 11 million litres of contaminated water every day.

Other types of mining pollute source water through acid mine drainage (the leaching that comes from rock and earth that has been disturbed) from exposure to heavy metals and the chemicals used to mine the ore. In just one three-year period, 2006–2009, reported Ecojustice, approximately 2 million tonnes of pollutants — including toxins such as lead and sulphuric acid, and known carcinogens such as arsenic, nickel and chromium — were released by mines in Canada into tailings and waste-rock dumps.[22]

Plastics ~
Microplastics, small particles of plastic less than five milli— metres in size, can be found in waters all over the world, both in lakes and rivers near large urban populations and in the oceans. Microbeads, a category of microplastics, are tiny plastic pellets found in sunscreen, toothpaste, makeup and body cleansers. A 2014 study of the Great Lakes by the

U.S.-based 5 Gyres Institute found an astonishing 43,000 microplastic particles per square kilometre; near cities, the number jumped to 466,000.[23]

Nutrient Overload ~

In addition to herbicide and pesticide runoff, there is also eutrophication (nutrient overload largely from fertilizers) harming many lakes in Canada and around the world. So extensive is the blue-green algae on Lake Winnipeg, for example, that it can be seen by satellite from space. In 2013, the Berlin-based Global Nature Fund named it the most threatened lake in the world. And, during the summer of 2014, the city of Toledo, Ohio, shut down the city's public drinking water system for three days due to the concentration of blue-green algae in Lake Erie.

Manitoba scientist Diane Orihel, affectionately dubbed the Lady of the Lakes by the science journal *Nature*, has studied the presence of microcystins (potentially fatal toxins found in blue-green algae) across Canada. In her 2012 report, she identified these toxins in lakes in every province, with the highest concentrations in the cottage and recreational areas of central Alberta and southern Manitoba. Her survey found conditions "of concern" in 246 lakes across Canada.[24]

Dams ~

Canada is home to more than 900 large dams (defined as ten metres or higher), a number of which have caused serious mercury contamination of local waters and fish. When land is flooded for dam projects, vegetation that has been suddenly submerged creates habitat for bacteria that absorb any mercury that happens to be in the underlying soil. It is released into the reservoir waters and is ingested by the local fish. This is one of the primary means by which mercury enters the freshwater food chain. By the time humans, at the top of that food chain, eat fish at their dinner tables, the mercury has bioaccumulated many times, increasing in concentration. Mercury poisoning can cause blindness, reproductive failure and brain damage. There really were "mad hatters," victims of the mercury poisoning that was the result of the hat-making process of the 18th and 19th centuries.

Mercury poisoning from the massive James Bay hydroelectric project in Quebec was one of the prime legacies left to the local Cree First Nation when its members ate the fish from diverted reservoir waters. And a 2015 study for the West Moberly First Nations and the McLeod Lake Indian Band of B.C. found that 98% of fish samples in their territories contain mercury levels above the provincial guidelines. The fish came from a reservoir that was created as part of the 1960s-era W.A.C. Bennett Dam.[25]

Methylmercury, a potent form of mercury most easily bioaccumulated, is especially high in Arctic marine life. Scientists from Harvard University undertook an environmental impact assessment for the troubled Muskrat Falls hydroelectric project in Labrador, which, in 2017, is scheduled to flood a large region upstream from an estuarine fjord called Lake Melville. The scientists were examining increases of this neurotoxin in Lake Melville after another dam was built further up the Churchill River. They collected soil cores from the inland areas slated to be covered by the Muskrat dam and simulated flooding. Within just five days, they found that methylmercury levels in the water increased 14-fold.[26]

In their report published in August 2015 by the U.S. National Academy of Sciences, the Harvard scientists predicted that increased methylmercury concentrations in the Arctic as a result of new hydroelectric projects will be greater than those expected from climate change.[27]

As we collectively turn serious attention to clean alternatives to fossil fuels, we cannot assume hydroelectricity is a benign choice. Protecting air by endangering water and human health is not the solution to our climate crisis.

The Fourth Threat: Ecosystem Degradation

Source waters don't exist in a vacuum. They are protected and purified by a complex filter ecosystem that includes wetlands and forests. By continuing to drain or build over wetlands and cut down forests beyond a sustainable level, Canadians are putting the waterways we rely on at grave risk.

Wetlands perform many important tasks. They recharge groundwater and filter out algae-causing nutrients that would otherwise flow into major lakes and rivers. They provide and protect habitat for wildfowl, animals, fish and plants. Wetlands are also important groundwater recharge areas. Their loss sets the stage for significant increases in greenhouse gas emissions as the land's ability to store carbon is reduced.

Canada still has one-quarter of the world's remaining wetlands, and an area covering over 130,000 kilometres has been set aside for protection. It's a good start. But like many other industrialized nations, Canada has also allowed widespread destruction of its wetland cover. It has dredged it, paved it over and converted it to agricultural production.

Ducks Unlimited, a conservation organization whose members are hunters, estimates that up to 70% of wetlands in Canada have been lost or degraded in settled areas. Wetlands near large urban centres are particularly at risk and have suffered the most severe losses. Natural Resources Canada estimates that as much as 98% of wetlands adjacent to major urban centres have been lost. Prior to European settlement, wetlands covered 25% of southern Ontario. By the turn of the 21st century, this had decreased to 7%.[28]

Scientists from the University of Birmingham studied an area of northern Alberta years after a wildfire had burned through a large fen wetland that covered thousands of kilometres in the northern boreal forest zone. They found that the part of the fen that had been drained for forestry before the fire had become a shrub ecosystem, no longer able to store large amounts of water. The part of the fen that had not been drained was once again a healthy wetland, storing water and carbon. Their research suggests that draining wetlands combined with climate change threatens to turn Alberta's huge northern wetlands into vast expanses of bush and shrub, altering the province's freshwater cycle and making it susceptible to the wildfires that are expected to increase in the boreal forest as climate change continues.[29]

Forests also filter and clean water through their root systems. They curb erosion and help to keep sediment and excess nutrients out of waterways. New York City saves billions of dollars by bringing in its high-quality water through aqueducts connected to protected areas in the nearby Catskill forest rather than using a chemical filtration system. Forests also capture rainwater, sending it through the soil and replenishing groundwater supplies. When forests are cut down and paved over, the rain often runs off to rivers and out to sea.

Cutting down forests devastates hydrologic cycles. The horrific droughts in São Paulo of the past several years have been linked by Brazilian scientists to the destruction of the Amazon rainforests. While El Niño rains of the winter of 2016 have eased the severe water shortage and partially refilled the city's reservoirs, many scientists believe that the water scarcity will soon return. The city has done little to curb demand or improve its systems as a result of the crisis.

Rainforests are critical climate regulators. They store carbon dioxide and absorb solar energy, serving as a large natural air conditioner. They also act as "biotic pumps," storing massive amounts of water, which they then release as water vapour. A mature rainforest tree releases 1,000 litres of water vapour a day into the atmosphere. The entire Amazon rainforest sends up 20 billion tonnes a day. The airborne current, or "flying river," over the Amazon River holds more water than the river itself and carries the water thousands of kilometres to provide rain for thirsty southern Brazil.[30]

Or at least it did. Over the past 40 years, 20% of the rainforest has been cleared for timber and farmland. On the day before the 2015 Conference of the Parties (COP) climate deal in Paris was announced, Brazil released 146,000 hectares of the Amazon rainforest to private contractors for logging and deforestation. A team of scientists for the University of Leeds says that if this pace of destruction keeps up, rainfall in the Amazon basin will decline another 12% in the wet season and 21% in the dry season by 2050.[31]

Antonio Donato Nobre is a highly respected scientist with Brazil's National Institute for Space Research. In 2014, he was part of a metastudy that massed the conclusions of 200 existing papers on the Amazon basin. It concluded that "the vegetation-climate equilibrium is teetering on the brink of the abyss." He believes that if deforestation continues at this galloping rate, the rainforest will convert to a much drier savannah, according to the *Guardian* newspaper. He also believes that the razing of the Amazon may be partially responsible for drought as far away as California and Texas, and that further destruction would have global climate consequences.

There are big lessons here for Canada. In 2014, scientists from Global Forest Watch, the University of Maryland, Greenpeace and the World Resources Institute reported that Canada now leads the planet in the degradation of previously untouched forests. Using satellite technology, the scientists found that, between 2002 and 2013, 8% of the world's forests were degraded — an area three times the size of Germany. Of that degradation, more than a fifth — 21.4% — occurred in Canada, substantially worse than Brazil, at 14%.

British Columbia's interior, parts of northern Ontario and Quebec and big swaths of northern prairie have been hard hit with forest loss due to logging, energy development and fire. Greenpeace says that over the past decade, logging companies cut down an area larger than 1,125 football fields every day in Quebec alone. The boreal forest in the tar sands mining area between Fort McMurray and Lake Athabasca has been almost totally devastated.[32]

If we continue to destroy and endanger Canada's forests and wetlands, the burden on our already stressed waterways will grow.

The Fifth Threat: Groundwater at Risk

In Canada, there is more water underground than there is on the surface. Dr. Alfonso Rivera, Canada's chief hydrologist, estimates that Canada has about 70,000 cubic kilometres of water sitting within 150 metres of the surface. He warns that much of it is fossil water trapped deep underground in aquifers that are not always rechargeable.

Canada's Tom Gleeson, a hydrologist with the University of Victoria, led an international team of scientists in a study that was released in November 2015. In it, the researchers reported that groundwater is mostly a non-renewable resource everywhere in the world. Just 6% of the global groundwater can be replenished and renewed within a span of 50 years and most groundwater tends to be found within a few metres of the surface, where it is most vulnerable to contamination by pollution and depletion.[33]

Environment Canada reported that groundwater is at risk from landfills, leaking gasoline storage tanks, leaking septic tanks, chemical farm runoff, livestock waste, petroleum products, industrial waste disposal sites and dense industrial organic liquids. And contamination is increasing in Canada primarily due to the number of toxic compounds used in industry and agriculture. Contamination can render groundwater unsuitable for use and the cost of cleanup is high. Once an aquifer is contaminated, reported the department, it may be unusable for decades. Some contaminants can still be in the system 10,000 years after they were introduced.

Importantly, pollution of surface water by groundwater is also serious because contaminants migrate as groundwater passes through the hydrologic cycle.

There is no systemic information on the amount of

contaminants in Canada's groundwater. But a study by ProPublica, a consortium of American investigative journalists, gives us an idea of how groundwater is being used as a dumpsite for waste. It found that U.S. industries have injected over 120 trillion litres of toxic liquid into American groundwater in just decades. There are more than 680,000 underground waste and injection wells, more than 15,000 of which shoot industrial fluids thousands of metres below the surface.

"In 10 to 100 years, we are going to find out that most of our groundwater is polluted," said Mario Salazar, an engineer who has worked as a technical expert with the U.S. Environmental Protection Agency's underground injection program. "A lot of people are going to get sick. A lot of people may die."[34]

Over one-third of Canadians rely on groundwater for their water supplies. Those depending on wells are particularly vulnerable to source water.

Citizens on southern Vancouver Island have been waging a fierce fight against a landfill for contaminated soil that sits above Shawnigan Lake, the watershed that supplies drinking water for the Shawnigan Lake community of 12,000. The landfill company has a permit to accept and store up to 100,000 tonnes of contaminated soil a year in an old quarry.

Assured by the B.C. environment ministry that the dump is safe, local residents felt validated in their concerns when, in November 2015, following a water overflow from the site, the island's health department issued an advisory warning people not to draw water from the lake for drinking, bathing, personal hygiene or food preparation. Earlier, in May 2015, B.C. MLA and climate scientist Andrew Weaver unveiled the results of his own tests of the site and reported that he found heavy metal concentrations up to 19 times greater downstream of the site than upstream. These concentrates included thorium, lead, niobium, zirconium, vanadium, chromium, iron, tin and cobalt.[35]

Further testing in March 2016 yielded better results, with contaminants within guidelines. But the testing shows that contamination can ebb and flow in source waters and concerned citizens still don't know what exactly lies at the bottom of the quarry.

On March 21, 2016 (the day before World Water Day), the hard work of the citizens of Vancouver Island's Shawnigan Lake in opposing the contaminated soil landfill paid off. The B.C. Supreme Court ruled that the province erred in granting a waste disposal permit near the lake. The judge also imposed an injunction on the company that bars further importing of contaminated soil, although current contracts totalling 106,000 tonnes of waste can still be fulfilled. The group is appealing to the Department of National Defence, the source of most of this tainted soil.

The political will to tackle groundwater contamination has been distressingly lacking. Perhaps the citizens of the Shawnigan Lake watershed can now press their government for full disclosure, setting a new benchmark for transparency in other jurisdictions. With the planned expansion of industrial development, particularly in the North, threats to both surface and groundwater are sure to increase and transparency becomes more critical than ever.

The Sixth Threat: Growth at All Costs

The rush is on in the Yukon. Not since the days when prospectors led pack trains upriver, hunting for the motherlode with picks and pans, said the *Toronto Star*, has there been such a rush to stake claims in the Klondike. Most are working for a handful of large corporations racing to stake out vast tracts of the Yukon, and in one year alone — 2010 — stakers filed a record 83,863 mineral claims across the territory.[36]

In 2014, the Yukon government announced it would open up a huge swath of the pristine Peel Watershed for mining, an area over half the size of New Brunswick. Shocked First Nations asserted this violates land claim agreements. They joined conservation groups to launch a legal challenge to the plan, saying it betrayed a previously negotiated agreement that would have conserved a much greater landmass and protected the watershed. The Supreme Court of Yukon agreed. In November 2015, the court set the planning bar back to 2011, before the development announcements. However, the government says this is not an end to the project, but rather a requirement for it to improve the consultation process with local First Nations. Intent on a more permanent answer, the First Nations and conservation groups sought leave to appeal to the Supreme Court of Canada. In June 2016, the court agreed to hear the case.

As Karen Baltgailis of the Yukon Conservation Society told *National Geographic*, the plan would allow mines and all-weather roads for industrial development along rivers that are major tourist destinations. "Given that most of the Yukon is already open for development," she asked, "do they not see the need to protect some large, last great wilderness areas?"[37]

A rash of mining claims has been staked throughout the northern half of Ontario's boreal forest since the provincial government opened the area for exploration in 2010.

Claimants are looking to cash in on the "Ring of Fire," a $50-billion deposit of minerals spread over 5,000 square kilometres of untouched land in the James Bay lowlands. It is potentially the biggest resource development Ontario has seen in more than a century.

Many Ontario conservation groups and First Nations of the area have deep concerns about the project's impact on water, forests and wetlands. As Brent Patterson, political director for the Council of Canadians, points out, along with the threat to water from the mining itself, which would include tailings ponds for the mining waste and hydroelectric dams to power the operations, a road would need to be built that would traverse ancient boreal forest and intersect several major waterways. These developments would pose water risks in the traditional lands of several First Nations communities. "Beyond the northern reaches of the forest lies tundra, which supports one of the earth's largest, continuous wetlands, and through which half of Canada's largest dozen rivers drain," said Ontario Nature.[38]

Quebec's Plan Nord would develop a piece of its remote northern region twice the size of France. The original plan predicted $80 billion in public and private spending over two decades and included major forestry development, several hydroelectric dams and mining activity. Northern Quebec is rich in deposits of nickel, cobalt, platinum, zinc, iron ore, lignite, gold, lithium, vanadium, diamonds and rare earths. In April 2015, Quebec premier Philippe Couillard announced a slightly scaled-down version of the plan, citing a deep slump in global metal prices. He said his government would invest about $1.3 billion in infrastructure over the next five years but still anticipated investments in the range of $50 billion by 2035.

With development plans like these and similar ones in other provinces, the question must be asked: have we learned anything at all from past mistakes? If we have not protected the water heritage of Canada in the past, how do we expect to protect endangered waterways from this style of development? How do we alter our industrial techniques so that these remote areas can gain much-needed economic growth without sacrificing the environment? This is the crucial challenge of the 21st century, for we cannot keep extracting and polluting as we have been doing.

two
A Federal Government Missing in Action

Water experts, scientists and environmental groups are voicing a singular message about Canada's water management: it is a patchwork of uneven and often inadequate regulations and standards in need of firm federal oversight and governance. For decades, reports from academics, universities and government watchdogs have called for a national plan of action that includes strong federal data collection, better and more enforced federal laws and more national cooperation and coordination with the provinces and municipalities.

Before the Harper government closed its doors in 2013, the National Round Table on the Environment and the Economy brought together leading water experts and scientists as well as hands-on water managers to discuss the state of Canada's water. In its report, "Charting a Course: Sustainable Water Use by Canada's Natural Resource

Sectors," the group urged the federal and provincial governments as well as First Nations to negotiate a charter whose goal is the collaborative care and management of water in Canada. This is only one of many collaborations, the vast majority of which have been ignored by successive governments.

Water Management, Falling through the Cracks

As it presently works, the federal, provincial and municipal governments share the responsibility for water management, although a great deal falls through the cracks. The provinces and one of the territories — Yukon — have the primary jurisdiction over most areas of water management and protection. Most delegate certain responsibilities to municipalities, especially drinking water treatment and distribution and wastewater treatment. Most major uses of water are permitted or licensed by provincial water authorities.

The federal government is responsible for fisheries, navigation and international relations relating to shared water boundaries. The federal government also manages water on federal lands, national parks and federal facilities such as military bases and prisons, on First Nations communities and in Nunavut and the Northwest Territories. The jurisdictions of provinces and federal government overlap, including areas such as agriculture, health and issues of national concern. The federal government runs the Water Survey of Canada that collects and distributes water data from monitoring stations across the country. Costs are shared among federal, provincial and territorial governments, except Quebec, which does its own monitoring.

Environment Canada lists a number of ways in which the federal and provincial governments cooperate. The Prairie Provinces Water Board, for example, manages the oversight for water quality problems as well as an agreement for the equitable apportionment of eastward-flowing rivers (an important consideration in the semi-arid prairies). The Mackenzie River Basin Board helps to implement the Mackenzie River Basin Transboundary Waters Master Agreement, which commits six governments, including the federal government, to work closely together to sustainably manage the resources of the whole basin. The Canadian Council of Ministers of the Environment provides an avenue through which the various levels of government can discuss and act on common approaches to water issues.[39]

Despite these and other water management institutions, the federal government has consistently passed on opportunities to provide leadership and assert its authority in ways that would give Canada a coherent freshwater management plan. In their book, *Down the Drain*, Pentland and Wood argue that the 1970 Canada Water Act, enacted by Pierre Trudeau, actually did give the federal government a great deal of authority to invoke its full constitutional powers to protect and manage our water resources. The act recognized the urgent need to deal with water pollution at a national level and empowered the federal government to unilaterally establish water quality agencies to restore distressed watersheds and levy fines against polluters.

But the provinces resisted this authority, and successive federal governments have given in to their demand for greater control and, preoccupied with other priorities, abdicated the crucial role they might have played.

This was not the only squandered opportunity. In 1987, the Federal Water Policy was introduced after the findings of the two-year Pearse Inquiry were tabled. It had a far-reaching vision for the future of water in Canada, and the government of Brian Mulroney pledged to provide more federal funding for research, establish better coordination of water management with the provinces, review major developments for their impact on water and introduce a national program to control toxic chemicals.

But as Alberta environmental journalist Hanneke Brooymans reports in her 2011 book, *Water in Canada: A Resource in Crisis*, the policy was never adopted into law and never enacted. She quotes Rob de Loë, research chair in water policy and governance at the University of Waterloo, who said of the Federal Water Policy, "It was a great policy. For its time, it was thoughtful and well developed and there was lots of consultation. But the policy was not implemented. So from my point of view, what is the federal government's water policy? It seems to be that the policy is not to have a comprehensive policy."[40]

Perhaps one of the problems is that water management has been looked at as a federal policy rather than a national one. In other words, it was thought of in terms of the limitations of the federal government's role rather than as an area of national concern that should rise above government turf considerations.

Another opportunity presented itself two years later with the passage of the Canadian Environmental Protection Act (CEPA) that made pollution protection the cornerstone of national efforts to reduce toxic substances in the environment. CEPA allowed the federal government to relinquish enforcement of pollution regulation to the provinces but with the condition that each agreed in writing that its standards will meet or exceed those of the federal government. As of 2016, over 20 years later, only Alberta and Nova Scotia have signed, and the federal government has not brought the provinces to task for failing to implement their undertaking. Pentland and Wood document the very different paths taken by both the U.S. and the European Union on water management. In both jurisdictions, ensuring the safety and security of the public's water lay with the highest level of government authority. But Canada's national leaders, down the decades and across party divides, have instead opted to shrug. "The federal Crown offers intelligence," they wrote, "a little coaching, some objectives, but leaves any actual on-field contact to its constitutional juniors."[41]

Arguably the strongest tool the federal government had was its oldest — the Fisheries Act, enacted at the time of Confederation and armed with the power to prosecute any practice that results in harm to fish habitat. While environmentalists have consistently praised the intent of the act (now dramatically watered down), they lament that there have been few instances of enforcement, especially against large industrial operations.

The federal government has consistently lacked the political will to enforce policy and has chronically underfunded inspection and enforcement. Brooymans points out that the federal government says it has no control over inland waters, beds of watercourses or inland shorelines, while the provinces claim to have no regulatory decision-making powers concerning fish habitat. A catch-22 indeed.

Starving Budgets for Water Protection

Resources for Environment Canada, created in 1971, have never been great. For most of its first 20 years, the department's budget was between 0.8% and 1.2% of the federal budget program spending. When Brian Mulroney left office in 1993, the level had slipped to 0.6%.

In the years that the federal government struggled to get Canada's debt under control, Finance Minister Paul Martin cut the annual budget again in 1995 — from $737 million to $503 million over three years. Dale Marshall, now national program manager with Environmental Defence, wrote in a 2004 analysis for the Canadian Centre for Policy Alternatives that, by 1998, Environment Canada had fewer personnel than any other federal government department and fewer than 70 environmental officers to enforce regulations right across the country. That is just over five officers per province and territory with a combined responsibility for Canada's nearly ten million square kilometres. How could spills, pollution or other problems be adequately handled with such a skeleton staff? By 2000, its budget as a percentage of overall government program spending stood at 0.5%.

Similar cuts were made to Parks Canada, Natural Resources Canada, the Department of Fisheries and Oceans, and Science and Technology.

Cuts to Environment Canada's Water Survey branch were so severe that the number of water monitoring stations had to be dramatically reduced. Susan Rowntree, a physicist who worked with the branch from 1984 to 1995, wrote that the remnants of the staff were relocated, mainly to universities, where they attempted to continue to provide data, collected by students. Rowntree left in 1995 after she was ordered to run scenarios with 90% cuts to her water-safety monitoring network. "I foresaw a Walkerton event happening in Canada and didn't want to be there when it did because our mandate was to protect the public. In 2000, Walkerton's deadly tainted-water nightmare struck."[42]

The cuts to the environment portfolios overall were so acute that then environment minister Sheila Copps stopped publishing the annual State of the Environment Report.[43]

The Harper Assault on Water Protection

But no government has been more of a threat to the long-term health of Canada's water than the government of Stephen Harper. The Harper government gutted the regulatory framework that — modest as it was — held the promise of protections for Canada's lakes, rivers and groundwater, and turned policy and practice upside down to advance the interests of extractive industries, largely the energy sector.

Early on in its mandate, in 2002, the Harper government allowed a loophole into the Metal Mining Effluent Regulations of the Fisheries Act, giving the green light to mining companies to dump their toxic waste into healthy lakes and creeks. Originally introduced under the former Liberal government and intended only to apply to lakes already dead, Schedule 2 allows for the reclassification of a lake as a "tailings impoundment area" no longer protected by the Fisheries Act.

Already, Sandy Pond on Newfoundland's south coast has been destroyed under this loophole. The once pristine, fish-bearing 38-hectare freshwater lake is now a dumpsite for Vale Inco's nickel operations at Voisey's Bay. The company moved about 1,400 fish, mostly trout, to other water bodies, built three dams to increase its dumpsite capacity, installed liners in the lake and is now filling the site with toxic waste. Environment Canada has since released the names of 23 other natural water bodies that have been approved as Schedule 2 toxic waste dumps.

With Bills C-38 (2012) and C-45 (2013), two notorious omnibus budget bills each more than 400 pages long, the Harper government made drastic changes to freshwater protection in Canada, with no public consultation.

The omnibus bills gutted the Fisheries Act further. The old Fisheries Act clearly stated that it was a criminal offence to deposit a deleterious substance into waters inhabited by fish. The new law no longer protects habitat and is limited to "serious harm" to fish that have commercial, recreational or Aboriginal purposes.

The new rules allowed the Minister of Fisheries and Oceans to authorize deposits of deleterious substances if the "whole of the deposit is not acutely lethal to fish." The regulation defines "acutely lethal" as a deposit that kills more that 50% of fish at 100% concentration over a 96-hour period. As Council of Canadians national water campaigner Emma Lui points out, this threshold does not take into account that sometimes the most damaging pollution is slow and chronic.

West Coast Environmental Law said that fish habitat protection is an internationally agreed-to obligation and a national Canadian priority. The provision in the Fisheries Act before the changes introduced in the budget bills clearly prohibited harm to fish habitat and was a "much-needed tool" to preserve marine biodiversity and maintain sustainable fisheries, said the group.[44] The Royal Society of Canada expert panel report on marine biodiversity stated that the current Fisheries Act is insufficient to fulfil Canada's obligations to sustain marine biodiversity and is in need of "extensive" revisions.

In Bill C-38, the Harper government also gutted the Navigable Waters Protection Act, legislation that dated back to 1882 and that gave the federal government the authority to control what was built on, under, over, through or across any navigable waterway. With the changes made to the act, federal protection of 99% of lakes and rivers in Canada was stripped. Shockingly, an *Ottawa Citizen* investigation found that of the water bodies earmarked for continuing federal waterways protection, 90% had shoreline in Conservative ridings.[45]

The changes exempted pipelines and interprovincial power lines that now have a green light to cross over and under more than 31,000 lakes and 2.25 million rivers without federal scrutiny. The few remaining protections of navigable waters were transferred to the National Energy Board (NEB), itself now only a body that can recommend a course of action. Federal decisions on major pipeline and extraction projects can now be made in Cabinet, although the Trudeau government has promised it will re-invigorate the NEB regulatory process.

The Canadian Environmental Assessment Act required an environmental assessment of all projects under federal jurisdiction, including waterways that cross provincial boundaries. In Bill C-38, it was replaced with a diluted version that immediately resulted in the cancellation of 3,000 active assessments. More disturbing, the new regulations gave Cabinet the right to determine which projects will be assessed and to ignore their findings.

As Lake Ontario Waterkeeper stated, "The Navigable Waters Protection Act no longer protects water. The Fisheries Act no longer protects fish. The Environmental Assessment Act no longer requires environmental assessments be done before important decisions are made."[46]

The Species at Risk Act was also amended during the Harper years. One of the changes removed mandatory time limits on permits that allowed activity with an impact on threatened and endangered species. Even before these changes, the government's record on upholding that law was abysmal, acting federal environment commissioner Neil Maxwell said in his 2013 annual report to Parliament. At that time, he said, Environment Canada had action plans for only seven of over 500 identified species at risk. Former environment minister Peter Kent had already signalled his intention in 2012 to "reform" the act to make it more "efficient" and "effective," code words for making it more industry friendly.[47]

The changes made were all to laws that the energy industry, in particular, didn't like. A December 2012 letter obtained by Greenpeace revealed that the oil and gas industry, through a lobby group called the Energy Framework Initiative, outlined six laws it wanted amended in order for it to do its work. Those laws included the Canadian Environmental Assessment Act, Fisheries Act, Navigable Waters Protection Act, Species at Risk Act and Migratory Birds Convention Act. All but the last, which is a treaty with the U.S. and therefore not easily broken, had been, or was slated to be, weakened.

The War on Science

Hundreds of research projects, facilities and institutes conducting scientific research were shut down during the Harper years. One of the most controversial was the decision to stop funding and shut down the Experimental Lakes Area (ELA), the world's leading freshwater research centre. Located in northwestern Ontario, the ELA was responsible for groundbreaking work on acid rain, household pollutants and mercury contamination, and the outcry against its shuttering was loud and widespread. Eventually the Manitoba and Ontario governments came forward with some funding and the International Institute for Sustainable Development undertook the management of the file. But without federal funding, its future is still precarious.

The ELA was perhaps the most high profile of the cuts, but it was by no means the only one. The Harper government also slashed staff at the Canada Centre for Inland Waters, the most important science-monitoring agency for the Great Lakes, and killed the Global Environment Monitoring System Water Programme, a Canadian research network that monitored the health of freshwater lakes around the world for the United Nations. Over $73 million was cut from the water protection programs of Environment Canada and the Department of Fisheries and Oceans (DFO). And more than 2,000 scientists, many of them working on water and climate protection, were laid off between 2009 and 2014.

The government also cut funding to independent voices, including the 24-year-old National Round Table on the Environment and the Economy, an independent source of expert scientific advice, and the Canadian Environmental Network. The national science advisor was let go and not replaced.

Cuts Already Felt

During the years of the Harper government, decades of neglect met deliberate destruction and the result is terrible for Canada's water.

In his 2012 — and final — annual report, then environmental commissioner Scott Vaughan strongly condemned the lack of oversight of Canada's mining, fracking, and oil and gas sectors. He also said that Canada is not prepared for a major offshore oil spill on its east coast and warned of a huge jump in tanker traffic on the west coast. "We concluded that the enforcement program was not well managed to adequately enforce compliance with the Canadian Environmental Protection Act," he wrote in the report. "There are serious questions about the federal capacity to safeguard Canada's environment," he told the *Toronto Star*.[48]

That same year, Ecojustice released "Getting Tough on Environment Crime?" which found that the number of inspections and warnings issued under the Canadian Environmental Protection Act had declined since 2005–2006, despite an increase in the number of enforcement officers. Average fines for environmental offenders amount to about $10,000 per CEPA conviction, too low to serve as a deterrent, especially to large corporations with deep pockets. It took Environment Canada more than 20 years to collect $2.4 million in fines under CEPA, said Ecojustice, and compared this to the Toronto Public Library, which collected $2.6 million in fines for overdue books in 2009 alone.[49]

In early 2013, reporter Mike De Souza, then of Postmedia, used access to information requests to find that Environment Canada was hitting polluters with warnings instead of fines. Violations are punishable by fines of up to $1 million or imprisonment of up to three years. But Scott Vaughan told De Souza that the department does not adequately track cases or follow up with companies about violations.[50]

Julie Gelfand, Canada's new environmental watchdog and Vaughan's replacement, reported in 2014 that under the new system put in place by the Harper government, there is no clear rationale for which projects will be evaluated and which will not.

In January 2016, Gelfand released her 2015 report. She strongly took Health Canada's Pest Management Regulatory Agency to task for taking years to remove confirmed pesticide risks from the marketplace while failing to evaluate many other products posing a serious threat to human health and the environment. The agency took between four and 11 years to remove some pesticides from the market even after it determined they posed "unacceptable risk for all use," said the commissioner. She singled out as pesticides of concern the 36 types of neonicotinoids in use in Canada for over two decades. These pesticides are widely believed to be linked to bee die-offs. Overall, she said, the agency is failing to properly re-evaluate many of the 7,000 pest control products used in Canada, many of which leach into adjacent waterways.

In September 2015, University of Calgary law professor Martin Olszynski released the findings of a statistical analysis that showed Ottawa has "all but abandoned" attempts to protect fish habitat. Analyzing data and development applications, Olszynski concluded that federal protection for fisheries and waterways has been sharply declining for over a decade, reported the Canadian Press.

It was apparent to Olszynski that the 2012 changes to the Fisheries Act were not intended to cut red tape, as was cited at the time, but to validate the fact that the DFO, whose budget had been cut by $80 million, was already doing less. By 2014, the number of projects reviewed by the government had dropped to fewer than 4,000 from more than 12,000 in 2001. After the gutting of the Fisheries Act, "enforcement fell off a cliff."[51]

No better authority exists to measure the impact of the Harper government decisions on the environment and science than the federal government scientists on the front line. In a fall 2015 survey, the Professional Institute of the Public Service of Canada revealed that nine out of ten federal government scientists believed that the cuts to federal science budgets have had a detrimental impact on the government's ability to serve the public. Seven out of ten Environment Canada scientists believed Canada is doing a worse job of environmental protection than in 2000, and 86% of scientists at the DFO believed that changes to the Fisheries Act are hampering Canada's ability to protect fish and fish habitat.

"In 31 years on the job, never have I witnessed such systematic destruction of the scientific capability of the federal public service," said one scientist. "Science has been cut to the bone; there is no way to reduce further without just stopping," said another. "Arbitrary changes to the Fisheries Act, the Environmental Assessment Act, the Navigable Waters Protection Act and cuts to Environment Canada and DFO have tilted the playing field toward industrial development to such an extent that environmental/fisheries regulations are practically non-existent or unenforceable for future developments," said another.

A DFO scientist lamented that the cuts to staff have severely reduced the quality of service DFO is able to provide to industry and the public. "The face of DFO is now virtually gone from communities, especially in the North where all the development is occurring. . . . The list of threatened and endangered species continues to grow. Salmon stocks are struggling all along the west coast of North America. The number of contaminated sites continues to grow and cleanup efforts are tied up in politicized bureaucracy."[52]

Gordon Owen, about to retire as head of Environment Canada's enforcement branch, issued a damning report to the new Trudeau government in January 2016. The report said the department and the Canadian Environmental Protection Agency are in such disarray, some enforcement officers ignore infractions to the act in order to keep in line with Ottawa's "priorities." In some cases, officers were actually breaking the law, fearing reprisals for doing their job. Said one, "I believe our organization lacks leadership, accountability, knowledge, confidence and care. There is no heart in the upper ranks."[53]

The dramatic gutting of water protection by the Harper government greatly exacerbates the long-standing issues facing Canadian governments as they try to meet the growing demands for action. Problems that have plagued water management, including the lack of national oversight, are still here and now are substantially harder to address.

Water Infrastructure Needs Still Not Dealt With

Like needing a new furnace in your home, water infrastructure upgrades are not sexy but they are essential. Systems in some Canadian cities are a century old and populations in most urban areas are growing, putting huge demands on aging pipes and treatment plants. Climate change is causing more dramatic storms and flooding, putting additional burdens on the infrastructure. The 2016 Canadian Infrastructure Report Card, compiled by the Federation of Canadian Municipalities and several other organizations, says that about 40% of wastewater pumping stations and storage tanks in Canada are in various degrees of decline and estimates that the cost of replacing them is about $61 billion.

There has been insufficient funding and coordination at the national level for decades. The Canadian Water Network, a collaboration of water managers, municipal representatives, researchers and regulatory bodies housed at the University of Waterloo, has created the Canadian Municipal Water Consortium to lead municipalities in water-management issues. One of its three major mandates is to "address the need for national coordination of leading knowledge to support improved decision making."[54]

In his 2013 report "Canada's Infrastructure Gap" for the Canadian Centre for Policy Alternatives, economist Hugh Mackenzie said Canada has an "infrastructure gap" as a result of decades of underinvestment. Consecutive federal governments have let the burden fall to lower levels of government. In 1955, the federal government owned 44% of the Canadian public capital stock, the provinces owned 34% and local governments 22%. (Public capital stock is the name given to government-owned assets such as highways, airports and transit systems.) By 2011, the federal government owned only 13%, the provinces 35% and municipalities 52%. The same pattern occurred with capital investment. In 1955, the federal government accounted for 34% of capital investment in infrastructure; by 2003, it had declined to just 13%, the provincial share remained constant at 39% and the municipal share increased from 27% to 48%.

The significance of this pattern, Mackenzie wrote, is that infrastructure responsibilities shifted from the level of government with the largest and most flexible revenue base — the federal government — to local government, the level with the smallest and least flexible revenue base. Transfer payments could have offset this imbalance, but they were cut to both the provinces and municipalities as a result of Ottawa's deficit-fighting efforts, forcing some local governments to raise local property taxes to pay for upgrades. In many ways, the federal government balanced its own budgets by passing spending obligations down to other levels of government.

Mackenzie believes that the province's long-standing reluctance to allow a direct financial relationship between the federal government and local governments should end, and he recommends that a mechanism be found for cost sharing to replace the "ad hoc, off-again non-system we have now." He also calls for a robust and transparent governmental structure for national infrastructure renewal that resists the tendency to use infrastructure spending as a "political pork barrel" or to promote costly and wasteful public-private partnerships.[55] The Trudeau government has promised to put substantial funds into Canada's water infrastructure.

Groundwater Still Not Protected

The Council of Canadian Academies conducted a study published in 2009 that estimated that more than 30,000 groundwater sources were contaminated. The scientists criticized the "fragmented and overlapping jurisdictions and responsibilities" and "competing priorities" of groundwater governance in Canada and also lamented that existing federal laws have either been little used or have failed to provide clarity of jurisdiction.

While stating that groundwater management is best achieved at a local level through municipal or watershed authority, the report identified the need for strong federal funding and standards if Canada's groundwater is to be protected.[56]

Not only is Canadian groundwater insufficiently protected, it is not even thoroughly mapped. Staff at Natural Resources Canada warned in a briefing paper that the federal government was taking too long to map Canada's groundwater and that key information needed to protect the water supply would not be available for almost two more decades. Dr. Alfonso Rivera is the head of the department's groundwater mapping program, and in 2013 he published *Canada's Groundwater Resources*, the most detailed compilation of information on the state of Canada's groundwater to date. In the introduction, he bluntly states, "Nationally we have no idea what our groundwater resources are. There is no national monitoring network to assess its quality and use."[57]

To date, only 19 of the country's 30 major aquifers have been properly mapped and the project is still a decade away from completion. In the meantime, said Adèle Hurley, director of the Program on Water Issues at the Munk School of Global Affairs (disbanded in April 2016 due to loss of funding), provinces are basically giving away this unmapped water to foreign-owned bitumen-miners, bottled-water companies and water-hungry shale gas fracking companies for little to nothing in terms of fees, rents or royalties. In many parts of the country, Hurley reported, long-term monitoring of vital aquifers is almost non-existent. No regulatory body in Canada has set up a program to trace methane and other contaminants in shallow and deep groundwater in areas of intense hydrocarbon drilling.[58]

New National Regulations on Wastewater Inadequate

For at least a decade, there have been calls for national, enforced regulations regarding the discharge of wastewater facilities in Canada. While the federal government had some real authority to require that effluent from wastewater plants meet a "deleterious substance" test, it rarely and inconsistently used it, choosing instead to track pollutants emitted from the biggest industrial and municipal source points. So plans for national wastewater regulations were welcomed.

In 2012, the federal government announced its Wastewater Systems Effluent Regulations under the Fisheries Act, claiming that it was stepping up to the plate on this issue. The act sets national minimum standards on a number of deleterious substances in the effluents of wastewater treatment plants. They list suspended solids, total residual chlorine and un-ionized ammonia as "deleterious" substances. Of the 3,700-wastewater facilities operating in Canada when the new regulations were adopted, almost one quarter did not meet the new standards.[59]

However there are some concerns with the regulations. The majority of the costs must be borne by municipalities, many of which will have great trouble raising funds to pay for the changes. The greatest concern is that operators of "high-risk" facilities — at least 136 plants — have until 2021 to upgrade while the compliance deadline for "medium-risk" plants is 2031 and "low-risk" plants, 2041.

Nor do the new rules set reduction targets or standards for combined storm sewer overflows (CSOs), a major source of sewage discharge in older cities. A loophole could see high- and medium-risk plants extend their compliance timelines from 2021 and 2031 to 2041 if they opt to deal with CSOs at the same time. And the new rules do not apply at all to systems in the Northwest Territories, Nunavut and north of the 54th parallel in Quebec and Newfoundland and Labrador.

Ecojustice says the new regulations will allow raw sewage to be legally dumped into Canada's water until 2041, jeopardizing lakes, rivers and groundwater. Canadians were expecting real leadership on this crucial issue, but instead many cities were given a 28-year free pass to continue dumping sewage into Canada's water. Ecojustice notes that the new regulations actually contradict the intent of the Fisheries Act under which they fall.[60]

Lake Ontario Waterkeeper's Mark Mattson says when the city of Montreal discharged almost 5 billion litres of raw sewage into the St. Lawrence in November 2015 (given the green light by the brand new Liberal environment minister Catherine McKenna), it became clear that the new rules were not working. For the same year that the Harper government brought in the Wastewater Systems Effluent Regulations, it also gutted the Fisheries Act. Under the new rules, it is much easier for a municipality to get permits for construction-related sewage releases, while responsibility for enforcing parts of the act can be downloaded to the provinces. While it is unclear whether Montreal had actually entered into an agreement with the federal government giving it this authority, it acted as if it was free to pollute the St. Lawrence River and no one said otherwise.[61]

Still No National Drinking Water Standards

Unlike most other industrialized countries, Canada still has no national drinking water standards. In July 2014,

Ecojustice released its latest national drinking water report card, the fourth since the terrible Walkerton *E. coli* outbreak in 2000. "Waterproof: Standards" is highly critical of Canada's drinking water standards and management. In its first report card, published in 2001, Ecojustice found that in most Canadian provinces and territories, laws were not strong enough to ensure drinking water safety. The report examined Canadian guidelines for drinking water quality and compared them to corresponding frameworks in the United States, Europe and Australia as well as the standards recommended by the World Health Organization.

"The findings are troubling," say lead authors Randy Christensen and Dr. Elaine MacDonald. While Canada has, or is tied for, the strongest standard for 24 substances, it has, or is tied for, the weakest for another 27. And in 105 others, Canada has no standard at all. Nor does Canada have any microbiological water treatment standards to ensure that we are protected from waterborne pathogens, such as the *E. coli* that caused the Walkerton disaster, killing seven and hospitalizing hundreds.[62]

Instead of national drinking water standards, the federal government has voluntary national guidelines. They list 75 contaminants that should regularly be tested for. However, in a June 2015 cross-Canada investigation, the CBC found that many Canadian cities are falling short of testing for all the contaminants recommended in the Health Canada guidelines. The broadcaster asked 18 cities in every province and territory to provide a list of the health-related contaminants they test in their water supplies. Only Ottawa tests for all 75. Several, including Calgary, Edmonton and Halifax, test for all but one. Quebec City tests for 62, Regina for 52, Winnipeg 49, St. John's 26 and Iqaluit for just 20.[63]

This is not good enough. Access to safe, clean drinking water is a health and human rights issue and our lack of strong, binding national water standards perpetuates inequity in water quality across the country, particularly in First Nations communities.

Saving ELA ~

The Experimental Lakes Area (ELA) is an internationally known research station in the Kenora district of Ontario whose 58 lakes are an open-air laboratory for research on what makes water sick and what makes it well again. Set up in 1968, the location was chosen by the Canadian and Ontario governments for its isolation, as it was important to find a site as unaffected by human and industrial activity as possible. The ELA was part of Canada's commitment to the International Joint Commission to study water pollution issues, such as eutrophication, that were beginning to plague the Great Lakes. The ELA attracted a stellar group of freshwater scientists, including the late John Vallentyne and David Schindler.

Early research showed just how badly nutrient overloads of phosphorus and nitrogen could affect a lake and helped explain the dead zone in Lake Erie. Research at the ELA produced crucial evidence about the effects of acid rain on lakes and led to the discovery that phosphates from household detergents caused harmful algal blooms. It studied the impacts of mercury on fish and showed how wetland flooding for hydroelectricity leads to increased production of greenhouse gases. Its research demonstrated the accumulative effect on boreal lakes of global warming, acidification and ozone depletion and showed that climate change is having severe and previously unrecognized effects on lakes and their habitat. Research on acid rain led to the air quality agreement between Canada and the United States in 1991.

Research from the ELA generated hundreds of scientific articles, graduate theses, contributions to books and papers and data reports. Many dozens of young scientists have done the research for their Master's and Ph.D. dissertations at the ELA. *Nature* magazine wrote, "The ELA has attracted scientists from around the world to its shores since research started there in 1968. It is possibly the only place where aquatic scientists can use lakes and their ecosystems as test tubes as well as having access to long-term environmental data and a decent place to sleep and eat."[64]

On May 17, 2012, the Harper government announced the cancellation of its funding for the ELA. The Department of Fisheries and Oceans said that the ELA doors would close for good on March 31, 2013, and ordered staff to start removing their equipment from the sites. The government also instructed the scientists and researchers not to talk to the media. The fallout was immediate. Years of neglect had left many ELA positions unfilled and a number of the remaining scientists packed their bags and dispersed.

Reaction in Canada and around the world was immediate and intense. Jim Elser, an aquatic ecologist at Arizona State University who worked at the site in the 1990s, told *Nature* that it was comparable to the U.S. government shutting down Los Alamos — the most important nuclear-physics site — or taking the world's best telescope and turning it off. David Schindler said that there would be no way to replicate the research done at the ELA in a university or a laboratory. "If you try to base policy on small-scale experiments, you miss some key ecosystem processes. And that can have huge implications."

Diane Orihel was one of Schindler's Ph.D. students and had spent a decade of summers at the ELA site. She was devastated by the news. Quiet by nature, she was not one to seek the spotlight or organize protests. She told the media that it was her obligation to step up because the gag order to staff did not apply to her as a student. She put her thesis on hold to fight the ELA closure. David Schindler was both upset by this disruption to her career and proud of her courage.

Within weeks, she set up Save ELA, a national organization made up of hundreds of the most prestigious scientists in the country. She brought in many environmental allies including Boreal Action, Ecojustice and the Manitoba Wilderness Committee, and grassroots social justice organizations such as the Council of Canadians, whose chapters organized for local action. In June, she brought a petition signed by almost 12,000 Canadians to Ottawa and was one of the organizers for the July "Death of Evidence" rally on Parliament Hill that brought out an unprecedented 2,000 scientists to demand an end to the Harper war on science. That petition would grow to more than 30,000 and be tabled 140 times in the House of Commons.

The Harper government was unrelenting. During the winter of 2013, work crews had started to dismantle the cabins and labs at the site. But the Save ELA team had come up with a solution. In April, with financial support from the governments of Ontario and Manitoba, the

International Institute for Sustainable Development took over the running of the ELA. While a great deal needs to be done to bring this world-renowned facility back to its former stature, and while it should never have been removed as a federal government research institution in the first place, the possibility is now there to rebuild the ELA.

Diane Orihel went back and finished her Ph.D. and is now engaged in postdoctoral studies at the University of Ottawa. Asked three years later how she feels about this fight, she says, "There was no question in my mind as to whether the ELA was worth saving. Like arriving at the scene of an accident, you help because every human life is precious and worth saving. So it was with the ELA — a one-of-a-kind living laboratory to study whole lake ecosystems. The lesson I took from the fight to save the ELA was the power of people coming together. I was amazed by how this cause mobilized people from across the country, even across the world. It was through the concerted effort of tens of thousands of caring people that the ELA lives on today."

three

First Nations on the Front Line

On a warm sunny day in April 2015, I did what countless others in the Shoal Lake 40 First Nation do every year and took my life in my hands. I crossed a large stretch of ice clearly melting in some places to reach an island where the community lives just off the Manitoba-Ontario border near Kenora. Every now and then, our group would hear a loud "crack" and steer away to find safer footing. In recent memory, nine people have died falling through the ice trying to cross in the fall and spring when the ice is unsafe, say the elders.

Shoal Lake 40 has been living with a Drinking Water Advisory (DWA) longer than all but one other First Nation in Canada — almost 20 years. Their ancestors lived not on this island but on the shores of Shoal Lake. A century ago, their land was expropriated and the band was forced to move to a peninsula when crews arrived to build a 140-kilometre aqueduct to provide water to the city of Winnipeg. The island was created when crews carved a channel through the peninsula that connected them to the mainland. Some of the band (now Shoal Lake 39) stayed on shore and some (now Shoal Lake 40) stayed on what is now an island. A dam was then built to divert the clean water of Shoal Lake to the Winnipeg aqueduct and the residents of Shoal Lake 40 were left with access only to the tannin-laden, boggy water of Falcon Lake.

We were there to see how the several hundred people of this community survive, cut off from the mainland with only an old barge to haul people, food, cars, medicines and water back and forth. As Stewart Redsky, a member of the band and our guide for the day, explained, "This body of water is like a time capsule. Shoal Lake 40 is many years behind in our development, yet we are 20 kilometres from the Trans-Canada Highway. Today you will see the results of what was done by humans to supply Winnipeg's drinking water — on the better side of the aqueduct."

Our first stop was the community centre where Cuyler Cotton, a policy analyst to the Shoal Lake First Nation, gave us a tour of the Museum of Canadian Human Rights Violations, a direct reference to the new Canadian Human Rights Museum in Winnipeg. There we learned that the first group sent out to assess whether the water of Shoal Lake would be good to provide Winnipeg with its drinking water reported that the area was largely uninhabited "with the exception of a few Indians."

We saw raw sewage running in the streets and hills of garbage and full septic tanks piled high in the woods. In the 1990s, water systems were installed in homes, but inadequate treatment makes that water unsafe to drink. The residents are forced to cook and bathe in low-grade

Falcon River water so contaminated that people have to put washcloths over their taps to catch debris.

Andrea Harden-Donahue, climate justice campaigner for the Council of Canadians, was on the tour as well and described what she saw and felt: "The tour ended in the recreational room off the community centre with two pool tables which also now house rows of large bottles of water after the previous building's floor collapsed under the weight." When Redsky said, "Imagine your family, your elder picking up one of these to make their tea every morning, to make their food," Harden-Donahue took it personally. "I lifted the heavy bottle. I imagined bathing my young son in that water."[65]

After years of struggle, finally there was a light at the end of the tunnel. On December 17, 2015, in the Manitoba legislature, then Manitoba premier Greg Selinger, Canada's Indigenous and Northern Affairs minister Carolyn Bennett and Winnipeg mayor Brian Bowman pledged the needed funding to build a "Freedom Road" to connect the band to the mainland. Shoal Lake chief Erwin Redsky said that a century ago, the thousands of acres of land taken from his people started a "cascade of human rights abuses" and he paid homage to "those who have brought us to this present opportunity for reconciliation."

And on April 28, 2016, Prime Minister Justin Trudeau spent seven hours with the Shoal Lake 40 community, hauling water and speaking to children. He was clearly deeply moved by the hardship he witnessed. Of his government's commitment to build Freedom Road, he said, "It's about doing the right thing, about doing the fair thing."

Shoal Lake 40 may have a terrible record for the length of time it has been under a water advisory (only the Neskantaga First Nation in northern Ontario has a worse record by a year), but it is far from alone. As of winter 2016, there were 163 Drinking Water Advisories in 119 First Nations communities, an increase from 2014. Most DWAs in indigenous communities are boil-water advisories. However there are a number of First Nations communities under a "do not consume" order.

Health Canada lists various reasons for the DWAs, including "unacceptable microbiological quality, inadequate disinfection or disinfectant residuals, operation of system would compromise public health, significant deterioration in source water quality, unacceptable turbidity (cloudiness) or particle count and equipment malfunction during treatment or distribution."[66]

An October 2015 CBC investigative report found that two-thirds of First Nations have been under at least one water advisory between 2004 and 2014. The numbers show that 400 of 618 First Nations in Canada have had some kind of water problem in that decade. Ninety-three percent of all First Nations in Saskatchewan and New Brunswick reported advisories. Alberta's was 87%. Moreover, the number of advisories climbed steadily in those years.[67]

But as Emma Lui of the Council of Canadians points out, even these statistics don't tell the whole story. The advisories only cover households with water piping or systems. Close to 2,000 First Nations homes are without any water system in their homes at all.[68]

The Nazko First Nation of interior B.C. was under a "do not consume" advisory for 17 years after high levels of arsenic and manganese were found in the water. Residents told the CBC that they could not even brush their teeth with their tap water and when they took a shower, it smelled like bleach. Nazko chief Stuart Alec said, "We live in Canada but on reserve it feels like Third World conditions. Drinking, bathing — it's pretty appalling these conditions exist in this country."

The Pinaymootang First Nation in Manitoba has dealt with years of brown baths and bottled water. The Kitigan Zibi Anishinabeg First Nation in western Quebec has been under a "do not consume" advisory since 1999 due to high levels of naturally occurring uranium in the groundwater.

For half a century, the First Nations of Grassy Narrows and Whitedog in northwestern Ontario have suffered terrible mercury poisoning caused by effluent dumping from a chemical company and a pulp and paper mill into the Wabigoon-English River system.

A January 2015 report found that mercury continues to rise in some lakes in the area. Freshwater scientist Patricia Sellers said that "staggering levels of mercury" are buried deep in the sediment at Clay Lake, which acts as a kind of settling pond for the contaminants. Remediation measures recommended 30 years ago were never implemented. The communities are still showing symptoms of mercury poisoning, including weakness in limbs, loss of motor function, difficulty speaking and swallowing and developmental delays and physical abnormalities in children.[69]

Sometimes the communities are in remote areas, but sometimes they are close to wealthy cities and the contrast is stark. Sometimes they are near water systems so clean, big transnational companies want to exploit them.

Nestlé is seeking to purchase the Middlebrook Well in Elora, Ontario, near Guelph. The well sits on the traditional territory of the Six Nations of the Grand River — the most populous in the country — where over 11,000 people have not had access to clean, running water for decades. As many as four out of five homes are not connected to water-lines and families depend on wells that in recent decades have become contaminated by runoff from local farms, sewage and industry. As Emma Lui said in the Council of Canadians' submission to the province, it is appalling that Ontario would consider allowing Nestlé to bottle water from the watershed and transport it out of the region when it is so desperately needed there.

Will the Trudeau Government Fix This Travesty?

The water crisis is but one plaguing First Nations in Canada. As the *Globe and Mail*'s André Picard reported, indigenous people are the most vulnerable in the country.

- ~ *Life expectancy*: they will live a decade less.
- ~ *Disability*: they have higher rates and live on average 12 more years with a disability.
- ~ *Infant mortality*: the children die at three times the rate.
- ~ *Suicide*: the rate is six times higher.
- ~ *Chronic disease*: three times the rate of diabetes, more heart disease suffered at a younger age.
- ~ *Infectious diseases*: tuberculosis rates are 16 times higher; HIV/AIDS growing fastest within this population; water-borne diseases like dysentery and shigellosis are common.
- ~ *Environment*: contaminants such as mercury,

PCBs, toxaphene and pesticides stalk the communities.[70]

Dr. Pamela Palmater, associate professor and chair in Indigenous Governance at Ryerson University, reminds us that the worst mistake Canadians could make about the travesty of residential schools is to historicize them. Indian policy is not a sad chapter in our history, she says, but a lethal reality for indigenous people today. There are more children in state care today than during the residential school era. Nationally there are 30,000–40,000 First Nations children in care and in some provinces, such as Manitoba, indigenous children represent 90% of all kids in care.[71]

The continuing lack of access to clean water in First Nations communities today is perhaps the greatest evidence of Palmater's assertion.

During the 2015 federal election, Justin Trudeau promised to end the crisis of tainted water on First Nations within five years. Citing the high level and chronic presence of boil-water advisories in First Nations communities, he said, "A Canadian government led by me will address this as a top priority because it's not right in a country like Canada. This has gone on for far too long."[72]

Will he be able to succeed? Certainly it is clear that repairing the troubled relationship between the Canadian government and First Nations is a priority for Trudeau. Among his first acts upon taking power was establishing an inquiry on murdered and missing indigenous women and promising implementation of the recommendations of the Truth and Reconciliation Commission. And he did set aside serious funding to address the water crisis in First Nations communities in his first budget (see chapter nine). But he will have his work cut out for him on this front.

For one thing, there are a number of jurisdictions involved. For First Nations south of the 60th parallel, responsibility is shared between the government of Canada and the First Nations themselves, explains Health Canada. Chief and council are responsible for planning and developing their facilities for drinking water, and they are responsible for the day-to-day operation of water and wastewater systems, including sampling and testing. Indigenous and Northern Affairs Canada (formerly Aboriginal Affairs and Northern Development Canada) provides funding for water services and infrastructure such as the treatment facilities as well as financial support for training and certification of operators. Many First Nations say that this responsibility is not being met.

Health Canada is responsible for ensuring that water quality monitoring programs are in place and monitored themselves. It is Health Canada that recommends Drinking Water Advisories. Environment Canada develops standards, guidelines and protocols for wastewater treatment and provides advice and technical expertise. The territories are responsible for First Nations and Inuit communities above the 60th parallel.

However, it is the provinces that manage and govern water resources, and that includes the source water from which First Nations draw their water supply. This creates a problem, said Lalita Bharadwaj, toxicologist and associate professor of public health at the University of Saskatchewan, because First Nations have their primary relationship with the federal government and there aren't the mechanisms in place in the provincial sphere to manage drinking water. First Nations get left in a vacuum, their water management support falling into the jurisdictional divides of the federal and provincial governments.

To add to the mess, there has not been consistent annual monitoring of First Nations water supply. "So when you think about it," she said, "water regulation and governance involves multi-institutions and is fragmented, because individual government agencies don't talk to each other." Bharadwaj said progress will require all the federal and provincial agencies coming to one table to build a new way forward.[73]

Recovering from the Harper Government's Decisions

Then there is the legacy of Stephen Harper. Water protection budgets were not the only ones gutted.

In 2010, the government cut all funding to the First Nations Child and Family Caring Society after it and the Assembly of First Nations (AFN) filed a complaint with the Canadian Human Rights Tribunal in 2007 over the fact that children who live on-reserve receive substantially less welfare than children living off-reserve. The AFN budget for child and family services was cut 85%.

The case dragged on for years, but in January 2016, the tribunal agreed with the plaintiffs and ruled that, indeed, the federal government has been discriminating against First Nations children in failing to provide the same level of care that exists elsewhere. The ruling is a wake-up call for a government also responsible for clean water in these same communities. "This historic decision could have a profound impact on how the government of Canada funds other on-reserve programs and services," said Marie-Claude Landry, chief commissioner with the Canadian Human Rights Commission.[74]

The 2012 budget also targeted projects aimed at improving

the health of First Nations communities. All funding was cut to the National Aboriginal Health Organization, which had been working to advance the health of First Nations, Metis and Inuit people since 2000. All of the Native Women's Association of Canada's funding for its health programs was terminated. The Pauktuutit (the national organization representing Inuit women in Canada) also lost all of its health-care funds, as did the Metis National Council. The Inuit Tapiriit Kanatami (the national Inuit organization) and the Assembly of First Nations each lost 40%.

What was the motive of the Harper government in drastically cutting these funds? Mohawk policy analyst and writer Russell Diabo believes that by destroying the infrastructure of those movements and organizations speaking for First Nations, the government was attempting to make protest and resistance harder. The Conservative government had a very aggressive resource development plan. The less collective clout First Nations had, the less power they had to stop, or even shape, resource development in their communities.[75]

The 2006 Conservative Party platform clearly stated its intention to replace the Indian Act and devolve full legal and economic responsibility to individual indigenous people for their own affairs. This would set the stage for the slow but inevitable removal of the federal government from its constitutional obligations to First Nations.

Federal Law Falls Far Short of Promise

In 2013, the Safe Drinking Water for First Nations Act was passed "to allow the federal government to develop, in partnership with First Nations, enforceable federal regulations to ensure access to safe, clean and reliable drinking water; the effective treatment of wastewater; and the protection of sources of drinking water on First Nations lands" — all good goals at first blush.

But there have been serious problems. The funds allotted to the project — $323 million over two years — were totally insufficient. The Assembly of First Nations criticized the government for imposing new responsibilities and costs on First Nations through the enactment of this law without the resources to finance them. It said that, at minimum, $4.7 billion was needed to properly address the water crises on First Nation communities.

And there is more. A clause in the act appears to weaken indigenous and treaty rights if it is necessary to ensure the safety of water on First Nations lands. The act contains an immunity clause against the federal government for any lawsuits for injury caused by poor-quality water and outlaws payments to satisfy claims against it. The act does not recognize First Nations entitlement.

The act allows the federal government to "enter into an agreement for the administration and enforcement of regulations" with the provinces or with corporations. This sets the stage for off-loading authority to the provinces and opens the door to the privatization of water management.

Given how strongly the Harper government promoted public-private partnerships in Canadian municipalities needing to upgrade their water infrastructure, it is no coincidence that a law establishing strong new regulatory standards unaccompanied by sufficient funding would offer the private sector a way in to this new arena.

Karen Busby, a law professor of law and the director of the Centre for Human Rights Research at the University of Manitoba, said, "The goal [of the act] is a laudable one, but the way the federal government has gone about it in this bill not only lacks substance and principle, but is doomed to failure without First Nations involvement, infrastructure support and access to capital. First Nations organizations are right to be concerned."[76]

At the Special Chiefs Assembly in December 2015, the Assembly of First Nations under its new leader, National Chief Perry Bellegarde, adopted a resolution calling for the complete repeal of the Safe Drinking Water for First Nations Act.

A Need to Break with Bad Laws and Practices

This is the situation the Trudeau government faces as it makes its plans to fulfil its promises. To move forward, it will have to repeal this law and replace it with one that recognizes the inherent rights of First Nations in Canada. It will have to commit serious funds to the process, backing away from the Harper plan to devolve responsibility away from the federal government. It will have to bring all the players together to clarify responsibilities and roles. It will have to undo the changes the Harper government made to the key water regulations — the Fisheries Act, the Navigable Waters Protection Act and the Canadian Environmental Assessment Act.

The Trudeau government will have to follow its instincts to curb runaway resource development and to consult in a true and meaningful way with First Nations about the type and speed of development in their territories.

It will have to give up its promotion of public-private partnerships (P3s) when it comes to water services. In a November 2014 speech to the Canadian Council for

Public-Private Partnerships, Trudeau talked about the need to fix the "shameful lack of investment" in First Nations communities and said their desperate need for infrastructure represents an opportunity for private sector investment and P3s. I believe that allowing for-profit corporations to run private water services in indigenous communities is a recipe for disaster.

Recognizing Inherent and Charter Water Rights

The Trudeau government will also have to recognize that, in light of the water and sanitation crisis in First Nations communities, Canada is violating its own Charter of Rights and Freedoms as well as the human rights to water and sanitation defined by the United Nations and the inherent water rights of indigenous people in Canada.

David Boyd, a law professor at Simon Fraser University and an expert on environmental and constitutional law, asserts that indigenous people have clearly established constitutional rights under two sections of the Canadian Charter of Right and Freedoms — 7, that guarantees the right to life, liberty and security, and 15, that guarantees the right to equality. As well, he points to section 36 of the Constitution Act of 1982 that obliges governments to provide "essential public services of reasonable quality to all Canadians."

Boyd calls for the recognition of the right to water as implicit in the Canadian Constitution, saying this would provide accountability, offer remedies and ensure non-discrimination. "If Canada's Constitution, including the Charter of Rights and Freedoms, cannot be extended to provide relief to individuals deprived of their human right to water, a deprivation that causes severe health effects, violates their dignity and flouts the principle of environmental justice, then the Constitution is not a living tree but is merely dead wood."[77]

In June 2016, Human Rights Watch released a damning report on water safety on First Nations reserves in Ontario, "Make It Safe: Canada's Obligation to End the First Nations Water Crisis." The report documents the impact of ongoing water crises across the reserves and lays the responsibility firmly at the federal government's feet for failing to build a regulatory framework that would set standards for water safety. Lead researcher Amanda Klasing said, "Despite significant investments in the sector, the Canadian government has failed to bring the water and sanitation conditions on reserves up to the standards most Canadians enjoy. Funding alone does not indicate success."[78]

In March 2016, the hereditary chiefs of two northern B.C. First Nations — the Nadleh Whut'en and Stellat'en — proclaimed the first traditional indigenous water laws in the province. No development will be allowed in their territories unless the proponents can assure the communities that surface waters will "remain substantially unaltered in terms of water quality and flow." They will have to enter into a complex set of consultations about each and every waterway, including collecting data on historical water quality and cultural use. The leaders said that frustration over the lack of protection from provincial and Canadian laws drove them to look to their own traditional laws.[79]

Merrell-Ann Phare, executive director and legal counsel to the Centre for Indigenous Environmental Resources at the University of Winnipeg, reminds us that the First Nations were here, occupying the lands and governing their traditional territories, when Europeans first arrived.

Their presence for thousands of years before European settlement combined with the existence of their distinctive cultures, traditions and social systems form the legal basis for the recognition of inherent indigenous rights today. Not only does the government have to recognize international human rights obligations in this regard, it must formally recognize traditional indigenous water rights as well.[80]

The land and care for the land and water is the founding source of First Nations identity and culture and is captured in each nation's laws, say the Chiefs of Ontario. These inherent rights were not "endowed" by any other state or nation, they explain, but recognized by oral treaties negotiated on the basis of mutual respect and trust. Treaties are living international agreements that to this day affirm the sovereign relationship between Canada and First Nations. This is why, say the chiefs, free, prior and informed consent is required before any development decisions are made that may have an impact on their inherent rights.

Free, prior and informed consent is the cornerstone of the UN Declaration on the Rights of Indigenous Peoples (UNDRIP) and is included in the outcome document of the September 2014 UN World Conference on Indigenous Peoples. The Harper government refused to recognize the UN declaration, saying that free, prior and informed consent "could be interpreted as providing a veto to Aboriginal groups and in that regard, cannot be reconciled with Canadian law as it exists. . . . As a result, Canada cannot associate itself with the elements contained in this outcome document related to free, prior and informed consent."[81]

However, on May 10, 2016, the Trudeau government officially adopted the UN Declaration on the Rights of Indigenous People "without qualification," a huge breakthrough on the long road to reconciliation. The announcement was made by Indigenous Affairs Minister Carolyn Bennett to a standing ovation at the UN Permanent Forum on Indigenous Issues in New York. Chief Wilton Littlechild, a Cree lawyer and former commissioner of the Truth and Reconciliation Commission, said that this move allows the government and First Nations to start a new journey together.[82]

The United Nations Adds Its Voice

It is not only in Canada, of course, that there are serious problems with the lack of access to clean water. Almost one billion people worldwide do not have access to clean drinking water and 2.5 billion do not have access to sanitation. For several decades, a growing chorus of voices has called for the UN to deal with this crisis and on July 28, 2010, the United Nations General Assembly adopted a historic resolution recognizing the human rights to clean drinking water and sanitation as "essential for the full enjoyment of the right to life."

Two months later, the UN Human Rights Council adopted a second resolution, adding that the human rights to water and sanitation are derived from the right to an adequate standard of living and, as well, from the right to life and human dignity. The council affirmed that governments have primary responsibility for the realization of these new rights and recommended that they pay special attention to vulnerable and marginalized groups, adopt effective regulatory frameworks for all service providers and ensure effective remedies for violations. In Canada, of course, this would refer to indigenous people.

The council's resolution went further than that of the General Assembly in that it specified that these new rights entail legally binding obligations and declared emphatically, "The right to water and sanitation is a human right, equal to all other human rights, which implies that it is justiciable and enforceable."

These two resolutions represented an extraordinary breakthrough in the international struggle for the right to safe drinking water and sanitation and is a crucial milestone in the fight for water justice.

Stephen Harper was in power that year. It is a sad reality that under his leadership, Canada led the opposition to the UN recognition of the human rights to water and sanitation. It wasn't until all countries adopted "The Future We Want," the outcome document of the 2012 United Nations Conference on Sustainable Development (Rio+20), that Canada finally agreed to recognize these rights.

Applying the Right to Water in Canada

Three obligations are imposed on states with this recognition of the human rights to water and sanitation.

The first is the "obligation to fulfil," whereby governments are required to adopt any additional measures directed toward the realization of the right to water and facilitate access by providing water and sanitation services in communities where none exist.

Canada must acknowledge that the systemic and long-running lack of access to clean water and sanitation for First Nations clearly violates this. The Canadian government, working in cooperation with First Nations and the provinces, must come up with a plan of action to meet its obligation to fulfil and adopt the necessary measures to do so.

The second is the "obligation to respect," whereby governments must refrain from any action or policy that interferes with the rights to water and sanitation. This means that no one should be denied essential water services because of an inability to pay.

The obligation to respect is a clear call to the federal government to clarify its fiduciary responsibly to ensure clean drinking water and sanitation on First Nations communities and not change the rules in a way that would interfere with these rights. Turning the running of water services over to for-profit corporations would change the rules in a profound way, as those who cannot pay for higher water rates could have their services cut off under a public-private partnership model. The recent crises in Detroit and other American inner cities are clear proof that cut-offs have not been exaggerated.

The third is the "obligation to protect," whereby governments are obliged to prevent third parties from interfering with the enjoyment of the human right to water. Governments must protect local communities from pollution and water destruction.

This means that the federal government has to prevent third parties from contaminating the water supplies of Canadian communities, including First Nations, and it means that assessments of all energy, mining, fracking and other industrial projects must be examined and judged within this context.

A rash of recent court cases show that First Nations are beginning to use the courts effectively to assert their right to water and to protect the waters in their territory.

In June 2014, four Alberta First Nations — the Tsuu T'ina, Ermineskin, Aundeck Omni Kaning and Blood — took the federal government to court over what they call the deplorable state of their drinking water. They are asking the federal government to upgrade their water systems, provide continuing support to keep them operating safely and refund money they have saved the government over the years by not doing so. The failure to ensure clean water is systemic discrimination, say the bands.[83] The challenge includes their concerns that the Safe Drinking Water for First Nations Act inflicts onerous new burdens on their people, saying it is not fair to transfer responsibility without the resources to back it up.

And in December 2014, the Mikisew Cree of northern Alberta won a challenge against the Harper omnibus bills that gutted freshwater protections. As Council of Canadians political director Brent Patterson reported, the federal court ruled that the government should have consulted with First Nations before bringing in these legislative changes that removed federal protection for hundreds of streams, rivers and tributaries on First Nations territories.

Mikisew Cree First Nations chief Steve Courtoreille said of the landmark decision that the "Mikisew now expects the federal government and all other governments in Canada to consult with First Nations early on with legislation that may affect our rights. The government should not be afraid of us. We have valuable information and contributions to make on these important issues."

The *Edmonton Journal* reported, "Their win will not affect the legislation that is already in effect, but it requires governments to seek input from affected First Nations in the future before the bills pass." Jessica Clogg, senior counsel with West Coast Environmental Law, added, "The case has the potential to fundamentally change the rules of the game. It was essentially a signal to the federal government — but really all levels of government — that they can't proceed unilaterally with legislation that has the potential to impact on aboriginal treaty rights."[84]

There have been losses. North Cowichan, an amalgamated district on Vancouver Island, planned to dig new wells to provide drinking water for the residents of the town of Chemainus. They were to be built on the edge of the Halalt First Nation and draw water from an aquifer that feeds the Chemainus River — the source of the Halalt's drinking water. In 2011, the B.C. Supreme Court ruled in favour of the Halalt, who opposed the project. The province appealed the decision and won, so the First Nation took its case to the Supreme Court, where it was dismissed in 2013. At issue, explained Halalt lawyer William Andrew, was the question of who owns the groundwater under the reserve and the level of consultation required with First Nations.

But innovative court challenges keep coming. In 2010, Ecojustice launched an important charter challenge on behalf of the Aamjiwnaang First Nation near Sarnia, Ontario, on the effect of industrial pollution on the 800 members of the community who live in "Chemical Valley," surrounded by the chemical companies and oil refineries that account for approximately 40% of Canada's petrochemical industry. The facilities emit tens of millions of kilograms of air pollutants each year and their water supply is so contaminated that it is affecting the endocrine balance of the people who must use it — two girls are being born for every boy.

A Suncor desulphurization plant was built right next to the community cemetery and close to the school. Its emissions stack was lower than the legal minimum height, causing the sulphur emissions to rain directly over the community and settle there, polluting the air, water and land. In 2011, the Ontario environment ministry ordered Suncor to reduce emissions, but the government subsequently allowed it to ramp back up to full capacity.

Ecojustice said that, with this charter challenge, community plaintiffs Ron Plain and Ada Lockridge were attempting to make the unprecedented claim that it is a basic human right to walk outside one's home and not breathe air that is harmful to human health. On the advice of the legal team at Ecojustice, the plaintiffs dropped their case in the spring of 2016, as the government of Ontario finally acknowledged that this situation is intolerable and the team decided to focus their energy on ensuring the government makes good on its new initiatives.

But this case highlighted the need for Canada to approve a constitutional amendment for a right to a healthy environment, as 90 other countries around the world have done. And while this case applied to air pollution, future cases could equally claim that clean water is a constitutional human right.

The last decade has witnessed an unprecedented attack on both water protection and First Nations, but it has also witnessed the blossoming of indigenous activism. Idle No More, a peaceful protest movement founded in 2012 by four women, sprang upon the political scene with force, energizing indigenous communities, inspiring First Nations youth and engaging with a larger civil society movement.

Voter turnout among First Nations in the 2015 election was at its highest ever and First Nations communities and organizations have taken a leadership role that has inspired Canadians across the country. The scene is set for unprecedented collaboration between First Nations and the rest of Canada.

Crystal Lameman, spokeswoman for the Beaver Lake Cree, says that indigenous rights are the last stronghold we have to stop the unmitigated and unregulated expansion of water-destructive extractive development. "But," she adds, "this is no longer an 'Indian' problem. If you breathe air and drink water, this is about you too. It is about the inherent rights of First Nations people, collective basic human rights and the rights of nature."[85]

Lois Frank is a member of the Kainai Nation Blood Reserve in southern Alberta, the largest First Nations territory in Canada. She has a Master's degree in education administration and is working toward her Ph.D. in leadership studies. Lois has had a distinguished career, serving as police commissioner and teacher in her community. She is a lecturer in the Native American Studies Department at the University of Lethbridge and a board member of the Council of Canadians. Her husband, Harley Frank, has held a number of key positions with his nation, including chief, councillor and economic development coordinator. They have four children and seven grandchildren.

On September 9, 2011, Lois Frank, Elle-Máijá Tailfeathers and Jill Crop Eared Wolf were arrested by tribal police while blockading fracking trucks on Blood land. Tailfeathers wrote, "Just got arrested. In the back of the cop car with Lois Frank. Texting with handcuffs." The women, calling themselves Kainai Earth Watch, were protesting a 2010 deal that the tribal council and chief made with U.S. energy company Murphy Oil to explore almost half the reserve land for oil and gas to frack in exchange for $50 million. The women, supported by many people in nearby Lethbridge, were very concerned about the impact such extensive energy exploration and fracking would have on their water, which is called "OhKih" in Blackfoot and means "the source of life."

Harley Frank explains that the Blood Nation's mineral rights were transferred to the federal government in 1910, which holds the authority to grant leases for resource extraction. An energy company wanting to explore on indigenous territory must obtain a permit from Ottawa and all royalties from these operations are held in trust by Indigenous and Northern Affairs. To access these funds, the tribal council must send in a detailed request.

Harley Frank says that many First Nations elected officials are not well versed in the complex world of oil and gas and have been quick to sign leases they later come to regret. The companies come, drill and leave when the oil and gas dry up. Frank says that many of the wells drilled on Blood land decades ago were illegally abandoned and some cannot even be located now.

Lois Frank says that indigenous people struggle with the legacy of an external, imposed governance system of resource management, including little or no control over waters or rivers flowing through their territories. At the time of her arrest, there were over 130 producing oil and gas wells on the Blood Reserve, she reported, with the possibility of another 200 wells in the next few years. "These projects are owned and controlled by energy companies with little or no regard to the conditions in our community and they are indifferent to the consequences of mass extraction. They exploit our lands and our people, poison our water and then leave," she told a Council of Canadians town hall meeting in Lethbridge a year after her arrest. It is reasonable to ask them to obey the law, she added, but it's a different thing to ask them to have a soul and care about her people's pain.

The three women were charged with criminal intimidation. Elle-Máijá Tailfeathers and Jill Crop Eared Wolf had their charges dropped after they agreed to complete a community service program. But Lois Frank pleaded not guilty, insisting she had committed no crime, using the constitution for her defence. She had to go to court seven times and was worried that if she were found guilty under Harper's anti-terrorism laws, she would be labelled a terrorist. But she persevered and in June 2012, all charges against her were dropped.

Asked her thoughts five years later, Lois said that her stand ended up educating many people about their rights. Her arrest went viral and she heard from supporters all over Canada and as far away as the U.K., Australia, the U.S. and Africa. She cites a time honoured "commandment" of her people to explain her commitment: enjoy life's journey but leave no tracks.

four

Where Oil Meets Water

In the fall of 2008, I joined a busload of Council of Canadians staff, board and local chapter members for a site visit to the tar sands of northern Alberta. We drove first to Fort McMurray, where we met with local workers and residents, toured the impressive Oil Sands Discovery Centre and met with Mayor Melissa Blake. Everywhere we were greeted with warmth and welcome. Everywhere we found hardworking people trying to build a liveable community. We also were made very aware that the jobs in the tar sands paid well and were unionized, something our organization supports.

Mayor Blake was gracious and welcoming, even though she knew of our opposition to the expansion of the tar sands. She was also open about her community's challenges. The energy industry was exploding, as was the population, and officials were having a very hard time meeting the need for infrastructure, police, firefighters, parks, schools, hospitals and social services. There were also deep concerns about the serious traffic accidents on Highway 63, the one and only highway leading into and out of the town. In spite of these problems, we all felt we were in a flourishing community where thousands of people from across the country, and even around the world, were building new lives.

Then we toured the tar sands operations themselves and several of us flew over them. I was overwhelmed by the sheer size of the operation and the devastation of the natural environment. It looked like we had landed on the moon. As far as the eye could see, gigantic extractive equipment was mining thick, gooey black tar. There was not a blade of grass or a tree to be seen anywhere. Massive pools of contaminated water sat next to the Athabasca River. From the air, the land separating them looked like thin ribbons. The smell of chemicals and oil was overpowering and gave me a headache within minutes. Every few seconds, gunshots rang out to warn birds not to land on the poisoned lakes. Our bus stopped at the Syncrude site, but when we got out to take a closer look, an executive of the company yelled at us and called her security personnel, who ordered us to move on even though we were on a public highway.

As I watched the horror of the May 2016 fire that destroyed so much of Fort McMurray, these memories — and the mixed emotions they stirred — came back to me. I remembered driving Highway 63 myself as I watched people fleeing, fire embers raining down upon them and felt the terror they must have felt. I hoped no one would be killed, that the town would not be destroyed, that lives so disrupted could one day get back to normal. But I also hoped that we could build future communities in Fort McMurray and elsewhere based on safer and healthier economies.

This is the legacy, and the conundrum, of building an entire economy on an energy source that is, at its core, dangerous to air and water, First Nations communities downstream and, yes, to the workers themselves and their families. To want to stop the expansion of the tar sands and find alternative, more sustainable sources of energy is not to judge those who work in the current system or hope for anything but the best for them.

Depending on Extreme Energy

Canada is the world's fifth largest oil exporter behind China, the U.S., Russia and Saudi Arabia. The country exported two-thirds of its oil production in 2014, 96% of that to the U.S. Oil exports increased 65% in the decade that Stephen Harper was in power. Between 2004 and 2014, Canadian exports soared from 2,148,000 barrels a day to 3,535,000 barrels a day according to British Petroleum's February 2016 annual report on world energy.[86] As conventional sources of energy are drying up in Canada — conventional oil production peaked in 1973 — new, more intensive and environmentally destructive energy extraction methods are being used to meet increased energy demand. They pose a great threat to Canada's waterways.

The University of London's Extreme Energy Initiative defines extreme energy as "a number of energy extraction methods that grow more intensive over time and that are strongly correlated with damage to both the environment and society."[87] This includes tar sands, open-pit mining, mountaintop removal, deep water and Arctic offshore drilling, hydraulic fracturing (fracking) for shale gas and coal bed methane extraction. Biofuels are often also considered extreme energy as they constitute a form of energy production that requires large amounts of water and the removal of land from food production.

This university's think tank warns that extreme energy poses a threat not only to environmental degradation but also to civil and human rights. We have certainly seen this in Canada in relation to vulnerable First Nations communities with their water contamination issues and their disputes with government over land and water rights. The environmental implications of extreme energy extraction methods are dire. For one thing, it requires much more energy to produce. As Canadian journalist and energy expert Andrew Nikiforuk points out, fuels that require lots of energy to make energy ultimately provide fewer returns to society.

At the beginning of the hydrocarbon era, it took one barrel of oil to find and liquidate 100 barrels, resulting in an energy return on energy investment ratio of 100 to 1. This ratio steadily dropped as the deposits of easily accessible oil and gas were depleted. The ratio for U.S. oil production is now approximately 11 to 1. For extraction of Alberta tar sands oil, the ratio is 7 to 1 and drops to 3 to 1 after it has been upgraded and refined into something useful, such as gasoline. This, says Nikiforuk, makes bitumen a "pathetic and tragic" source of energy.[88]

The threat of extreme energy to Canada's vulnerable waterways is real. Large-scale water consumption combined with pollution from the extraction and the risky shipment of chemical-laden energy supplies by pipeline, rail and marine transport jeopardize Canada's lakes and rivers.

Tar Sands Production Threatens Alberta's Water

The Canadian tar sands operation is the largest industrial project on earth. Tar sands (or oil sands) are a type of petroleum deposit of sand, clay and water saturated with a dense form of petroleum called bitumen. It has the consistency of cold molasses and the challenge is to remove the oil from the rest of the mixture. While there are deposits in other countries, over 70% of known reserves are found in Canada, most of it in northern Alberta.

The deposits around Fort McMurray, Peace River and Cold Lake lie under 141,000 square kilometres of boreal forest (an area bigger than Scotland) and contain about 1.7 trillion barrels of bitumen, over 2.3 million of which were processed every day before the spring 2016 fire. The process of extracting the oil from the bitumen is energy intensive and produces 3.2 to 4.5 times more greenhouse gas emissions than conventional oil.

It takes astounding quantities of water to steam-blast oil from the sands. For every barrel of oil recovered from the tar sands, three to five barrels of water are used, according to the Pembina Institute. Currently, approved tar sands operations are licensed to remove a volume of water from the Athabasca River that is more than twice the amount required to meet the annual needs of the city of Calgary. This removal accounts for three-quarters of the river's water, whose summer flows have declined by 30% since 1970.

Environmental Defence, a respected Canadian environmental law NGO, reports that more than 95% of the water drawn from the Athabasca River and used in tar sands operations is too toxic to return to the natural water cycle. After it is used, the water is dumped into lagoons that have become so polluted, birds die on impact. The tailings lakes contain heavy metals and other hydrocarbon pollutants acutely dangerous to aquatic life and human health. Two hundred and twenty square kilometres of these poisoned lakes leach over 11 million litres of toxic water into the watershed every day, reports scientist David Schindler, enough toxic waste to fill Toronto's Rogers Centre two and a half times.[89]

In its 2013 report "Reality Check: Water and the Tar Sands," Environmental Defence said that oil companies are spending millions of dollars on glossy public relations campaigns in the hope that most Canadians won't notice that their operations are having a devastating impact on the province's water. There has been little provincial oversight of toxic tailings and those few regulations that exist have been inadequately enforced. In one year, 2011–2012, for instance, not one company was in compliance with Alberta's 2009 Directive 74, which required modest progress in accelerating the cleanup of the tailings waste.[90]

In March 2015, the provincial government introduced new guidelines on how much water the tar sands companies can extract from the Athabasca River and on the management and production of toxic tailings waste. The Tailings Management Framework and Surface Water Quality Framework claim to set limits on the amount of tailings that can be accumulated and ensure they are treated and reclaimed throughout the life of a project. But environmental watchdog groups slammed the new rules, saying they bowed to corporate interests and favoured oil over water. In fact, they said, the new regulations were a step backward from Directive 74.

The new rules did not include a plan to protect the Athabasca River from catastrophic damage during low-flow events. And it gave a major exemption to Suncor and Syncrude to extract water directly from the river even when water levels are dangerously low. Furthermore, the water management framework is voluntary. The government admitted that the plan depends on companies coming up with solutions and technologies that don't yet exist.[91]

Only months later, with unseasonably low water levels and wildfires raging through Alberta, First Nations and environmentalists north of Fort McMurray asked the government to limit water withdrawals by oil companies on the Athabasca River. Keepers of the Athabasca is a broad alliance of concerned people and groups that live and work in the Athabasca watershed. Its coordinator, Jesse Cardinal, said that the new rules don't take into account the effect of climate change on weather patterns and river flows and that there should be no exemptions from the regulations. "We're beginning to see water crisis situations happening where corporations have access to water before communities do," she said.[92]

Little help appears to be on the way from the federal government. In January 2015, it blocked an investigation into the tailings ponds by the Commission for Environmental Cooperation, NAFTA's watchdog set up to ensure governments follow their own environmental rules. Representatives from the Mexican, American and Canadian governments met behind closed doors and denied the commission's application to look into whether the federal government is failing to enforce the Fisheries Act.[93]

Before the crash in world oil prices, there were plans to expand the tar sands threefold. This, in turn, would consume and poison as much as 20 million barrels of water per day. While some observers are predicting that lower world oil prices will put a halt to growth in tar sands production, a February 2016 report by RBC Capital Markets still posited that production would grow by a further 760,000 barrels a day between 2016 and 2020, to peak at 3.1 million barrels. That means that Canada's overall oil production will climb to 4.6 million barrels a day by 2020. While this growth will be 40% lower than previously expected when oil prices were soaring, this is still a remarkable leap in volume from the two million barrels a day produced in 2000, said the report.[94]

Crude Oil Spills Pose Another Danger

Global News tracks oil spills in Alberta and reported in 2013 that the province has averaged two crude oil spills a day for almost four decades. That is 29,000 crude oil spills and more than 31,000 spills of other substances, including liquid petroleum, to that year. If the rate of spills has remained constant, the number of crude oil spills over the last four decades is now more than 31,000 by 2016 — or 7,750 crude spills per decade.

In July 2015, five million litres of bitumen wastewater and emulsion were found to have leaked from a one-year-old Nexen pipeline south of Fort McMurray. Company officials admitted the spill had actually started earlier and was undetected for at least several weeks. The damage from thousands of smaller spills is unknown, but that does not mean they don't still pose a huge threat to water. Nexen was simply the latest in a long line of horrifying spills.

~   In April 2011, almost 4.5 million litres of
    crude oil leaked near the First Nations com-
    munity of Little Buffalo in northern Alberta,

the largest spill in 35 years, contaminating more than three hectares of beaver ponds and muskeg.

~ In June 2012, almost half a million litres of sour crude leaked into a creek that flows into the Red Deer River about 100 kilometres north of Calgary.

~ Also in June 2012, a pumping station north-east of Edmonton spilled about 230,000 litres of crude and a pipeline spill released 100,000 litres of wastewater, oil and gas near Rainbow Lake, north of the Peace River.

~ In April 2014, an aboveground pipe failure caused 70,000 litres of oil and processed (contaminated) water to spill near Slave Lake.

~ A few months later, about 60,000 litres of crude oil leaked near Red Earth Creek in the northern part of the province.[95]

Global News is critical of the Alberta government's regulatory body, saying its database is messy and missing data. It doesn't include any spills from some of the biggest pipelines, the ones that cross provincial or national borders. And for spills that come from somewhere other than a pipeline, such as oil wells and pumping stations — which represent over half of all spills — anything under 2,000 litres doesn't get counted at all.[96]

Diluted Bitumen — A Very Dirty Oil Source

Alberta energy companies and the Alberta government are promoting new pipelines to get their crude to the coasts where it can be exported. While conventional oil spills are a serious environmental problem, many pipelines are now carrying diluted bitumen as well as conventional oil. Dilbit, as it is also known, is dangerous and toxic, and all proposed new pipelines plan to carry some dilbit.

Since tar sands bitumen is thick and heavy, chemical diluents such as benzene and toluene — known carcinogens — are added to liquefy the bitumen enough to flow through a pipeline. Dilbit will float briefly in water but it then sinks as the light components evaporate, leaving the heavy components behind. This makes dilbit substantially more difficult to clean up and poses a greater danger to watersheds than conventional crude.

On July 25, 2010, an Enbridge pipeline ruptured outside of Marshall, Michigan. It took the company 17 hours to stop the flow, allowing almost 4 million litres of chemical-laced Alberta tar sands bitumen to spill into the nearby Kalamazoo River. Air pollution from the evaporation of the chemicals forced the evacuation of local families and businesses. The heavy oil inundated local marshes and wetlands and sank to the bottom of the river. Enbridge tried to remediate the area but the Environmental Protection Agency said that the damage of dredging the river was worse than the effects of the spill. The cleanup expense has topped $1 billion yet the damage remains widespread.[97]

A Canadian government–commissioned study obtained in February 2015 by Greenpeace through an access to information request admitted that very little is known about the impacts of bitumen spills and laid out ten "knowledge gaps" that should be researched. "Very little information is available on the physical and chemical characteristics of oil sands–related products following a spill into water," it said. "Research on the biological effects of oil sands–related products on aquatic organisms is lacking . . . A better understanding of the fate and behaviour of these products is critical for assessing the potential risk to aquatic organisms." The authors reported that Orimulsion, a Venezuelan bitumen product, is 300 times more toxic to embryos than heavy fuel oil and is "highly toxic to fish."[98]

The U.S. National Academy of Sciences recently concluded the most comprehensive review of diluted bitumen spills to date. It confirms the experience of the Kalamazoo spill that bitumen sinks quicker than conventional oil. The scientists further concluded that first responders and companies are not prepared to handle diluted bitumen spills.[99]

The Energy East Pipeline

In spite of the low price of oil, the energy industry and most governments in Canada are still trying to build or convert existing pipelines to take bitumen to an ocean where it can be shipped by tanker around the world. Pipeline proponents were taken aback when President Obama vetoed the Keystone pipeline and lobbied hard to promote two western pipelines: Northern Gateway, which would carry dilbit across 800 rivers and streams to the northern B.C. coast, and Kinder Morgan Trans Mountain pipeline, which would pass across dozens of waterways, five provincial parks, Jasper National Park, through critical salmon-bearing watersheds and across the Fraser River to the B.C. coast at Burnaby. If built, it would result in six times more oil tankers off Canada's fragile and difficult-to-navigate west coast.

For a while, because of fierce opposition led by First Nations and communities along both routes, it appeared these projects were unlikely to move ahead. In November 2015, the Trudeau government announced a moratorium on oil tanker traffic on the northern coast of British Columbia, and on June 30, 2016, the Federal Court of Appeal over-turned the government's approval of Enbridge's Northern Gateway Pipeline after finding that Ottawa failed to prop-erly consult the First Nations affected. In January 2016, the B.C. government said it would oppose Kinder Morgan (which would be a twin to an existing pipeline) before the National Energy Board because the company has not pro-vided a plan to prevent or respond to an oil spill.

However, negotiations appear to be underway between the governments of B.C. and Alberta to export Site C power to Alberta (with federal subsidies) in exchange for allowing a western pipeline to be built. As well, in May 2016, the National Energy Board recommended that the federal government approve the expansion of the Kinder Morgan pipeline, albeit with a number of conditions. A panel has been set up to consult with the public before the Trudeau government makes its decision later in the year. If this project is given the green light, opposition in B.C. that includes the municipalities of Vancouver and Burnaby will be strongly reactivated.

Many pipeline proponents are banking on Trans-Canada's Energy East, a 4,500-kilometre pipeline that would stretch from Hardisty, Alberta, to Saint John, New Brunswick, and possibly Cape Breton, Nova Scotia. Energy East would carry up to 1.1 million barrels per day of west-ern crude, including tar sands bitumen and fracked Bakken shale gas, making it the largest tar sands pipeline in North America. The project would consist of converting one of

TransCanada's existing 3,000-kilometre, 40-year-old natural gas pipelines to carry oil and connecting it with a new pipeline through Quebec to the east coast.

Energy East would pose a grave risk of dilbit spills to the thousands of waterways it would cross on its path, as documented in a report by Andrea Harden-Donahue and Emma Lui of the Council of Canadians.[100] In January 2014, one of TransCanada's mainline pipelines, the same system that will see a pipe converted for Energy East, experienced a massive natural gas explosion close to Winnipeg that left over 4,000 people without heat. A month later, CBC reported that it had unearthed a critical report the National Energy Board had effectively buried. The report detailed a July 2009 rupture on the company's Peace River mainline that sent 50-metre flames into the air and razed a two-hectare wooded area.[101]

Evan Vokes was a pipeline materials engineer with TransCanada for five years before he was fired in May 2011 for taking his concerns about the company's pipeline safety to the National Energy Board and then the public. He had already brought his concerns about the competency of some pipeline inspectors, the company's lack of compliance with welding regulations and what he called a "poor safety culture" to the executives of TransCanada, but his warnings fell on deaf ears.

At its October 2014 annual general meeting in Hamilton, the Council of Canadians gave Vokes an award for whistleblowing. In his acceptance speech, Vokes talked about the toll this process has taken on his personal life. He said that he had seen "dangerous and blatantly illegal practices you should never see" on TransCanada pipeline sites and wept when he described several pipeline disasters, including the July 2011 rupture of the brand new TransCanada

Bison pipeline in Wyoming — a danger he had warned the company about. He told the audience that he loved his job and is having trouble finding work because of his decision to go public. TransCanada "has fought me to the ends of the earth," said Vokes.

In February 2014, the National Energy Board released an audit of Vokes's complaints and found that the company was not in compliance in several key areas, including hazard identification, risk assessment and control, and inspection and management review. In February 2016, the board ruled that TransCanada had put substandard materials in a pipeline that blew up in 2013, again vindicating Vokes. As the *National Observer*'s Mike De Souza reported, Vokes had correctly identified a safety issue that contributed to the rupture that happened within a few hundred metres of a hunting cabin owned by a Cree family, a move that made him a pariah in the energy industry. "It was only an act of God that multiple members of the Cree family didn't wind up in a barbecue," said Vokes.[102]

In his September 2015 report, "Quantifying Risk," the Council of Canadians' Mark Calzavara quotes National Energy Board statistics that show that TransCanada has the worst safety record in Canada, with 17 full-bore ruptures since 1992, eight of these since 2009 and four between July 2014 and September 2015. Based on the company's Canadian record, if the Energy East pipeline is built, it would have a 15% chance per year of rupturing. Up to 30 million litres of crude could spill from a rupture and leaks as large as 2.6 million litres per day would not be detected by the company's electronic leak detection system.[103]

The threat of these pipelines is made worse by the gutted federal water-protection laws detailed in chapter two. Changes to the Navigable Waters Protection Act allow pipelines to carry crude oil adjacent to and over 99% of all lakes and rivers in Canada. Changes to the Canadian Environmental Assessment Act allowed the Harper government to cancel 3,000 ongoing environmental assessments, including 678 involving fossil fuel energy and 248 involving a pipeline.[104]

Energy East Threatens Thousands of Waterways

The biggest danger of the Energy East pipeline is that it would carry diluted bitumen across at least 2,963 waterways — more than 1,200 in Ontario alone — putting the drinking water of more than 5 million Canadians at risk.[105] It would carry dilbit through ageing pipes across four major watersheds in Alberta — Battle River, Sounding Creek, Red Deer River and the South Saskatchewan River. It would cross another four in Saskatchewan — South Saskatchewan, Qu'Appelle, Souris and Assiniboine. The pipeline runs alongside the sole aqueduct feeding Winnipeg's drinking water, even running two metres below it at one point. A spill there would be catastrophic.

Energy East would traverse the northern tip of Lake Superior. The most remote part of the pipeline — some 75 kilometres of roadless forest — is close to the Nipigon River crossing. A rupture there could go undetected for a long time and see millions of litres of chemical-laced bitumen flow down the Nipigon into Lake Superior. In 1990, a large section of the Nipigon's bank failed at the point where the pipeline crosses the river, leaving a 75-metre stretch of pipeline hanging in mid-air with no support. If the pipeline had been full of oil instead of natural gas, it would have been broken by the sheer weight of the crude. Such a rupture could produce the largest oil spill in Canada's history.

The Energy East route would continue across the top end of the Great Lakes–St. Lawrence River Basin watershed, eventually crossing the St. Lawrence River itself, the source of 50% of Quebec's drinking water and home to the endangered beluga whales. The drinking water sources of North Bay, Ottawa and Montreal all run near the pipeline. It would cross over 800 waterways in Quebec and another 300 in New Brunswick, including the Saint John River, which would threaten the drinking water of Edmundston, Fredericton and Saint John. The number of super tankers in the Bay of Fundy would increase dramatically, and a spill there could destroy the fishery, tourism and farms.

When oil prices make a rebound, the pipeline would make increased production in the tar sands more viable. Experts estimate that production could increase by up to 40%, making it impossible for Canada to meet its climate promises. Alberta's Pembina Institute reports that the crude production needed to fill this pipeline would generate the equivalent in greenhouse gas emissions of more than seven million new cars on the roads each year.[106] It would have Canada producing 1.1 million barrels per day well beyond 2050, the deadline for countries like ours to aim for a transition to 100% renewable energy as recommended by the recently signed Paris climate agreement.

Politicians of all stripes are telling Canadians that they have to support Energy East because it is a "national unity" issue and that this is western energy for eastern Canadians. Nothing could be further from the truth. Canada does not have the capacity to refine tar sands bitumen. "The Oil Price Intelligence Report" explains that it costs about $10 billion to build a new refinery just for conventional oil and takes years to construct. A new one has not been built in Canada since 1984. Upgrading current refineries to deal with tars sands bitumen is cost prohibitive, said the news source. In any case, there is no economic incentive to build new refineries, as Canada already refines more oil than it consumes. Even if Canada could refine Energy East bitumen, it would be for export.[107]

In a 2014 report, several organizations, including the Council of Canadians, Environmental Defence and Équiterre, showed that almost all of Energy East's crude oil would be exported and very little would remain in Canada. Of the 1.1 million barrels a day, between 750,000 and 1 million barrels would be exported to places like the United States, Europe and India.[108]

Nor would building this or any other pipeline reduce the number of rail cars carrying dangerous energy sources. The choice between rail and pipeline is a myth. It is true that there are serious risks associated with transporting oil by rail as the tragic Lac-Mégantic disaster that killed 47 people attests. There must be more regulatory control of this mode of energy transport. But rail in Canada largely carries fracked oil from the Bakken fields of North Dakota, Saskatchewan and Manitoba. It is fracked oil, not tar sands bitumen, that exploded at Lac-Mégantic. The quick production and decline peak of fracked oil makes the faster and more flexible transport by rail desirable to the fracking industry. Therefore, building a pipeline that primarily carries a different form of energy and depends on more stable long-term supplies will not cut down on the use of rail.

The premiers and major political parties have lined up to support the pipeline, but community resistance along the route is fierce and growing. Energy East would pass through 180 different First Nations communities and opposition among many of them is strong.

Red Head is a small New Brunswick community on the Bay of Fundy, not far from Saint John. It is here that the pipeline is proposed to end and where a new deep water marine terminal for up to 115 super tankers a year would be built. A massive oil storage "tanker farm" that would hold over 13 million barrels of bitumen is also planned. In May 2015, over 700 people protested against the Energy East pipeline proposal. Residents said it is inevitable that there would be an accident at some point and they predicted that a major spill would put 5,000 fishery jobs at risk.

The Great Lakes and St. Lawrence River —
Canada's Newest "Carbon Corridor"

Energy East is not the only tar sands threat to the Great Lakes and the St. Lawrence River. This watershed holds over 20% of the world's surface freshwater and 95% of North America's, is home to more than 3,500 species of plants and animals and is the drinking water supply for over 40 million people. Crude oil and fracked gas and oil are being transported around, under and over these waters, posing a risk to this watershed like nothing that has come before.

Canada exports about two-thirds of its oil, including tar sands crude, to the United States. If current expansion plans in the tars sands are realized, an additional 14,000 kilometres of pipeline will be needed to carry the crude to market. Many current and proposed pipelines are in the Great Lakes Basin because the refining of tar sands crude at American refineries has exploded. There are now 66 U.S. refineries processing Alberta bitumen, 19 of them in the Great Lakes states and nine located right on or very near the Great Lakes.[109]

The Flint Hills refinery in Pine Bend, Minnesota, owned by billionaire right-wing advocates Charles and David Koch, refines more tar sands crude than any other refinery in the U.S. Almost 80% of the fuel purchased at gas stations in Minnesota now comes from this Albertan source. The U.S.-based Natural Resources Defense Council says that by 2020, almost one-fifth of the gasoline supply of the northeast and mid-Atlantic states could be derived from tar sands crude.

While TransCanada's Keystone pipeline and the presidential decision to veto it have received widespread media coverage, Enbridge has been quietly building a network of lesser pipelines in the Great Lakes region and, in doing so, getting around American environmental permits and regulations.

The Alberta Clipper pipeline transports Alberta crude, including bitumen, to a refinery in Superior, Wisconsin. In December 2015, the U.S. State Department granted the company the right to double its capacity to 800,000 barrels of bitumen a day at this and other U.S. refineries — about the same volume as Keystone would have held. In a complicated sleight of hand, using its broader network of pipelines, Enbridge avoided the scrutiny to which the single-pipeline Keystone project was subjected.

Inside Climate News, a Pulitzer Prize–winning non-profit news organization, reported that Enbridge is building an 8,000-kilometre network of new and expanded pipelines — called the Lakehead System — that will bring even more tar sands oil into the U.S. than Keystone would have. These plans have escaped public scrutiny and media attention largely because the expansion has proceeded in many segments and phases.[110]

Other pipelines are aging dangerously. One of them is Line 5, a twin pipeline that runs under the Straits of Mackinac in northern Michigan and carries almost 80 million litres of oil and gas each day from Superior, Wisconsin, to Sarnia, Ontario. Built in 1953, it has been described by the U.S. National Wildlife Federation as an "ever present threat" to the Great Lakes. Powerful storm-driven currents in that area make the straits one of the most dangerous places in the Great Lakes for a spill, as the oil would spread quickly and widely.

A significant rupture of Line 5 would be catastrophic. A March 2016 report published by the University of Michigan Water Center warned that 1,160 kilometres of Lake Michigan and Lake Huron shoreline are at risk. The study used hundreds of computer models to mimic a spill and said that an oil slick could travel as far as Manitoulin Island and the South Bruce Peninsula on Lake Huron.[111] Enbridge's own emergency response plans show it would not be possible to shut off the flow of oil immediately and that it would take company crews at last three hours to respond. The National Wildlife Federation said a serious spill would cause an Exxon Valdez–like disaster that would spread and "cause unimaginable damage in the Great Lakes and cripple economies that depend on the lakes."[112]

FLOW, For Love of Water, is a Michigan-based organization founded by environmental lawyer Jim Olson and devoted to protecting the Great Lakes. In 2015, FLOW assembled a team of experts, including several from the energy industry itself, to counter Enbridge's argument that decommissioning Line 5 would disrupt Michigan's crude oil supply. "Our work to date has led to the conclusion that Line 5 in the Straits of Mackinac can be shut down, without resorting to additional oil trains, tank trucks or lake tankers to serve regional refineries, as Enbridge would have you believe," said Gary Street, a retired chemical engineer and former director of engineering at Dow Environmental — AWD Technologies.[113]

The BP refinery in Whiting, Indiana, was recently upgraded to process tar sands oil, and BP asked the state government to allow it to continue its dumping of toxic waste into Lake Michigan. In 2007, the Indiana government had originally permitted the dumping on a temporary basis, citing the need for jobs as its justification. This temporary permit was never rescinded, and in July 2013, the state actually gave BP permission to increase its toxic dumping into Lake Michigan — up to 54% more ammonia and 35% more toxic sludge. BP is also now permitted to dump 20 times the amount of mercury allowed under U.S. federal law.[114]

On May 15, 2016, more than 1,000 protesters, including well-known activist and 350.org founder Bill McKibben, marched several kilometres through the strong stench of tar and sulphur to the Whiting refinery, where police in riot gear arrested 41 of them. It was one of the biggest protests in Indiana history.

Shipping Tar Sands Bitumen on Water

Transporting energy over the Great Lakes is not new. Nearly four million tons of oil and petroleum products are shipped every year to and from American Great Lakes ports[115] and over 19 million metric tonnes to and from Canadian ports in the Great Lakes and on the St. Lawrence River.[116] The St. Lawrence Seaway moves a great deal of energy traffic every day. There is twice as much petroleum tanker traffic on Canada's east coast than on its west coast.

But there is growing pressure to increase the flow of tar sands bitumen through existing and new pipelines and to transport it by barges and ships across the watershed to waiting refineries. Shipping tar sands crude by tanker is considerably cheaper than by rail. Officials at Calumet LLC, owners of a refinery in Superior, Wisconsin, estimate that vessel transport is about one-third of the cost of rail.[117]

The Alliance for the Great Lakes is a Chicago-based conservation and education organization that has been devoted to protecting the Great Lakes for over 40 years. It reports that proposals are in the works that could make the Great Lakes the next frontier for moving tar sands crude to this network of local refineries: "With more tar sands crude coming to Great Lakes refineries, the pressure is mounting to find economical ways to move it out. Shipping it across the Great Lakes is a strong possibility."[118]

In fact, tar sands transport by ship has already begun. Between 2011 and 2012, oil from the fracking fields of North Dakota and the tar sands of Alberta delivered to U.S. refineries by barge increased 53%.[119] An estimated 40,000 barrels of heavy Canadian crude is loaded daily from pipelines onto barges at Wood River, Illinois, and travels down the Mississippi River to the Marathon Petroleum Corporation's refinery in Garyville, Louisiana. There are plans to expand this operation.[120]

The American Petroleum Institute predicts that between 2014 and 2025, capital investment in marine transport of liquefied petroleum gas and natural gas liquids will increase by 32%, liquid natural gas by 36% and crude oil by 73%.[121]

On September 24, 2014, Suncor shipped 700,000 bar-rels of tar sands bitumen from a port east of Montreal down the St. Lawrence River and across the Atlantic to Sardinia, Italy. Another vessel transported bitumen down the eastern seaboard to the Gulf of Mexico. These were the first ship-ments of bitumen to be transported on the open sea. The federal government approved these shipments without any environmental assessment. Until the price of oil dropped, there were plans for 20 to 30 vessel shipments each year. While these plans are not currently being pursued because of the low price of crude, it is safe to bet they will restart once it is economically viable again.

Writing in *Maritime Executive*, a journal for leaders in the shipping industry, Canadian transportation journalist Harry Valentine speculates on a future water connection between Lakes Superior and Winnipeg to transport Alberta tar sands oil to the American inland waterway system at Chicago and Cleveland and then to move it to markets via the St. Lawrence Seaway.[122]

Not Prepared for Bitumen Spills

According to the Alliance for the Great Lakes, the U.S. Coast Guard acknowledges that current methods for find-ing and recovering submerged oils are inadequate and that their "worst case" discharge scenario is based upon a spill of conventional oil. Great Lakes ports were not designed to load and ship heavy tar sands crude and the U.S. Environmental Protection Agency does not have the resources to fulfil its responsibility to inspect and moni-tor facilities that have a reasonable chance of a discharge into navigable waters — about 64,000 of them. The last survey of petroleum-refining facilities was undertaken in 1995 before the tar sands era and, at that time, only about 39% met EPA criteria.

Several reports in Canada cite similar flaws in the country's ability to deal with major oil spills. A strongly worded 2010 audit authored by then environment and sustainable development commissioner Scott Vaughan said that the Canadian government is not ready to handle a major oil spill. He worried that the Canadian Coast Guard had not done a national risk assessment of oil spills from ships since 2000, before tar sands oil started to be moved in bulk across the continent. He further warned that the volume of hazardous and noxious substances being transported in Canadian waters is growing quickly, but said that the Canadian government has no plan to deal with the consequences of accidents.[123]

In December 2013, a panel set up to examine preparedness for tanker traffic carrying oil off the west coast found that Ottawa's oil spill response lacks federal leadership and is not prepared for disasters in high-risk areas.[124]

One such area is Lac Saint-Pierre, a UNESCO World Biosphere Reserve on the St. Lawrence River recognized as a wetland of international importance. Lac Saint-Pierre is a drinking water source for its surrounding communities and is home to 27 species of rare plants, 79 species of fish and 288 species of waterfowl. In the event of a spill, emergency response would be limited by ice conditions if it happened in winter, and by the inadequate capacity of the small private company responsible for oil spill cleanup on the river. Under normal conditions, a spill would travel the length of Lac Saint-Pierre in eight hours — far quicker than a response could be mounted.

In their January 2015 report, "Doubling Down on Disaster," the Council of Canadians and Équiterre found that costs and damages from a spill in this area of less than 10% of the cargo of an Aframax-class supertanker — the size of tanker that Suncor uses on the St. Lawrence River — would cost $2.14 billion. The federal limit to liability for oil spills is $1.4 billion, leaving taxpayers to cover the difference.[125]

Sierra Club Wisconsin said this tar sands shipping system severely threatens the Great Lakes and is "sneaking in under the radar." Brent Patterson, political director of the Council of Canadians, noted that the proposal to ship tar sands crude on the Great Lakes and down the St. Lawrence is "a dangerous equation for those of us who see the Great Lakes as a commons, not as a tar sands and fracked oil shipping route."[126]

Andrew Slade, former program coordinator for Minnesota Environmental Partnership, said that trying to curb tar sands shipments from Alberta is like trying to stop lava flowing from a volcano. He wondered whether the people of the region are prepared to see the gales of November threaten a floating tank of tar sands oil and asked if the Great Lakes will be the next front in the global fossil-fuel war.[127]

Nowhere in Canada is opposition to the Energy East pipeline stronger than in Quebec. This is because three powerful movements — students, First Nations and environmentalists — came together to fight the pipeline and their position has had a huge influence on elected officials in that province. They remember the effectiveness of the student strike of 2012 involving a quarter of a million students over tuition hikes. The issue was crucial in the defeat of the Jean Charest government that fall.

Many of these students went on to join the campaign against Energy East. Gabriel Nadeau-Dubois, one of the leaders of the student protest, donated the money he won from the Governor General's Literary Award in 2014 to Coule Pas Chez Nous, one of the key Quebec coalitions fighting the pipeline. (His book, *Tenir Tête*, won $25,000 for non-fiction in French.) Within 12 hours of his announcement, Quebeckers donated another $143,000.

Earlier that year, on Earth Day, 250,000 people turned out for a Montreal march to demand a healthy environment — the biggest protest in the city's history and the biggest environmental march ever held in Canada. The Quebec environmental movement is solidly opposed to the Energy East pipeline.

First Nations in Quebec have also voiced their opposition to Energy East. The Assembly of First Nations Quebec and Labrador, representing 43 chiefs, officially opposes the pipeline. In March 2016, Mohawk

Kanesatake grand chief Serge Simon said his people would do "everything in their power" to block Energy East, calling it a threat to their way of life.

One particularly intense fight that brought together all these and others was the plan by TransCanada to build a marine oil tanker terminal in Cacouna just north of Rivière-du-Loup on the St. Lawrence River. From there, Alberta crude, including diluted bitumen, carried by the Energy East pipeline would be shipped by tanker down the river and out to sea. The port is located at the heart of the river's endangered beluga whale habitat. Fewer than 900 beluga whales are found in the river, and they are recognized under the Species at Risk Act.

In late summer 2014, four Quebec environmental groups sought and were granted a temporary injunction to stop construction of the port. Karine Péloffy, an administrator with the Centre québécois de droit de l'environnement, said the main concern was the belugas and the fact that the females move closer to the Cacouna area, where the water is shallower, in order to feed their newborns. Over the spring and summer of 2014, protests and marches against the port intensified. An online petition calling for a permanent ban collected more than 30,000 signatures.

In September 29, 2014, Robert Michaud, the scientific director of Quebec's Group for Research and Education on Marine Mammals, warned of a "looming catastrophe" after several summers of record baby beluga deaths. If the population is to recover, he said, there must be a concerted effort to reduce the sources of stress on the animals, particularly the areas frequented by beluga mothers and their calves.[128] This is precisely the threat of building this port, said David Suzuki. The expert scientific advice was unanimous: a deep tanker port at Cacouna would deliver a fatal blow to the whales.

On October 12, 1,500 people from all over Quebec gathered on the Cacouna waterfront to demand a halt to exploratory drilling for TransCanada's port site. Martin Poirier, a young spokesperson for the group No Oil Spills in the St. Lawrence (now known as Stop Oléoduc), said there was no social mandate from the people of Quebec for this port and accused the Couillard government of behaving like a lobbyist for TransCanada. "We have a duty to protect the common good," he told the crowd. "We do not accept this agenda of transforming Quebec into a provincial petro-power as part of a larger Canadian petro-power project."

In April 2015, with protests escalating and at the urging of Quebec's premier — who had withdrawn his support after a federal government report sounded alarm over the dwindling beluga population — TransCanada confirmed it was pulling out of the project in Cacouna. Russ Girling, president and CEO of the company, said it was over concern for the belugas. The company was clearly in damage-control mode, said Keith Stewart, climate and energy campaigner for Greenpeace Canada. "There is no chance TransCanada will find a place in Quebec where they will find the social licence to operate," he told the *Globe and Mail*.[129]

five

Hewers of Wood, Drawers of Water

As a percentage of gross domestic product in Canada, manufacturing has declined from 26% in the 1960s to about 11% in 2016, and much of the country's manufacturing has moved offshore. Since 2000, Canada has lost over 540,000 manufacturing jobs, many of them to low wage states in the U.S. and the Maquiladora free trade zones of Mexico. During Stephen Harper's decade in power, this trend accelerated and his government looked increasingly to the energy and mining sectors for growth. Most premiers are now doing the same. In spite of the global downturn in commodity pricing, leaders of all political stripes are promoting the growth in resource exports, with calamitous results for the country's water.

Fracking Frenzy

Fracking is a water-intensive and polluting process in which a mixture of sand, chemicals and water is injected deep underground at high pressure to release natural gas from rock formations. Over the past decade, fracking has exploded in North America and transformed the politics of energy.

Since 2005, there have been over 140,000 wells drilled or permitted in the U.S., says Food & Water Watch's Wenonah Hauter in her 2016 book *Frackopoly*.[130] Canadian journalist Andrew Nikiforuk reports that both Encana and Chesapeake Energy, two of the largest shale gas players, have assembled land bases equal to the size of the state of West Virginia for shale drilling alone.[131]

Shale gas fracking helped the U.S. to become the world's largest natural gas producer, and the exponential growth led to expansive capital investment in oil and gas infrastructure, from pipelines and railways to terminals and marine transport.

With the drop in oil prices worldwide, it is unclear where the fracking industry will go, but many analysts believe that it will try to hold on to existing operations, hoping for a price recovery. There is strong political will in the United States to wean the country off Middle Eastern energy, so North American energy sources of all kinds are encouraged even though fracking is wreaking havoc on water.

Water is by far the largest component of fracking fluids. Generally, 8 to 32 million litres of water are used to frack a well, but some wells use much more, and many wells are fracked more than once. Fracking not only uses water, it contaminates the surrounding groundwater with the chemical cocktail used in the process. Every year, fracking wells in the U.S. produce over three trillion litres of contaminated water.[132]

While the chemicals are under trademark protection and therefore considered trade secrets, a 2011 American study identified more than 600 chemicals used in fracking, at least a quarter of which have been linked to cancer and mutations and half of which can affect the nervous, immune and cardiovascular systems.[133] They include arsenic, lead, barium, strontium, toluene, xylene, radium-226 and benzene. The amount of benzene from a single fracked well can contaminate almost 400 billion litres of drinking water.[134] These chemicals can leak into groundwater as a direct result of the fracking as well as from waste "stored" permanently underground.

Under the Chemicals Management Plan, Environment Canada reviewed 265 chemicals used in the fracking process in both Quebec and the U.S. and found that only 13 have been assessed under the Canadian Environmental Protection Act. At least half did not meet the department's criteria for further assessment and would therefore not receive "further attention," Environment Canada announced in a March 2011 memo to the environment minister.[135]

It's not just the groundwater. Surface water, too, gets contaminated from the treatment and disposal of the wastewater. Flowback water (water that "flows back" during the fracking process) contains large amounts of brine; toxic metals and chemicals such as mercury, lead and arsenic; radioactive material such as radium and uranium; organic acids, polycyclic aromatic hydrocarbons and chloride, which can cause acute harm to aquatic insects, fish and frogs. Flowback is hard to treat, as standard municipal water treatment plants are not designed to handle this kind of contamination. If it is released into surface waters after improper treatment, it poses a direct threat to water, as do disposal wells that can leak, leading to the migration of contaminated water into local groundwater and drinking water sources.

Since 2005, fracking in the U.S. has produced 8 billion litres of toxic chemicals.[136] Between 2011 and 2013, nearly 300 oil spills occurred in North Dakota alone, and recent reports confirm that radioactive sludge is brimming back to the surface of many of the fracking sites, mixing with freshwater across the state.[137]

Some fracking is for oil. In early 2014, the U.S. Department of Transportation issued a safety alert on the transport of fracked oil from the Bakken fields of North Dakota, saying that this type of crude may be more flammable than traditional heavy crude oil. It was fracked Bakken oil carried on Canada's poorly regulated rail system that resulted in the catastrophic explosion in Lac-Mégantic. Major derailments have terrified rural communities in North Dakota and Alabama as well. A fiery December 2013 train collision near Casselton, North Dakota, set off a blaze that engulfed at least 21 cars.

Fracked oil has unusual properties and its explosive flammability may in part be related to the large number of volatile chemicals and frack fluids such as diesel and kerosene that are used, in some cases illegally, to release the oil from the deep shale formations. The oil may also have a high hydrogen-sulphide content in such perilous amounts that even Enbridge itself recently applied to restrict shipments on its pipelines over concern for worker safety.[138] Hydrogen sulphide is poisonous, corrosive, explosive and flammable.

Dr. Scott Smith, a scientist with actor Mark Ruffalo's organization Water Defense, has tested oil samples he collected from the Bakken fields and said they contain unprecedented levels of explosive volatiles such as benzene, toluene and xylene. "We must work to better understand the risks involved with the transportation of unconventional crude oil," he said, "whether diluted bitumen or Bakken fracked oil."[139]

Fracking has brought environmental devastation and declining property values to many areas; it has polluted drinking water supplies, contaminated groundwater and spilled into rivers and lakes. There are myriad reports of livestock illnesses and deaths on farms near fracking operations, as well as reports of earthquakes near sites of intense operations.

Even Rex Tillerson, CEO of ExxonMobil, the world's largest drilling company and heavily invested in fracking, took to the courts to try to stop a fracking water tower near his $5 million horse ranch in a wealthy enclave of Texas. In his 2012 lawsuit, the executive cited his concern over heavy truck traffic, noise, the devaluation of his property and the adverse impact the tower would have on the "rural lifestyle" he and others "sought to enjoy."

Most people affected by fracking lose more than a rural lifestyle. Dimock is a small community in northeastern Pennsylvania where over 600 fracking wells were drilled in a 12-square-kilometre area between 2008 and 2010. Craig and Julie Sautner's modest home and property are now worthless because their water supply has been contaminated. The water coming out of their tap is brown and they can no longer take showers or cook with the water in their home, as the chemicals in the water make them dizzy and cause sores on their bodies. "Our land is worthless," Craig told journalist Christopher Bateman. "Who is going to buy this house?"[140]

People living downwind from fracking sites have reported eye, throat and nasal irritation, frequent nosebleeds, hair loss, unexplained rashes, chronic coughs, lung congestion and extreme fatigue. Children have developed asthma and tumours. The Fracking and Health Awareness Project of Nova Scotia warns that children are less able to metabolize some toxic substances and are more vulnerable than adults when they are exposed.[141]

Fracking has been directly linked to earthquakes. Until 2008, Oklahoma, where there has been major fracking activity, experienced an average of one to two earthquakes of 3.0 magnitude or greater a year. In 2009, there were 20. The next year, there were 42. In 2014, there were 585. And in 2015, there were 907 earthquakes in the state. William Ellsworth is a research geologist at the United States Geological Survey. Here is what he had to say to the *New Yorker*: "We can say with virtual certainty that the increased seismicity in Oklahoma has to do with recent changes in the way that oil and gas are being produced. . . . Disposal wells trigger earthquakes when they are dug too deep, near or into basement rock, or when the wells impinge on a fault line. Scientifically, it's really quite clear."[142]

Western Canada's Fracking Experiment

In January 2016, the small northwestern Alberta community of Fox Creek had the dubious distinction of the largest fracking-related earthquake to date anywhere in the world, a magnitude of 4.8. The same month, a "swarm" of at least 15 earthquakes was reported in the area where at least 25 earthquakes ranging in magnitude from 2.5 to 3.5 had taken place the year before. Encana, Talisman, Apache,

Chevron Canada and ExxonMobil had been steadily intensifying drilling for their fracking operations, cracking rock in the Duvernay Shale at a depth of 3,000 metres.

The earthquakes took place in the province's first "play-based regulations pilot," an area where the provincial regulator has given blanket approval to the development of a whole area rather than approving one well at a time, reported the *Tyee*.[143] While the province says that this practice cuts red tape, critics say it is a dangerous form of deregulation. Following the 4.8 earthquake, the Alberta Energy Regulator ordered the fracking operation at Fox Creek to be shut down.

In 2013 alone, the number of licences for shale gas fracking soared 647%. The water loss due to fracking in that same year was over 17 billion litres. "This is an enormous amount of groundwater," said Brian Mason, NDP party leader at the time in Alberta: "It's pumped into the ground, it's polluted by chemicals and it's never seen again."[144] The mayor of Fox Creek said the fracking operations there have caused severe and persistent water shortages, forcing the town to pay $300,000 to bring in bottled water in 2015.

The energy industry and governments continue to claim that fracking is safe. On its website, the Canadian Association of Petroleum Producers states that "hydraulic fracturing is a safe activity regulated by governments." But the experience of people and communities near fracking sites says otherwise.

Jessica Ernst is an environmental consultant with a Master of Science degree and 30 years of experience in the oil and gas industry. She lives on a rural property near Rosebud, Alberta, and depends for water on a well fed by the Rosebud Aquifer. Between 2001 and 2006, the gas company Encana dug dozens of fracking wells adjacent to her property. Soon after operations started, Ernst's well water became so severely contaminated with hazardous and flammable levels of methane and other toxic chemicals, the water coming out of her taps could be lit on fire. It is too dangerous to even use her toilets, as one spark could ignite and cause a serious explosion.

In 2011, Ernst filed a lawsuit against the Alberta government, the province's energy regulator and Encana. In its defence statement, the company denied all her allegations and blamed her for any pollution she was encountering. In 2013, the Alberta Court of Queen's Bench ruled that the regulator is immune from private legal claims, so Ernst took her case to the Supreme Court of Canada on the grounds that her charter rights have been violated by the Alberta regulator's refusal to deal with her case. The Supreme Court heard her case in early 2016 and its decision is pending.

British Columbia has ambitious plans to expand its northeastern gas fields exponentially, requiring thousands of new fracking wells and as well as the construction of new pipelines to carry the fracked gas to terminals where it will be liquefied and stored. Major liquid natural gas (LNG) terminals include Petronas's Pacific Northwest on Lelu Island; Woodfibre in Squamish, approved by the Trudeau government; and the Tilbury facility in Delta — about 30 kilometres from downtown Vancouver. The liquid gas will then be loaded onto mega-tankers the size of three football fields and exported to Asia. The Clark government has been promised a $100 billion windfall from the industry.

In 2012, B.C.'s fracking industry used more than seven billion litres of water; if its plans come to fruition, the water needed to get the shale gas out of the ground will increase 500% or more.

In May 2015, geoscientist David Hughes, a 32-year veteran with the Geological Survey of Canada and a fellow with the Post Carbon Institute, published a report for the Canadian Centre for Policy Alternatives on B.C.'s plans for natural gas expansion. The export licences granted by the National Energy Board for 12 new LNG terminals means that B.C. will produce more natural gas than the rest of Canada and will require massive new fracking operations to supply them. (Hughes explained that so many new wells are required because of the steep decline in production of fracking wells. On average, production from a fracked well declines by 69% in its first three years, a far sharper decline than for conventional gas.)

This in turn will require drilling as many as 43,000 new wells by 2040, to be added to the 40,000 already drilled in B.C. and Alberta since 2007. In the ramp-up phase, the water demands of 3,000 new wells per year would be equal to about half the annual water consumption of Calgary.[145]

And this is just the water needed for the fracking itself. LNG conversion also uses an enormous amount of water. The Shell LNG project in Kitimat, which has received its licence, proposes to use 70 million litres of water a day from the Kitimat River. This equates to the daily domestic use of a city of 225,000 people.[146]

One of the largest fracking operations in the world is in the Horn River Basin in northeastern British Columbia, where an entire wilderness area has been turned into an industrial site in just a decade. Multiple earthquakes have rocked the area for the last few years. Water use in the Horn Basin fracking operations is double the average for North America; each fracked well there consumes and poisons almost 64 million litres of water over its lifetime. The Fort Nelson First Nation calls it "Shale Gale" and says the lakes and rivers in the area have become terribly polluted.

Fort Nelson chief Liz Logan worries that no one is looking at the cumulative effects of this industry that is destroying their traditional ways of living off the land. "My family's cabin and dock is at a lake that people used to come from miles away to fish at," she said. "Now the water is yellow. You can't swim in it, you can't drink it, there are no fish in it anymore."[147]

The community won a small but important victory in September 2015 when the B.C. Environmental Appeal Board cancelled a licence to extract water from a small lake north of the community. The licence was held by Calgary-based Nexen, owned by Chinese state-controlled CNOOC.

No one yet knows how much shale oil and gas there is in the Yukon, Northwest Territories and Nunavut. The government of the NWT estimates that the Canol shale underground deposit, which extends from the Mackenzie Mountains along the Yukon/NWT border near Great Bear Lake, contains two to three billion barrels of recoverable oil, as much or more than the Bakken formation of North Dakota, reported environmental writer Ed Struzik. Scientists are concerned that the fragile northern ecosystem will be especially susceptible to seismic activity and pollution and the Mountain Dene people are worried about their way of life, which depends on the pristine free-flowing rivers of the region.[148]

The drop in the price of oil and the fierce opposition has limited development in the North so far. There is breathing room to develop better policy.

Fracking the Great Lakes

Shale gas reserves underlie vast areas of the Great Lakes region including Michigan, Ohio, Pennsylvania, New York, Ontario and Quebec. Pennsylvania accounts for nearly 40% of U.S. shale gas production. Between 2011 and 2015, the state approved more than 12,000 fracking permits even though the government admits that this industry damaged the state's water supplies in 209 separate incidents in those same years.[149] Pennsylvania has developed its shale gas industry so quickly that its rural areas — once vast, dark expanses viewed from space — are now lit up like a Christmas tree in satellite images.

Michigan is the centre of fracking close to the Great Lakes. There are 12,000 fracking wells in Michigan now, and major plans to drill several hundred thousand acres of northern Michigan, south of Traverse City. Water withdrawal for oil and gas operations in that state is exempt from water withdrawal statute requirements.

While New York has banned fracking within its own jurisdiction, upstate New York disposes of radioactive fracking waste from the Marcellus shale projects in Pennsylvania, putting local watersheds, Lake Ontario and the Great Lakes Basin at risk. And while there are no natural gas deposits in Wisconsin and Minnesota, both states are being mined for silica sand, used in the fracking process and which itself uses large amounts of water.[150]

If the land area of just four Great Lakes states within the basin experienced shale development similar to that of the Marcellus shale, total water withdrawals could be over 148 billion litres a year.[151] While U.S. federal law prohibits water from being diverted directly out of the basin, many fracking operations and other bulk water users withdraw from ground and surface water sources that feed the Great Lakes.

In its February 2014 report, "Trouble Brewing in the Great Lakes," Washington-based Food & Water Watch reminded us that when an aquifer is overpumped, the water levels of a connected surface water body can fall and water flows can change: "With millions of gallons of water needed to frack a single well, withdrawing water from around the Great Lakes could affect local supplies and have cumulative impacts on the basin, further straining already stressed water sources."[152] Moreover, says the National Wildlife Federation, almost all of the water withdrawn for fracking in the Great Lakes Basin will not be returned to the source watershed to replenish resources; instead, the water will be sealed underground for disposal.

On the Canadian side of the Great Lakes, strong community resistance to fracking has slowed down industry boosters. Over 70 Quebec municipalities adopted bylaws protecting source water from fracking. There had been exploratory drilling in 31 locations in the St. Lawrence River Lowlands in Quebec, but in 2011, the government placed a moratorium on fracking in the area until further study and, in December 2014, Premier Philippe Couillard affirmed that the moratorium would stay in place.

While Ontario has not yet granted fracking permits, pending a promised review, in March 2015 the government of Kathleen Wynne defeated a private member's bill to ban fracking brought forward by NDP environment critic Peter Tabuns. Tabuns had urged the government to follow the lead of Quebec, Nova Scotia, New Brunswick, Newfoundland and New York, where there are bans or moratoriums, but the government left the door open.

Even if there is no fracking on the Canadian side of the lakes, the sheer size of the industry on the American side poses a great risk to the whole basin. And now, there are plans to transport fracking wastewater by ship.

In 2013, under pressure from the industry, the U.S. Coast Guard announced it would allow shale gas companies to ship fracking wastewater on the nation's rivers and lakes. In January 2015, Greenhunter Resources, a wastewater management company, announced it had received approval from the Coast Guard to haul tens of thousands of barrels of Marcellus shale wastewater from its Ohio storage and shipping terminal down the Ohio River to dump sites in the southern part of the state. Each barge could transport approximately 10,000 barrels of wastewater, becoming a floating time bomb.

Atlantic Canada Says No

The eastern provinces have largely rejected fracking. Nova Scotia and New Brunswick have placed indefinite moratoriums on the practice, and a May 2016 report of an independent study on fracking in Newfoundland concluded that a "pause" the government called in 2013 should stay in place until further study is completed. The report's authors, who include Ray Gosine, Memorial University associate vice-president, made it clear that a 25-kilometre buffer zone must be built around the fragile Gros Morne National Park.

But that doesn't mean there are no issues with natural gas in the region. First Nations, local residents and environmentalists have come together in Colchester County, Nova Scotia, to oppose the Alton Gas Storage Project, which would develop salt caverns for natural gas storage along the Shubenacadie River, a tidal bore river that flows into

Cobequid Bay. Local people are deeply concerned about the dangers this project poses to the river ecosystem, local residents and climate.

In January 2016, the Nova Scotia government gave approval of the project, leading Chief Rufus Copage of the Sipekne'katik First Nation to launch an appeal and promise to initiate rolling protests. "Our band members want to shut the project down," he said. "They don't want that brine going into the river."[153] The appeal caused a temporary halt to the project, pending a summer 2016 hearing by the Nova Scotia Supreme Court.

Mounting Mining Concerns

Mining operations pollute source water through acid mine drainage, which happens when sulphide minerals are exposed to both water and air, causing them to oxidize, producing acid. If this acid leaks into waterways, it can have devastating effects on the water and aquatic life. Mining exposes heavy metals occurring naturally in the rock. Chemicals used in the extraction process are a further threat. MiningWatch Canada reports that bodies of water around the world, including Canada, are threatened by the toxic chemicals and heavy metals released into tailings ponds. These can include as many as three dozen dangerous substances, including arsenic, lead, mercury and cyanide.

Mining is the second largest industrial user of water after power generation. Industry journal *Global Water Intelligence* says that every year, mining uses as much as 9 trillion litres of water globally, about the same amount of water used every year in Malaysia, with a population of over 30 million.

And every year mining companies dump 180 million tonnes of hazardous waste into lakes, rivers, groundwater and oceans, 1.5 times the amount of municipal solid waste the U.S. dumps into its landfills. Even though most Canadians think our mining operations are safer than those in other parts of the world, MiningWatch and Earthworks report that a Canadian company — Cliffs Natural Resources' Wabush Scully mine in Labrador — is one of the top four mines in the world that account for 86% of that 180 million tonnes of hazardous waste.[154]

The Wabush Scully mine is not the only one. Newfoundland and Labrador is home to a number of highly polluting mines. Vale Inco's use of Sandy Pond (the legally dead lake mentioned earlier) is another one, and MiningWatch lists a number of other mines that are destroying lakes in the province. Canada Fluorspar is planning on using Shoal Cove Pond, a coastal lake, when it reopens its mine. Teck has already destroyed Trout Pond and Gills Brook tributary for its copper-zinc mine. Rio Tinto has been dumping around 30,000 tonnes of iron ore tailings a day from its Labrador City mine for 40 years. Cliffs dumps 13 million tonnes of tailings annually into Flora Lake and tributary streams.

Near Sudbury, Ontario, Glencore's Strathcona mill dumps nickel and copper tailings into Moose Lake, and Vale operates the Copper Cliffs mine that dumps into the remains of Meatbird Lake. In October 2015, Environment Canada announced it is investigating Vale for leaking toxic runoff into local waterways for over 50 years. In its warrant, the government accused the company of allowing "acutely lethal" seepage into water frequented by fish, and of knowing about this leakage since at least 1997. The investigation was triggered after a resident noticed a "foamy, lime-green coloured substance" in a local creek. An independent environmental study found that contaminated water from the mine site was seeping onto a local school property, at times at a rate of 180 litres a minute.[155]

In December 2015, the Ontario auditor general released its first environmental liability report in a decade and found that operations and abandoned mine site cleanup costs for the province rose 300% in that decade to over $3.1 billon. However, the real cost is likely well over double that amount, said Ugo Lapointe, MiningWatch's Canada coordinator. These costs are paid for by the taxpayers, not the mining companies.

With 4,412 active and abandoned mine sites and 5,000 recorded mine hazards, Ontario now ranks highest for environmental liability in the mining sector and it is the only province in Canada that does not require environmental assessments before mines are developed.[156] Environmental groups urged the premier to reform water-use fees, saying that they are alarmed that most heavy industries in Ontario — especially mining — continue to get a free ride for the millions of litres of freshwater they use every day. Joan Kuyek of Ontarians for a Just Accountable Mineral Strategy said that large water users are only paying 1.2% of the $16.2 million it costs to run the water-permitting program.[157]

In November 2015, Vale announced it had put its plans for a controversial $3.5 billion potash mine in a rural community north of Regina on hold due to low world prices. The company predicts that the mine could produce 3 to 4 million tonnes of potash a year for 40 years and many feared the impact of the project on water. The Kronau mine would have been a solution mine, which requires water to separate the potash from other minerals. Since there are not enough local water sources, Vale proposed building a 70-kilometre water pipeline to Katepwa Lake in the Qu'Appelle Valley and pumping more than 40 million litres of water out of the lake every day.

Uranium mining in northern Saskatchewan makes Canada the world's largest exporter of the ore. The Athabasca Sandstone is a geological formation that spreads from northern Alberta to northern Manitoba and contains the world's highest-grade uranium. In April 2015, Stephen Harper and Indian prime minister Narendra Modi signed a deal to confirm the export of 3,220 tons of uranium from northern Saskatchewan.

In a scathing March 2015 report, the Saskatchewan Environmental Society calls for an end to the expansion of this industry. Radioactive contaminants from uranium mines have done great damage to many Saskatchewan waterways, with watersheds contaminated by the millions of tonnes of waste left behind at mined-out sites. Remediation is totally inadequate. The report cites numerous examples of toxic lake sediment buildup as well as waterway contamination in levels well above provincial water quality standards. The authors are critical of the federal government's abandonment of its water quality standards enforcement and the limited remediation work it is undertaking.[158]

The taxpayers of NWT may have to pay almost $1 billion to clean up the toxic dust buried under Yellowknife's Giant Mine, one of the richest gold mines in Canadian history. From 1948 to 2004, 200 tonnes of gold was mined from the site, leaving a highly toxic byproduct called arsenic trioxide. Global News called the amount of this contaminant "unfathomable," and quoted environmental advocate Kevin O'Reilly saying there is probably enough of it underground to kill every person on the planet several times over. If it escapes or leaches into Great Slave Lake, it could flow down the Mackenzie River with catastrophic results. He noted that the company is not around anymore and the public must foot the cleanup bill.[159]

In January 2016, B.C. premier Christie Clark announced that her government would open a Major Mine Permitting Office to handle the estimated ten major new mines expected to enter production in the next few years. She wants to jumpstart the province's mining activity following several years of downturn due to slowed global demand. Her budget also earmarked an additional $6 billion to the Mines and Mineral Resources division of the Ministry of Energy, bringing its budget up to $17.1 billion. She also announced several other measures to boost the industry, including a generous tax credit program to support investment in the sector.

Five new mines have been opened and seven major mine expansions were approved in the province since 2011, the year Clark announced her intent to build much of B.C.'s future prosperity on mining, a promise she plans to keep.

The Wilderness Committee and other environmental activists had the recent Mount Polley accident clearly in their minds when they worried aloud about the expansion of the industry not accompanied by strict regulations. In August 2014, the tailings impoundment of the Mount Polley Mine Corporation, owned by Imperial Metals, collapsed, sending 24 billion litres of mining waste into the pristine waters of Quesnel Lake, the cleanest deep water lake in the world, the source of drinking water for the local community and a major sockeye salmon spawning ground. The company has a history of operating its tailings pond beyond capacity, and for years before the disaster, environmentalists warned the provincial government about a possible breach.

The controlling shareholder of Imperial Metals is billionaire N. Murray Edwards. He has donated to the B.C. Liberal Party since 2005 and helped organize a $1 million private fundraiser for Premier Christy Clark's re-election bid in 2013.[160] In December 2015, following an investigation of the spill, the Clark government announced that the mine had operated "within existing regulation" and that there would be no charges laid.

But an independent May 2016 report by B.C.'s auditor general challenged these findings. In a scathing indictment of the government, Carol Bellringer concluded the government is not properly prepared to protect the environment from potential disasters in the mining industry. She said that almost all expectations for government compliance and enforcement in this sector are not being met and particularly noted the lack of adequate and regular inspections of mining sites. The auditor general reported that the collapse of the Mount Polley tailings dam was triggered by weakness in the foundation and too much water buildup. B.C. grand chief Stewart Phillip said Mount Polley will be remembered as one of the most disastrous environmental events in the province's history, one that could have been avoided with vigorous governmental oversight.

In another case, Canadian mining giant Teck Resources admitted in a U.S. court in 2012 that effluent from its smelter in southeast B.C. had been polluting the Columbia River in Washington for more than a century. American Native tribes claimed that Teck had dumped slag containing arsenic, cadmium, copper, mercury, lead and zinc directly into the river, contaminating the surface and groundwater of the Upper Columbia and Lake Roosevelt. Judge Lonny Suko ruled that the company knowingly dumped almost 10 million tonnes of slag between 1935 and 1995 alone.

The cost of the cleanup, to be borne by the company, is estimated to be around $1 billion.[161]

There are also serious concerns about B.C.'s expanding coal mining industry that contaminates surface and groundwater with its wastewater. The proposed Raven Coal Mine on Vancouver Island would have removed 44 million tonnes of coal over 20 years but strong resistance from local residents, combined with the loss of its corporate partners, forced the company to retreat in June 2015.

Even the U.S. Environmental Protection Agency has sounded the alarm over B.C.'s decision to expand coal production. It has threatened to take the province before the International Joint Commission over the Elk River Valley mines at the request of Montana's senators, who are worried about the impact of current and future coal mining in southeastern B.C. on their watersheds. The senators have complained that Canadian authorities are examining coal projects on a piecemeal basis and are not considering overall impacts, including the "significant and continuing" increases in selenium leaching into rivers and lakes, reported the *Vancouver Sun*.

"Drainage from the Elk Valley mines present serious risks to the Kootenai Basin water quality and valued trout fisheries," the senators wrote. "It is imperative that international scrutiny be applied to the mines' downstream impacts."[162]

In November 2015, the Clark government acceded to Taseko Mines' request to increase effluent discharges of its Gibraltar copper mine, located near Williams Lake, into the Fraser River. The company now discharges 3.5 billion litres of toxic mining tailings and seeks to double that amount. In its Monty Python–esque explanation for allowing the increase, the B.C. government said that the Fraser

River already has metals such as selenium, iron, lead, mercury, aluminium, copper, sulphates and nitrates, and these new discharges will be diluted so that, further along, the river will meet water quality guidelines. The Tsilhqot'in First Nation disagreed, saying the new effluents will further harm their fisheries and their inherent right to clean water.

In their January 2016 report, "Cleaning Up B.C.'s Dirty Mining Industry," the Wilderness Committee, MiningWatch Canada and Clayoquot Action called on the B.C. government to invest in better industry practices and implement stronger regulations to protect the environment, communities and taxpayers from further environmental liability related to mining. They called for a ban on massive toxic tailings ponds; legislated "no-go" zones to protect critical ecosystems, waters and livelihoods; a stop to industry self-regulation in favour of strong government oversight; a levy on operating mines to ensure zero public liability as well as a multibillion-dollar cleanup fund; and required consent from local communities and First Nations before a mining project can proceed.[163]

Who Is in Charge?

The Canadian government assumes ownership of the majority of mineral rights, although this is disputed by many First Nations who have not yet had their land claims settled. The regulation of mining activities on publicly owned mineral leases falls under provincial and territorial jurisdiction, and there is separate mining rights legislation for each jurisdiction. Despite this, Environment Canada assures Canadians that the federal government has legislation that covers key aspects of the sector.

These laws include the Canadian Environmental Assessment Act, the Metal Mining Effluent Regulations of the Fisheries Act, the Canadian Environmental Protection Act, the Migratory Birds Convention Act, the International Rivers Improvement Act and the Species at Risk Act.

While it is technically true that the department has these powers, successive Canadian governments have not used their full authority to enforce them, as discussed in chapter two. When the Harper government gutted federal water laws and inflicted deep cuts to the department's budget, Environment Canada's ability to protect watersheds from mining activity was further severely compromised.

The changes to the Fisheries Act and the Navigable Waters Protection Act are of particular concern because of the limits they place on Environment Canada in regulating this industry. And while most major mining projects are still covered by the federal government, the amended Canadian Environmental Assessment Act limited the scope of what government can consider and restricted the public's right to participate. In 2013, Ottawa did move to increase its presence over the dumping of certain substances, such as selenium, but only because American governments expressed concerns over our shared boundary waters.

Some of the 3,000 federal environmental assessments that were dropped involve mining-related activities such as mining waste cleanup and disposal facilities. And some smaller mines were turned over to the provinces, many of which have themselves cut back on their environmental budgets and assessment oversight.

Ontario's environmental assessment process has been criticized for years. In 2013, the Canadian Environmental Law Association called for reform of the 1976 Act, which it says is dated and unenforced. Ontario's lax assessment standards for mining projects combined with the changes to the federal assessment process make it difficult to hold the mining industry in that province accountable, according to MiningWatch. This abdication on the part of both the federal and provincial governments means that the large majority of operating and proposed mines in Ontario have not undergone a thorough environmental assessment.[164]

Gwen Barlee, policy director for B.C.'s Wilderness Committee, spoke out on the changes to the federal assessment process in the province: "I knew this was coming but it blows my mind. If you care about clean air, fresh water and wild salmon, you should be very, very concerned. This approach by the federal government is a blueprint for environmental degradation and future lawsuits and an abdication of federal responsibility."[165]

The Trudeau government must reinstate the laws and regulations gutted by the Harper government, and it is past time to enforce these laws. In light of the major mining activity planned in many parts of Canada's north, it is urgent that federal, provincial and territorial governments, in consultation with First Nations and the wider public, determine how to regulate mining in Canada and protect the health of Canada's water.

MiningWatch's Jamie Kneen says the federal government clearly has the power to protect the environment, but it also has the duty to do so: "The laws that were gutted in 2012 were far from perfect and poorly enforced, but they were strong and well understood. We need to force all levels of government to do their duty to Canadians in protecting and rehabilitating our waters, lands and ecosystems, not continue to degrade them. The federal government has a special responsibility given both its power and its position as the national authority, not only to act and enforce minimum standards, but to take leadership in moving toward real sustainability."

Building Canada's future on tar sands energy, fracking and mining poses a clear and present danger to Canada's water. It is also bad economic policy, as the current downturn in world markets demonstrates.

In 2010, the government of New Brunswick granted
a licence to Texas-based Southwestern Energy (SWN)
for over a million hectares (2.5 million acres) of land
for fracking exploration. Soon after, a movement built
over concerns for the safety of New Brunswick's ground
and drinking water and public health. It demanded
that the government cancel this licence and other shale
gas licences and place a moratorium on the practice.
A number of lawsuits were launched, and protests
and demonstrations sprang up across the province at
government buildings, test sites and public meetings.
Leadership came from a number of First Nations, in
particular the Mi'kmaq Elsipogtog First Nation and its
chief, Aaron Sock, in Kent County, where the company
was slated to start seismic testing.

By the summer of 2011, opposition had grown so
strong the company abandoned its operations for a year,
citing a "campaign of misinformation." But opposition
continued to mount and the Conservative government
of Premier David Alward was forced to withhold the
company's permits, causing it to cancel seismic testing
again in the summer of 2012. In February 2013, the
government adopted new regulations governing the oil
and gas industry that it claimed met the concerns of the
public for stricter controls and granted SWN its permits
to continue exploration. Thus began the long, hot and
confrontational summer of 2013.

In June, the people from Elsipogtog, along with hundreds of others, including Acadians, Anglophones

and members of the Mi'kmaq Warrior Society, set up camp on the initial seismic testing route. The company contracted by SWN to do the seismic testing had their trucks seized and their work interrupted with peaceful highway blockades. The RCMP moved in and started arresting dozens of people, including a 16-year-old boy and 44-year-old Lorraine Clair of Elsipogtog. "Now they know what we mean when we say we are going to protect our Mother Earth and our treaty rights," she said.

Elsipogtog's Chief Sock urged caution: "Tensions have escalated. We must never be afraid to raise our voice to protect our rights and interests but we must resolve to do it peacefully."[166] But tempers flared. The company claimed some equipment was torched, the blockade intensified over the summer and more arrests followed. In October, the New Brunswick government got a court order imposing an injunction against the blockade.

It was clear a serious confrontation was coming. On October 17 near the town of Rexton, over a hundred RCMP officers and emergency police personnel from Quebec, Nova Scotia, New Brunswick and PEI moved in at dawn, guns drawn, to dismantle the encampment. The aggressive style and shocking amount of force took the encampment by surprise. In the hours that followed, more activists and supporters arrived. Several police cars were set on fire and police arrested 40 people, including Chief Sock. There were widespread accusations of police brutality, including beatings, the use of tear gas and rubber bullets. Lorraine Clair said she was attacked in the woods and suffered multiple injuries while being arrested.

Former Elsipogtog chief Susan Levi-Peters said the police moved in aggressively on unarmed people: "The RCMP is coming in here with their tear gas — they even had dogs on us. They acted like we were standing there with weapons when we were standing there as women, with drums and eagle feathers. This is crazy. This is not Canada."[167] Miles Howe, a journalist with the Halifax Media Co-op and author of 2015's *Debriefing Elsipogtog: The Anatomy of a Struggle*, wrote that the situation was provoked by the Irving Oil–owned private security forces who provided the main security for the compound where the company's equipment was held, heightening the crisis and allowing the RCMP to move in on a planned raid.

Within 24 hours, Idle No More and other networks organized over 100 solidarity actions across Canada and in over half a dozen other countries, according to Clayton Thomas-Muller, then with the Indigenous Environmental Network.

The September 2014 provincial election was held almost exclusively on the issue of fracking. Liberal leader Brian Gallant ran on a promise of a moratorium until the full risks of fracking were known. Premier Alward stood steadfastly by his support of the industry and was soundly defeated. In December that year, good to his word, Premier Gallant announced a moratorium on all shale gas fracking pending a commission to study the issue.

On February 26, 2015, the three-volume report of the New Brunswick Commission on Hydraulic Fracturing was tabled. It clearly stated that the shale gas industry had not met the conditions necessary to lift the moratorium. On May 27, 2016, the New Brunswick government announced an indefinite extension on its fracking moratorium, a victory for the courageous people who stood up for their rights.

six

Agribusiness Imperils Water

The 2015 movie *The Big Short* tells the story of Michael Burry, the market genius who saw the 2008 financial crash coming. The last line of the movie, printed on a placard, is "Michael Burry is focusing all of his trading on one commodity: Water." When asked in an interview to explain what he means by this, Burry talked about the world's water crisis and said that it had become clear to him that food is the way to invest in water. "That is, grow food in water-rich areas and transport it for sale in water-poor areas. This is the method for redistributing water that is least contentious and ultimately it can be profitable."[168]

Anthony Turton, a South African scientist and resource manager, says that the water wars of the future will not be fought on the battlefield between opposing armies, but on the trading floors of the world's grain markets, between virtual water warriors in the form of commodity traders.

These are important signals to Canada, with its relative water abundance, fertile soils and vast tracts of farmland. Canada's agriculture sector is becoming more and more geared to export, and this changes the way food is produced. Corporate dominated, export-oriented, chemical-reliant factory farming is posing a great danger to Canada's freshwater.

Factory Farms on the Rise

Every year in Canada, 700 million animals are slaughtered for food. The vast majority of them are raised and die in factory farm conditions where animals are seen as production units and receive the least possible space for the shortest time and the least amount of feed. Producers are under pressure to supply animal products at rock bottom prices for a globalized market and they face little scrutiny. Canada's federal government has no national policies that include compliance penalties when voluntary codes of practice for animal welfare are not followed, and Canada lags far behind the European Union in this regard.[169]

Factory farms are a growing threat to our lakes and groundwater. As Beyond Factory Farming, a national Canadian organization promoting sustainable and socially responsible livestock production, explains, at one time in Canada, crop and livestock production were complementary enterprises on mixed family farms, with the number of animals kept in proportion to the number of acres that grew crops for the animals' food. Most of the nutrients originating from those animals were returned to the soil in the same area.

Today most cattle, hogs and poultry are concentrated

in large holdings: giant feedlots of 20,000 cattle, mega hog farms of 5,000 to 20,000 hogs and poultry batteries of 100,000 birds on small land areas. Their feed is often grown far from the farms and their manure is spread onto fields and pastures as raw, untreated liquefied slurry in quantities that exceed the nutrient needs of crops. One 5,000-hog factory producing 2,400 piglets per week, 52 weeks of the year, uses over 200 million litres of drinking water per year, most of which will be flushed out of the barns to holding lagoons, then spread on fields.

Beyond Factory Farming reports that as well as hog urine and feces, compounds in hog manure, many of them toxic or pathogenic, may include hormones; human waste; hog carcasses; cleaning chemicals; insecticides; weed seeds; volatile organic compounds; salts; nitrogen; phosphorous; potassium; calcium; metals such as cadmium, zinc, nickel, lead, iron, boron, copper and manganese; vaccines; antibiotics; antibiotic-resistant bacteria; parasites; and other bacterial and viral pathogens such as *Cryptosporidium*, *Salmonella* and *E. coli.*

Many farms are located near water, and when this waste is spread on fields or held in unsecured lagoons, much of it finds its way into local lakes and aquifers, where it does great harm. In February 2016, the University of Victoria's Environmental Law Centre asked the B.C. health authority to order a permanent moratorium on the spread of liquid manure on a dairy farm above a drinking water aquifer that serves the North Okanagan community of Spallumcheen. The demand came after two years of a water quality advisory that warned residents of the high nitrates in their water supply. Calvin Sanborn, director of the centre, said that nitrate levels of 10 parts per million are considered unsafe and that this aquifer is testing at over 19 parts per million.[170]

Nutrient overload from fertilizers and human and animal waste causes eutrophication, the excessive enrichment of water, as well as blue-green algae, some forms of which produce harmful toxins. *The Weather Network* explains that the vibrant green colour of the algae comes from a growth explosion of algae known as cyanobacteria. It is touched off by a combination of warm water, sunshine and effluent runoff. Cyanobacteria can occur naturally, but in the past they were controlled by the natural processes in lakes. The rapid increase in industrial agriculture and human population, combined with the removal of wetlands and natural shorelines, encourages growth in amounts lakes cannot tolerate.

As a bloom spreads through the surface layer of lake water, the cyanobacteria release toxins known as microcystins into the environment. Simply swimming in water with high concentration of microcystins can cause vomiting, diarrhea, fever, headaches and muscle and joint pain. If these toxins enter the drinking water supply, they can cause liver and kidney damage and life-threatening gastroenteritis.

The bacteria live only a short time, so as the bloom spreads, millions of them die. The death and decay of the bacteria strip oxygen from the water and the dead organisms form a layer of surface scum. This combination creates oxygen-deprived "dead zones" where nothing can live, starving important species.[171]

Phosphorus and nitrates are 1,000 times more concentrated in sewage effluents than in lakes unaffected by humans or farmed animals. Their addition to natural water is like turning up the volume on an amplifier, says scientist David Schindler, and it takes only a small concentration to do a great deal of harm. With the output of phosphorus from a cow equivalent to that of 11 humans, the waste of a feedlot with 30,000 head of cattle can be equivalent to a city of over 300,000 people. But unlike human sewage waste, which is treated, there is no treatment in Canada for animal waste.

Climate change adds another problem. Ice-free seasons are longer and summer temperatures are higher, causing evaporation that silently removes water from lakes. The reduced water renewal makes it more difficult for a lake to recover from nutrient overload.

In their seminal book, *The Algal Bowl,* Schindler and John Vallentyne say we are creating the conditions in western North America for water degradation comparable to what happened to the land during the Dust Bowl. The Algal Bowl is the result of the mismanagement of both water and land because the runoff from mismanaged land generally leaches into the catchment of a lake or stream.[172]

Lake Winnipeg — Most Threatened Lake in the World

While hundreds of lakes across Canada are suffering eutrophication contamination, Lake Winnipeg and Lake Erie stand out.

Lake Winnipeg is dying, says Robert Sandford, fellow at the University of Saskatchewan's Centre for Hydrology, and we are having trouble figuring out just what to do about it. In his 2013 book, *Saving Lake Winnipeg,* Sandford calls this lake one of the largest open-air sewers in the world. In the last 40 years, nutrient loading in Lake Winnipeg has increased 70% and algal blooms of up to 15,000 square kilometres form on it every summer.

Despite the relatively small human population around

the Canadian side of the lake, the total excrement load is estimated to be equivalent to that of a human population of 50 million, so aggressively have the factory farms grown in size and number. The basin's rich soil is ideal for food production and 99% of the region's natural prairie landscape is being farmed or otherwise used by humans. Global demand for meat has created a market that has made the region one of the world's top pork producers.

Spring floods, magnified by climate change, wash the farm effluents and fertilizers into Lake Winnipeg. The area's once-abundant wetlands have been reduced by 90%, Sandford reports. (The Manitoba government says it is closer to 75%.) This matters because wetlands not only store water in times of flood, they act as a sink that collects the nitrogen and phosphorus and filters the runoff, purifying it. The concentration of cyanobacteria in Lake Winnipeg has increased 1,000% since 1990.[173]

Gimli is a lovely community of just over 1,900 located on the west side of Lake Winnipeg. Originally settled by Icelanders, Gimli holds a celebrated Icelandic Festival every August. With its beaches, parks, inns, shops and restaurants, Gimli is a hub for the thousands of cottagers and tourists who flock to that part of the lake every year.

In July 2015, I visited Gimli and the nearby village of Dunnottar for a community gathering and a "Walk for Water" put on by groups worried about the future of their beloved Lake Winnipeg. I had read about the Gimli beach signs warning people not to swim, posted when the green slime moves in. That day, there were people in the water, but several told me they no longer let their children or pets in the lake, while others said they still went swimming but always took a shower immediately after. All mourned the loss of a time when they could let their children in the water for hours at a time, knowing the water was clean and safe.

Citizen groups and communities are working to save Lake Winnipeg. Founded in 2005 as a volunteer coalition of "concerned lake-lovers," the Lake Winnipeg Foundation has become a leader in bringing together all sectors to restore the lake. Guided by its Science Advisory Council, the foundation focuses on research, public education, stewardship and collaboration.

In 2015, the foundation became a signatory to the Lake Friendly Accord, a commitment by the Manitoba government, a number of mayors and municipalities, and communities and agencies to the shared goals of reducing nutrient pollution "through engagement of all." It also launched an activist program called Aquavist to engage individuals and to certify municipalities for good water management practices. All these projects are blessed to have research support from scientists and researchers at the University of Manitoba as well as the world-class Freshwater Institute of the Department of Fisheries and Oceans located on that campus.

In 2014, the Manitoba government introduced the toughest wetland protection in Canada in an attempt to help Lake Winnipeg. The Surface Water Management Strategy deals with drainage issues, wetlands management and flood prevention. The plan is welcome, but we still need strict regulation on the prolific use of chemical fertilizers and the conditions on factory farms that create the effluent.

The province can't do it alone. For any plan to work, the federal government will have to be a key player. Waterways from four Canadian provinces and four U.S. states drain into the Lake Winnipeg Basin. Even though the Canadian side is over four times the size of the American side of the basin, nearly half of the contaminants come from the U.S.

through the Red River Basin. International negotiations are essential if Lake Winnipeg is to be saved.

Lake Erie — Sick Again

In the late 1960s, parts of Lake Erie were declared biologically dead because of algae infestation. *Time* magazine warned that the lake was in danger of dying by suffocation. Canada and the U.S. signed the Great Lakes Water Quality Agreement in 1972 and invested billions of dollars to reduce phosphorus flows into the lake. Phosphates were banned in detergents and sewage treatment was greatly improved. The lake recovered.

But the problem is back with a vengeance. In 2011, blue-green toxic algae returned to Lake Erie, covering 5,000 square kilometres, or about one-sixth of the lake's surface. In the summer of 2014, Toledo, Ohio, had to shut down its water system and provide bottled water for its 400,000 citizens because the contamination was so severe. The toxic bloom on Lake Erie in the summer of 2015 was the worst this century, according to scientists at the U.S. National Oceanic and Atmospheric Administration. While smaller in size than the 2011 bloom, the density of the blue-green algae was much higher, making it more dangerous. Big storms that rolled through the area in June that year caused a huge amount of runoff into the lake. In one month, phosphorus levels nearly tripled.

Scientists with the International Joint Commission's Lake Erie Ecosystem Priority said that phosphorus runoff from agricultural lands was to blame, feeding nutrient growth in the warm shallow waters of the lake. They said the practice of applying manure on frozen ground between

November and January is a huge problem, for when the snow melts, the effluent is washed into the lake. Lawn fertilizers add to the problem and the commission is pushing to have them banned.[174]

Around the Great Lakes Basin, 174,000 square kilometres — one-third of the area and larger than most of the bordering states — are devoted to agriculture. Wheat, corn, oats, barley, grapes, cheese, milk, fruits, vegetables and livestock are produced for domestic and export consumption and their effluent footprint is huge and deadly. Two thirds of the lower Great Lakes wetlands have been lost and the runoff flows unimpeded into the lakes.

It is not just happening in Manitoba and the Great Lakes area. Many farming communities are suffering nitrate contamination from fertilizer and animal manure in their groundwater, and thus in the wells they depend on for their drinking water. High nitrate levels in drinking water can cause skin rashes, hair loss and birth defects. Fertilizers are a growing problem across North America and the leading cause of nitrate pollution in California's groundwater.

At least one-fifth of the groundwater Californians rely on for their water supply is contaminated with nitrates, reports the U.S. Geological Survey, and 96% of the contamination is caused directly by the use of synthetic fertilizers in farming. The Community Water Center, an advocacy group in the state's Central Valley, estimates that because of the high cost of bottled water, at least 1.36 million people living in the valley could be drinking tainted groundwater.

Chris Kemper is the principal of an elementary school in the town of Seville in the Central Valley. He decided to shut off the water to the school to protect the health of his students. Now he has to spend at least $600 a month providing them with bottled water. He told journalist Alissa

Figueroa that many of his students are the children of immigrants working on local farms and cannot afford bottled water at home. "We're not talking about boxes," he said. "We're talking about human beings that we're delivering this water to. And people in this day and age find that acceptable? I think it's sad."[175]

Prince Edward Island's Endangered Waters

Prince Edward Islanders depend completely on groundwater for their water supplies because there are no major lakes on the island. Concerns over farming practices in that province centre on the contamination of groundwater, rivers and ponds. The island has become a potato monoculture in a few short decades, with one out of every six hectares devoted to potato production. Almost half a billion kilograms of potatoes are processed every year at the potato plants. And with the growth in the industry came an exponential increase in the use of pesticides, 571% since the year 2000.

Sharon Labchuk, former leader of the Green party of PEI, says that virtually all of PEI's groundwater is contaminated with nitrates, mostly from chemical fertilizers applied to potato fields. A PEI potato destined for the dinner table is subjected to about 20 applications of pesticides in order to protect it from blight. The primary pesticides used — mancozeb, chlorothalonil and metiram — are classified as carcinogens by various agencies and jurisdictions, including the state of California. Islanders know about this, but little has been done. As far back as 1990, a Royal Commission on Land called nitrates in PEI water "a ticking time bomb."[176]

Labchuk says the industry has so much power on the island that successive governments won't deal with the issue. In fact, in 2014, the potato growers sought permits to access deep water wells to irrigate their crops and end the ten-year moratorium that prevented them from using this water source. They argue that PEI has groundwater to spare. They also argue that they cannot compete with other potato-growing areas such as Wisconsin, where growers are allowed to use deep-well irrigation, giving them greater yield.

But in central Wisconsin, high capacity wells have caused water levels in dozens of lakes and streams to drop as the groundwater has been overdrawn, much to the dismay of farmers who bought into the abundance myth and planned their expansion accordingly. Wisconsin potato farmer Justin Isherwood said, "We were all raised with the sense that this is Lake Superior underneath us and it's not."[177]

And, as in PEI, the Wisconsin industry has been allowed to expand, dumping its nitrate effluent near streams and rivers with devastating effects. According to state authorities, one in five wells in agricultural areas is now too polluted with nitrates for safe drinking and the rate of contamination is growing in extent and severity. There are a number of reports of Blue Baby Syndrome: infants, exposed to nitrates in their milk formula, who develop bluish skin caused by lack of oxygen in the blood. All have recovered after hospital care.

"Nitrate that approaches and exceeds unsafe levels in drinking water is one of the top drinking water contaminants in Wisconsin, posing an acute risk to infants and women who are pregnant, a possible risk to the developing fetus during very early stages of pregnancy, and a chronic risk of serious disease in adults," according to the 2015 Wisconsin Groundwater Coordinating Council report.[178]

The Prince Edward Island government has set up a task force on the island's drinking water with the goal of writing a new water act for the province. Well-known PEI activist Leo Broderick says there is real urgency. "Many wells have been condemned and people are being poisoned," he says, adding that holding the corporate players, farmers and government to account is almost a full-time job. But it is imperative that the government act soon to protect the island's groundwater for future generations.

Commodity Exports Drawing Down Lakes and Groundwater

The now-disbanded National Round Table on the Environment and the Economy said, in a 2011 report, that by 2030 water use by the agriculture industry in Canada would increase by 54%, putting great stress on our surface and groundwater supplies.

This is exacerbated by the drive for agricultural export. According to Agriculture and Agri-Food Canada, this country exports more than half the food it produces, making Canada the fifth largest agricultural exporter in the world. The country produces 80% of the world's maple syrup, and it is the largest exporter of flaxseed, canola and durum wheat. Canada ships more than half the peas, lentils and linseed in the world and is the third largest exporter of pork. While the United States is by far Canada's largest customer, China and other Asian countries are importing more of our food commodities, particularly meat.

Canada's meat exports have grown rapidly in recent years. According to the Canadian Meat Council, exports of beef have risen from 100,000 tonnes in 1990 to 322,000 tonnes in 2015, at a value of $2.2 billion. Exports of pork have increased from 200,000 tonnes to 1,171,000 tonnes in those same years at a value of $3.42 billion. In 2015, Canada exported meat to 125 countries.[179]

It is crucial to understand that exporting food also exports the water it took to produce the food. It takes a great deal of water to grow food: 140 litres for a cup of coffee; 2,400 litres for a hamburger. The water used to produce food is called "virtual water," and when this food is exported, the water embedded in it is exported too, right out of the watershed and the country.

Canada is a net virtual water exporter, second only to Australia, meaning that we export more virtual water than we import. Our net annual virtual water exports would fill the Rogers Centre stadium in Toronto 37,500 times. Every year, Canada exports virtual water stored in wheat, barley, rye and oats equivalent to twice the annual discharge of the Athabasca River.[180]

Food production is a consumptive use of water; that is, the water used to produce transported crops is not returned to its original source. Agriculture uses about 8% of Canada's freshwater but, unlike other volume users of raw water, almost 70% of that is not returned to the watershed. The more food Canada produces, the more water it consumes. Growing so much food for export is an alarming exploitation of Canada's water supplies.

Some see an opportunity for Canada to use its water resources to increase its bottom line and profit from a planet running out of water. They promote global trade through the World Trade Organization and regional trade agreements to open more doors for Canadian food exports. But no one in either the government or industry appears to be taking water into account or asking if Canada has enough water to continue to expand indefinitely. For instance, under the Canada-EU Comprehensive Economic and Trade Agreement (CETA), Canadian producers would be allowed to sell an additional 50,000 tonnes of beef a year to Europe — the current quota is 15,000 tonnes — and even more pork.

Much of the increased pork production will come from Manitoba, where Lake Winnipeg is already in crisis with the current level of pig farming. And most of the beef will come from Alberta. As it takes over 15 million litres of water to produce one tonne of beef, it is clear that the expanding beef industry is going to place a huge strain on Alberta's fast-dwindling water supplies. With just 2% of Canada's water supply, Alberta accounts for two-thirds of the water used for irrigation, much of it for export.

No one is suggesting that Canada should not be exporting some of its agricultural production. But there are clear ecological limits that must be faced. David Schindler expects Alberta to become the first water "have not" province in Canada. Its water supply is already fully allocated, he reminds us. Yet, even without these trade agreements, livestock water use in Alberta is set to double in the next decade. No one knows where that water will come from. And few are asking.

Is Drought Here to Stay?

Alberta, along with Saskatchewan and British Columbia, is the epicentre of a new drought trend in Canada. The summer of 2015 was devastating for these provinces, with record-breaking temperatures and extremely low rainfalls causing chaos for farmers and waterways across the region. An investigative report for the *Edmonton Journal* said the hot and dry conditions led to a jump in wildfires and tight water restrictions that put pressure on farmers whose crops remained stunted. About 60% of the agricultural landscape within the prairie region received very low or record low precipitation, affecting 27,000 farmers and six million cattle.

In B.C.'s Fraser Valley, farmers were hit by hot, dry conditions, with crops ripening so fast they could not be harvested and unirrigated fields burned brown by the unrelenting sun. Farmers left whole fields of berries, corn, peas and beans to rot. With most of the mountain snowpack long melted and little rain, water flows in B.C. hit record low flow and higher water temperatures led to salmon deaths. Some river flows were the lowest recorded since measurements began a century ago. Metro Vancouver banned outdoor sprinklers, washing cars and filling swimming pools as the water supply in the reservoirs dipped below 70% of normal levels.[181]

Conditions in Saskatchewan were so dire, the government allowed grazing in 90,000 acres of its wildlife development land, reported the *Journal*. Parts of the province experienced a Level Four drought, the most extreme rating. The whole province of Alberta was declared a state of disaster by the end of that summer. The driest area was around Edmonton, with crop problems widely reported. Only about 15% of Alberta spring wheat, barley, canola and dry peas had fair conditions for harvest.

The horrific wildfire that devastated Fort McMurray in May 2016 has been directly linked to climate change, global warming and overextraction of rivers and lakes. Because the winters are not as long and cold, the trees are drier, infested with pine beetles and more prone to fire, says

University of Lethbridge health sciences professor Judith Kulig. Mike Flannigan with the University of Alberta's Western Partnership for Wildland Fire Science reports that the area burned to ash by wildfires has doubled since the 1970s. "In a warmer world, there will be more fire. That's a virtual certainty," he told reporter Stephen Leahy of Inter Press Service. "I'd say a doubling or even a tripling of fire events is a conservative estimate."[182] B.C.'s snowpack reached record lows in May 2016 and by the end of that month, there were so many forest fires, the province had spent half its firefighting budget for the whole season.

A landmark study published in April 2016 in *Remote Sensing of Environment* used 87,000 NASA satellite images over 29 years to show unequivocally what previously research had posited: that, with climate change, the Arctic is greening while the boreal forest becomes browner. The study showed that the Arctic grasslands are becoming shrubland and the boreal forest vegetation has declined by 3% over the period of the study.[183] The terrible Fort McMurray fire was fed by this boreal browning.

David Schindler has been predicting drought for years and says it is here to stay. In 2006, he and Bill Donahue, a former student now with the Alberta conservation organization Water Matters, gathered decades of flow records for all Alberta's rivers. Their findings showed that river volumes had been reduced by more than half over that time. Climate change, melting glaciers and receding rivers are now permanent features of the Canadian west, he says, and the issue demands the attention of our elected leaders. The California drought is moving north and it gives us a glimpse into our future.

Government Policies Fail Rural Canada

Facing these realities, provincial governments of every political stripe continue to create economic plans based on the growth of export agriculture and extractive industries. They react to individual crises with emergency and relief programs, but have no long term plans to deal with the possibility that Canada's west may be in for a long period of drought. While the Trudeau government is clearly taking the issue of climate change more seriously than did its predecessor, greenhouse gas emissions in Canada continue to rise, lakes continue to warm and recede and glaciers continue to melt.

As with many other sectors, the Trudeau government is dealing with the legacy of cuts and changes Stephen Harper made to Canada's farmers and farmlands. Funding cuts to Agriculture and Agri-Food Canada of 14% in 2014 and 20% in 2015 caused 700 employees, many of them researchers, to be laid off. The Professional Institute of the Public Service of Canada said the targeting of scientists and researchers for layoffs showed the Harper government did not want to listen to the independent voice of research when making policy regarding agriculture.

In his infamous 2012 omnibus bill, Stephen Harper killed the Prairie Farm Rehabilitation Administration (PFRA), created in 1935 to stop erosion of prairie land in the wake of the widespread drought, farm abandonment and land degradation that was the legacy of the Dust Bowl. The agency rehabilitated vast areas and introduced sustainable farm practices and land utilization, including tree culture, grassland preservation, soil conservation and enrichment, biodiversity and watershed protection. It has been called one of Canada's greatest success stories. The

PFRA created and protected 85 community pastures — collectively twice the size of Prince Edward Island — to provide grazing land for farmers and the protection of the prairie ecosystem.

Saskatchewan naturalist and writer Trevor Herriot says that just 20% is left of the original prairie landmass and that these pastures are protecting ecosystems that go back 8,000 years. The PFRA has been a bulwark against the forces now consolidating and globalizing the beef industry. "With large feeder cattle operations and foreign-owned meat processors tilting the marketplace their way, community pastures have helped to sustain smaller operators, keeping our national livestock herd connected to local economies," he wrote.[184]

Unless this policy is reversed, provincial governments are free to put this protected land up for sale. And it is feared that much of it will go to the oil and gas industry. *Canadian Cowboy Country Magazine* says the move to hand over this land to the provinces was a brilliant stroke on the part of the Harper government, given that it will be the provinces that take the heat for allowing the public land to become private.[185]

Added Herriot, "Once grassland is ploughed to grow crops, the appropriation is total. The public values and natural capital found on the prairie — its capacity to store carbon, foster biodiversity, stabilize fragile soils, filter and hold water, and provide recreation for hunters, hikers and naturalists and stirring beauty for the rest of us — do not survive."

Corporate Farms on the Rise

This loss of public land parallels another disturbing trend, namely the decline of the community-based family farm and farmer co-ops and the rise in corporately owned industrial food production and absentee farmer owners.

Statistics Canada reports that between 2006 and 2012, the number of farms in Canada decreased 10% but the average farm size grew by 7%. In some regions, such as Saskatchewan, the number of farms fell by 17% while the average farm size increased by 15%. Farms with $1 million or more in annual revenue represent the fastest growing sector of Canadian agriculture, jumping 36% in those years, reported the *Globe and Mail*. While those farms still make up less than 5% of the total number of producers, they account for nearly half of Canada's food production.[186]

In its March 2015 report, "Losing Our Grip," the National Farmers Union (NFU) posited that the kind of agricultural community that best protects land and water is one in which farmland is owned and worked by local people — farm families, producer co-ops and communities deliberately designed to have a high degree of social cohesion and teamwork. Long-term community thinking over short-term profit-driven foreign-investor thinking is more likely to protect the land, water and atmosphere by acting now to slow and reverse climate change.[187]

A good example of such local control was the Co-operative Development Initiative, a project that promoted people-centred local development and farmer-driven projects for sustainable rural development. The Harper government killed its funding and put at risk 9,000 co-operatives across Canada. Farmers' organizations protested that the decision cut off the lifeblood of locally run rural businesses in Canada.

Established in 1935, the Canadian Wheat Board was a pro-farmer marketing monopoly that guaranteed farmers a base price for their grain and protected them from the vagaries of the market. It was also one of the world's largest, longest-standing and most successful farmer-run trading enterprises. In 2012, the Harper government privatized the Wheat Board and put it on the open market. In April 2015, the Global Grain Group bought up a majority stake in the company and changed its name to G3 Canada. In February 2016, the Canadian Wheat Board Alliance, a group of grain farmers supportive of farmer-run grain trading, announced that the loss of their marketing monopoly meant a loss of $6.5 billion in income to farmers over the preceding two years.

The new owners are a partnership of Saudi investment giant SALIC and American agribusiness giant Bunge. SALIC was established by the rulers of Saudi Arabia in 2011 with a mandate to secure stable food supplies in other parts of the world. It has bought up large swaths of farmland in Europe and elsewhere. The company considers Canada a "prosperity destination" as it seeks water-secure places to grow commodities, according to the *Globe and Mail*.[188]

The Harper government also enacted an omnibus Agriculture Growth Act that included changes to the Plant Breeders' Rights Act. The changes gave more power to transnational seed companies to claim property rights in their seed, reducing the ability of Canadian farmers to save and reuse seed themselves. The change gave multinational agribusiness much more money and control while increasing farmers' costs and reducing farmers' autonomy and Canadian sovereignty, said the National Farmers Union.

Land Grabs Growing in Canada

Over the last decade, other changes to agriculture-related laws have also benefitted agribusiness corporations, weakened farmers' market-power and increased farmers' costs. Now, corporations and investment funds far from the farming communities are moving in to take advantage of rural Canada's rich soils, abundant space and freshwater supplies in a world of increasing land and water scarcity and rising demand for food.

Rising prices for farmland in Canada are making it very difficult for young farmers to make a living off the land. Farm Credit Canada says the price of farmland in Canada rose by over 75% between 2010 and 2015. A group of farmland investment funds have sprung up to buy up farmland for wealthy investors and lease the farms back to the former owners to operate. In 2013, the Canada Pension Plan bought up over 465 hectares (115,000 acres) of prime farmland in Saskatchewan, raising calls for stricter rules in that province.

Some farmers are selling, cashing in on a windfall. Others want to stay on the land but they are no longer competitive. To stay, they must become, essentially, "tenant farmers." Farmers who want to stay in business, Western University agriculture professor David Sparling told the *Globe and Mail*, are going to have to figure out how to scale up or sell their farms to corporations with enough capital to drive up productivity. The deck is stacked against those who would maintain the family farm.

Investment companies such as Bonnefield, Pike Management, Agcapita and Assiniboia have bought up hundreds of thousands of acres of prime farmland across the country in the last decade. The NFU explains that these companies are banking on global trends in hunger, drought, flooding and soil erosion for their future profitability.

They are also responding to decades of federal government policies that have promoted concentration and consolidation — "get big or get out." Farmers are overleveraged and feel they have no choice but to sell their land and lease it back to operate. Calgary-based Agcapita explains the appeal: "Investors are provided with the comfort of a direct investment in farmland combined with a non-operational model of front-end loaded cash rents." The NFU reports that in 2014, the company sold a parcel of farmland holdings at twice the buying price to a financial agency that manages the investment portfolio of one wealthy family.

Former NFU president Terry Boehm warns that this trend is dangerous for farmers and farm communities: "When you shift land ownership, you move into a new feudalism where those that work on the land become labourers. In the prairie region and many parts of Canada, we have land resources that other countries can't imagine having. Who do people want producing their food and under what kind of methods do they want it done?"[189]

Foreign investment in Canada's prime farmland is increasing, making it much more difficult to protect local communities and land and water protection regulations. Indeed global capital is circling Canada, clear in the knowledge that the world will need a huge increase in food production to feed a global population of almost 10 billion by 2050.

Canada's provinces vary in their rules about foreign ownership of farmland. British Columbia, Ontario, Nova Scotia, New Brunswick and Newfoundland and Labrador have no restrictions on foreign ownership although some require acquired land to remain as productive farmland. In Quebec, non-residents must get a permit to own farmland,

and while permits restrict the size of acreage at first, investors can apply to expand every year. Prince Edward Island, Alberta, Saskatchewan and Manitoba all have restrictions on the size of acreage allowed to be acquired by foreign owners, although all are under pressure to open up their farmlands to more foreign investment, as younger farmers find it increasingly hard to make a living off the land.

Information on foreign ownership of Canadian farmland is almost non-existent. "Are non-farmers snapping up too much Canadian farmland?" asks *Country Guide*, Canada's oldest farm publication. Its answer? "Nobody knows." This is because, says farmer-writer Gerald Pilger, no one is actively tracking it.[190]

But the NFU warns that foreign control can come in through the back door when Canadian investment companies buy up farmland. Calgary-based Walton International purchases farmland near cities in Alberta and Ontario in order to convert farmland to urban designation ready for development. Because Ontario does not restrict foreign ownership of farmland and Alberta does not restrict foreign ownership of farmland being converted to residential or industrial development, the company can and does seek international investors for its properties. AGInvest Canada has bought $70 million worth of farmland in southwestern Ontario, which it is marketing to investors in the United Arab Emirates.

Land Grabs Are Water Grabs Too

To learn what these land grabs in Canada might mean for water, it is important to look at the issue internationally. In the last decade, wealthy countries and international investors have bought up at least 70 million hectares (175 million acres) of land — an area almost triple the size of the UK — in Asia, Latin America and Africa to either feed their own populations or as speculation.

These include hedge funds, investment banks, agribusiness interests, commodity traders, pension funds and the investment funds of countries such as Saudi Arabia, Japan, Qatar, South Korea and the United Arab Emirates. Populous China and India are major players as well. Investors are getting incredible deals, some leasing vast tracts of land for 99 years for as little as 40 cents per acre per year in countries like Thailand and Nigeria. Some of the land purchases are so large, Food & Water Watch reported, that it would be like foreign investors buying up and owning all the farmland in Oklahoma. Many millions of small farmers and peasants have been displaced.[191]

The model is one of intense agro-industrial farming, using huge amounts of pesticides and chemical fertilizers, and guzzling local water sources, including groundwater extraction. The San Francisco–based Oakland Institute that studies land grabs in the global South reports that if the rate of land acquisition in Africa continues to grow at its current level, demand for freshwater on that continent will overtake the existing supply of renewable water by 2019. This will jeopardize Africa's fragile river systems by diverting even more water from rivers and lakes already under stress, such as the Niger River.[192]

Many of the most aggressive land grabbing countries are facing severe water shortages at home. Saudi Arabia's foreign-land-acquisition funds are openly meant to help that country preserve its limited domestic water supplies. It has bought large tracts of land in parched California in order to produce alfalfa for its livestock back home. In some countries such as Mali and Sudan, unlimited local water sources have been guaranteed to the foreign land investors and water is being dammed or diverted to their use.

Land grabbing is essentially control grabbing, explains the European-based research organization Transnational Institute. What is at stake is the power to decide how and for what purposes land and water can be used now and in the future. "Land grabbing needs to be seen in the context of the power of national and transnational capital and their desire for profit, which overrides existing meanings, uses and systems of management of the land that are rooted in local communities," said the group in their 2015 primer, "The Global Land Grab." This is the epitome of an ongoing and accelerating change in the meaning and use of the land and water toward large-scale, capital-intensive, resource-depleting industrial agriculture.[193]

The WorldWatch Institute says that this model of industrial farming is fouling our waterways and consuming far too much water. Governments and transnational food and seed companies promote a system of food production that pits farmers in one country against farmers in another to keep the system "competitive." The system squeezes out family- and community-based farms and has a negative impact on the biodiversity needed for healthy watersheds.

Land and water grabs in Canada, whether they are done by wealthy Canadian investors who have no stake in the community or by foreign investors, is an additional burden on Canada's already burdened freshwater heritage. And given the influence of money in politics, they pose an additional challenge to local governments trying to protect water.

The Alliston Aquifer is a subterranean lake that stretches from Georgian Bay to the Oak Ridges Moraine in southern Ontario. As well as being the source of drinking water for the region, the aquifer provides water for the Wye River and surrounding wetlands and feeds creeks and rivers that eventually flow into Georgian Bay, Lake Simcoe and Lake Ontario. The aquifer is located in Simcoe County north of Barrie, a land of incredible diversity and beauty, prime farmland and a popular destination for tourists seeking the lovely waters of Georgian Bay. In 2006, the water of this aquifer was tested by Dr. William Shotyk at his lab in Heidelberg, Germany, and pronounced among the cleanest water ever tested.

In 1990, before the Clean Water Act, the government of Ontario gave the go-ahead to build an industrial waste dump right atop the Alliston Aquifer on a parcel of land in Tiny Township known as Site 41. As David Suzuki has said, how this site got an approval boggles the mind. Up to 225 million litres of pristine groundwater was to be pumped out and disposed of before construction. And, over the life of the landfill, even more groundwater would have to be pumped out to maintain the dump's structural integrity. The province promised that its top-of-the-line plastic liner (with a two-year warranty against leakage on its seams) would protect groundwater, but the local residents were understandably skeptical.

Thousands of STOP SITE 41 signs sprang up. Farmers, seniors, students, First Nations and environmentalists formed a coalition to wage a long battle to stop the dump. It was led by people like "citizen scientist" Steve Ogden, local farmers Anne and John Ritchie Nahuis and Ray Millar, Aware Simcoe's Kate Harries and indigenous leaders Vicki Monague, Danny Beaton and Elizabeth Elson. Council of Canadians staff made stopping Site 41 a priority campaign, and I visited the site many times.

The summer of 2009 was pivotal. All the legal and political avenues for stopping the dump seemed exhausted and the local county council, made up of the mayors of all the small towns and villages in the area, had given the green light for the heavy excavation equipment to start digging the first of four "cells." Members of the nearby Beausoleil First Nation set up camp on the Parnell family farm across the road from Site 41 and lit a sacred fire that they promised would not go out until the dumpsite was stopped. They and others held morning prayers and blockades every day on the road to Site 41, delaying construction for five weeks and ultimately forcing a new vote on the matter at the council.

Seventeen people were arrested for blocking construction, including a number of indigenous protesters and farmers Ina and Keith Wood, then 76 and 82. When they received the call to present themselves to the Midland OPP detachment later that day, Ina was baking butter tarts for the local church. Keith, who died in early 2016, was not fazed by his first arrest. "I like to look after my heritage — which is land and water," he said. "My grandparents lived here 150 years ago, and I have seven grandchildren."[194]

While Steven Shrybman fought the blockade injunction in court on behalf of the Council of Canadians, activists went door to door in key communities across Simcoe County, seeking support for independent scientific studies and a moratorium on Site 41, which would mean no construction until 2011. The campaign was successful and a date was set for the council to vote on whether or not to place a moratorium on the project.

Hundreds descended on the county council meeting on August 25 that summer, filling the public gallery, while others waited outside, listening to the debate on loudspeakers. This was democracy in the raw, with feelings running high and tempers flaring on both sides. The *Globe and Mail*'s Joe Friesen was there and reported, "Shame, they shouted at Warden Guergis. He sipped his coffee impassively, his great warden's chain draped around his chest. It had been a bruising battle, but he was unbowed. He provoked the crowd periodically by threatening to remove the unruly, eliciting boos."[195]

Tiny Township mayor Peggy Breckenridge led the speakers in favour of the moratorium and gave a passionate defence of the need to protect the area's water. She was greeted with a standing ovation. But the day was probably won when Scott Warnock, mayor of Tay Township and a staunch supporter of Site 41, rose to speak. The vote was going to be close and his words would help sway the undecided.

Warnock started to speak but had to catch his breath, as he choked up with tears. He explained that when he went into his home office that morning, his grandchildren had taken one of the STOP SITE 41 signs and written the word "Poppa" on it. Warnock said in that moment, his job description changed and he was now a steward of the waters of Simcoe County. He urged his fellow councillors to oppose the dump. The moratorium was adopted 22–10.

Less than a year later, the county council voted to rezone the landfill for agricultural use and the province revoked the certificate of approval for Site 41. The land has been sold to a farmer and is once again producing food. Aware Simcoe helped defeat most of the councillors who had supported the dump in the next election. The precedent of the Site 41 victory was key in defeating the opening of a mega quarry in nearby Melancthon Township several years later.

seven
Water for Sale

American economist Richard Sandor is widely credited with inventing financial futures and has been called the "Father of Carbon Trading" by *Time* magazine. In a June 2015 lecture at the University of Chicago's law school, Sandor said that the drought in western North America would soon lead to the launch of a U.S. water futures market. Water will replace crude oil as the most important commodity of the 21st century, he predicted, and said that the U.S. Commodity Futures Trading Commission is now developing an algorithm to separate the price of water as a life necessity from the price of water as a commodity. The drought crises in California and China will lead to water quality and water quantity trading, he added.

The recent evolution in wealth creation can be summarized by "different eras of commoditization," he said and asserted that market signals — which he calls a "field of dreams" — from water traders would lead to the infrastructure investments needed to make it work: "We are on the verge of breaking into water markets in the world."[196]

Sandor is not alone in his advocacy of the market to solve the world's water problems. In business schools throughout the world, students are taught that where governments have failed to protect water, the market can take up the slack. Put a price on water, let it be bought and sold on the open market, and water will find its place, like running shoes and cars. They are told water markets and water trading are part of a trend to privatize and commodify the world's water resources.

Nestlé chairman Peter Brabeck-Letmathe, who also advises the World Bank on water policy in the global South, says that the market should determine the fate of the vast majority of the world's water: "Give the 1.5% of the water, make it a human right. But give me a market for the 98.5% so the market forces are able to react, and they will be the best guidance that you can have. Because if the market forces are there, the investments are going to be made."[197]

Putting a Price on Nature

Sandor and Brabeck-Letmathe are proponents of "ecosystem services" — basically putting a price on nature, ostensibly to save it, but in reality, to control and profit from it. The United Nations estimates that the planet's ecosystems and the biodiversity that underpins them generate services to humanity worth $72 trillion U.S. every year. Proponents of ecosystem services say that if we can prove that nature has a concrete monetary value, it can compete in its natural state with other uses to which it might be used.

There are real problems with this approach. For one thing, how is nature to be protected under this system if it can be proved that the land or water in question can make more profit if developed than if saved? For another, redefining nature as "natural capital" allows the control and management of natural resources to move from people and their governments to financial markets. Corporations would get to profit by locking natural-resources management into capital markets that would, in turn, dramatically curtail the power of local communities to claim and protect their water commons.

This kind of thinking is being incorporated into policy in various parts of Canada. In an assessment of the evolution of Canadian water policy, the law firm Gowling WLG cites a flurry of new provincial laws across the country. Some are regulatory in nature, recognizing that healthy ecosystems are vital to all life and that governments have a role to protect them. But there is an underlying openness to allowing the market to play a larger role in determining who gets access to water.

Most provinces have adopted a "mitigation and offset" approach to water resources, Gowling reports. Harm to a stream or wetland in one place can be offset by environmental remediation in another, much like the practice of allowing a country or an industry to continue to emit greenhouse gases in exchange for planting trees in a country far away.

Gowling gives the example of Alberta's 2013 Wetland Policy, which evaluates wetlands in terms of their "relative wetland value," that is, the contribution of the individual wetland to water-quality improvement, hydrology, biodiversity and various human uses. Wetlands of the highest value are protected in the long-term whereas wetlands with lower relative value are permitted to be developed if the "lost" wetland is offset somewhere else. This is similar to the changes made to the Fisheries Act, where fish habitat near commercial fisheries has more protection than fish habitat elsewhere.[198]

Water Markets in Alberta

Alberta is the first province in Canada to develop a market for water. (B.C. did briefly flirt with the idea when it was first preparing its new water legislation but backed off under strong opposition.) Since 2006, portions of the South Saskatchewan River Basin have been closed to new water licence applications (permits given by the province to take a certain amount of water) except for First Nations, water storage and some conservation projects. This moratorium set the stage for separating water rights from land rights and allowing the trading of licences. Under the old rules known as First in Time, First in Right (FITFIR), older licence holders had access to almost unlimited amounts of water during a shortage. Rather than challenging a system that favoured large users and discouraged conservation, the Alberta government decided to allow historic licences to be traded, setting the stage for a market based on who would pay more to redistribute water without reworking water title or ownership.

Within the first year of water trading, reported the *Calgary Herald*, millions of dollars changed hands and the price of water soared from $133 per acre-foot to $7,500. The Municipal District of Rocky View paid $15 million to secure water for a $1.6 billion entertainment and racetrack development complex, transferring water from the stressed

Red River. Local farmers and environmentalists were outraged that a for-profit development had set the priorities for the region's scarce water supplies.

In 2009, the provincial Conservative government announced that it wanted to extend the concept of water markets throughout the province, setting off a storm of opposition. Critics warned that this plan would give water resources to the highest bidder, forcing cash-strapped municipalities to compete with big oil and other large industries for increasingly scarce water.

In 2012, the University of Alberta set up a water advisory board to bring together international experts so that the university could make policy recommendations to the government. Included in the "experts" were a number of water investment funds, energy companies such as Total and Nexen, and Nestlé's Peter Brabeck-Letmathe, who said he was actively dealing with the Alberta government to think about setting up a water exchange where water could be bought and sold in Alberta the same way as other commodities are traded.

There has been little movement on this issue since the Notley government came to power. While critical of water markets in opposition, it is unclear which direction the government will take to deal with the province's growing water problems. It would, however, be very wise for the Alberta government to examine what has happened in other jurisdictions that have allowed water trading and water markets.

The drought in California has opened up a new source of revenue for farmers. In the summer of 2015, a number of rice farmers decided that, instead of using their protected water allocations to grow crops, they would sell their water to cities, developers and the state at record prices. Several years before, Texan billionaire oilman T. Boone Pickens sold 16 trillion litres of water rights he had bought from the Ogallala Aquifer to a Texas water supplier for $103 million. His company, Mesa Water, has come under strong criticism for hoarding water and selling it for profit in an area desperate for water. Pickens said the deal felt like "buying and selling a motor boat."[199]

In water-stressed Spain, farmers are buying and selling water on a rapidly growing black market, mostly from illegal wells, reported the *New York Times*. The hundreds of thousands of wells — most of them illegal — have depleted groundwater to the point of no return. Land-use changes now allow grass on a golf course to be labelled a crop and planted trees on a vacation home to be labelled a farm, thus making developers eligible to receive water marked for irrigation.[200]

Australia has had water markets since 1994. They have created an unregulated system of exchange involving hundreds of fly-by-night "water brokers." Big industrial farm operations swallowed up the small local farms and then the banks and investors — domestic and foreign — moved in to reap big profits. Governments encouraged bidding wars. In just a few years, Australia created an annual $2.6 billion largely unregulated water market that involves hundreds of brokers, buying and selling water on the open market. Not surprisingly, since the introduction of water trading, water prices have skyrocketed, going from $2 a megalitre in 2000 to over $1,500 a megalitre in 2014.

This has made it very expensive for the federal government to buy back enough water from these private interests to save the Murray Darling River, badly hurt by the recent decade-long drought. The government has pledged billions to buy back the very water it gave away for free just two decades ago. Australia is the driest inhabited continent on earth, but its people have lost control of their scarce water supplies. As one farmer told me, in the driest inhabited continent on the planet, the only way for the price to go is up.

It would be a terrible mistake to allow the expansion of water trading in Alberta or Canada. Water trading fails to give water priority to municipalities, local farmers, human needs and ecosystem preservation. It allows governments to abdicate their role in allocating dwindling supplies of water according to community values they should be upholding, allowing allocation decisions instead to be made based on the ability to pay. It also doesn't address the reality that in some places, water has been extensively overallocated and governments need to step in with new priorities for their water resources.

Water trading promotes speculation and diminishes the right of the public to know where local water supplies are going and gives a small group of people and corporations undue control over water sources. It gives corporate farms and hedge fund investors a reason to take prime farmland out of production, lay off farmworkers and make huge profits on water that should be safeguarded as a public trust. Sometimes it even results in the permanent dislocation of water, drawing down aquifers and altering rivers.

Pollution Trading in Ontario

Sustainable Prosperity, whose members include former Reform politician Preston Manning and several executives with energy companies, calls itself a national green economy "think tank/do tank." It promotes "environmental markets" — basically pollution trading — that would replace government fines by allowing a polluting company to trade its way around regulation and permit it to exceed its allowable pollution level by purchasing credit from another entity that has not yet exceeded its limit.

"The logic of this is to achieve a particular environmental objective in a more cost-effective way than a regulation," explains senior researcher Alex Wood. In a trading system for water, for instance, he told the *Globe and Mail*, a company can decide to limit its pollution at a certain cost or decide instead to buy a credit from another company or operation that can limit its pollution footprint more cheaply.[201]

Ontario has introduced what it calls "water-quality trading" to deal with the pollution and nutrient loading of its lakes, including the Great Lakes, and is open to the trading of pollution permits among farmers, industry and municipal sewage operators. The conservation authorities of South Nation River and Nottawasaga Valley have set up water quality trading experiments and a third is being considered for the Lake Simcoe watershed.

Increasing population in those communities necessitated the expansion of local sewage treatment plants. The municipalities were allowed to discharge phosphorus above allowable limits by financing some rural landowner stewardship projects — offsets that saved them millions. Lake Simcoe's plan would allow land developers in the watershed to purchase offsets generated by pollution improvements achieved elsewhere in the watershed. In its October 2015 Great Lakes Protection Act, the government of Ontario set targets to restrict the amount of phosphorus entering the lakes and opened the door to allow water quality trading strategies to be used to meet this goal.

In a November 2015 report to the Ontario government, Sustainable Prosperity touted these trading projects and urged the government to expand the program.[202] This pro-market group has found some important environmental allies. In their August 2014 report, "Clean, Not Green: Tackling Algal Blooms in the Great Lakes," Environmental Defence and Freshwater Future opened the door to the Ontario government exploring the use of market mechanisms — what they call nutrient trading — to give farmers the tools they need to reduce their nutrient runoff.[203]

Water Pollution Brokers in the U.S.

While it is understandable that environmental groups are frustrated with the slow pace of government action, promoting a market mechanism to protect water could give more control to polluters, open the door to water-trading brokers and reduce local democratic control over local water. Scott Edwards and Michele Merkel, the legal team at Washington-based Food & Water Watch, have studied similar water quality trading schemes in the U.S. and have a warning for others going down this path. In their November 2015 report, "Water Quality Trading: Polluting Public Waterways for Private Gain," they state that after over 40 years of effective Clean Water Act control of the biggest sources of pollution in the U.S., industries have found a way to evade meaningful and enforceable limits on their discharges through such "pay-to-pollute" schemes.

Pennsylvania has the longest-running pollution-trading program in the country. In 2014 alone, agriculture-related operations — largely factory farms — bought credit to dump more than 800,000 kilograms of nitrogen and over

50,000 kilograms of phosphorus into local waterways. The pollution trade was negotiated by "nutrient credit brokers," such as Red Barn Trading Company, that charge high fees for their services. Using information gathered from government documents, Food & Water Watch reported that in this case, as in others, industries are free to pollute under a "sky's the limit" permitting system that sees manure from agricultural operations trucked from one impaired watershed to another to generate profits.

Nutrient credit brokers like Red Barn work with "manure brokers" such as J&L Hay, a single farm in the southwest part of the state, where 90% of Red Barn's thousands of tons of manure end up. When Food & Water Watch lawyers asked state authorities where the manure went after it was transported to this farm, they couldn't say. "A significant number of pollution credits in Pennsylvania are being generated through what can only be described as a shell game, whereby piles of manure move from place to place to pollute local waterways while middlemen brokers skim profits from sales of highly questionable credits," said the authors.

In Ohio, the Alpine Cheese Company was allowed to increase its phosphorus-containing wastewater discharge by 200% to 145 million litres per year. The company has been cited for over 1,000 permit violations, but continues to dump its waste undeterred.

Food & Water Watch said that reporting and oversight in most states that allow pollution trading is almost non-existent, leaving the application and credit verification process largely in the hands of the pollution brokers. In fact, in Pennsylvania, much of the trading process is directly outsourced to the brokers such as Red Barn, which is a "one-stop shop" for farms that want to sell pollution credits to other industries. Red Barn puts together the proposals, and once they are given the go-ahead by the state, Red Barn and other brokers sell their "verified" credits on auction. "The lack of agency oversight and the degree to which companies like Red Barn control the trading process from cradle to grave create significant potential for abuse," warned the Food & Water Watch report.

Water pollution trading has not improved water quality and, in fact, has allowed industry to discharge more pollution in America's waterways. It represents a clear rollback of the Clean Water Act that industry has been seeking since the act was introduced and is being implemented in a way that is most favourable to industry — as a mechanism to avoid permit compliance and expenditures for pollution reduction. "People who care about water quality should never support water pollution trading," the authors concluded.[204]

Where it might be tempting to think that in Canada, water pollution trading could be used as a transitional tool for good, especially if overseen by governments, the reality is that most of those promoting it are doing so in order to get government out of the way and allow the market to set the rules. The story of water pollution trading in the U.S. is a cautionary tale.

Pollution "Fees" Permit Continued Waste Dumping

Another market instrument being promoted in many quarters is pollution fees or taxes. A new organization, Canadians for Clean Prosperity, advocates free market solutions to environmental problems and promotes pollution fees in Canada. Mark Cameron, former policy director to Prime Minister Stephen Harper, is the group's executive director. Cut from the same anti-regulation cloth as the former PM, Cameron insists that Canada can build pipelines *and* meet reduced greenhouse emissions targets by charging oil consumers, but fails to explain how this practice will result in reduced emissions. Polluters paying to pollute, says the group, will allow governments to lower taxes — clearly a political goal.

As in water pollution trading, polluter fees simply give big industry licence to keep on polluting, paying a nominal fee to do so. The Global Water Partnership (GWP) is an international network of players, including the World Bank and big private water operators, that has a major influence on global water policy. It is a promoter of pollution fees and is open about the fact that they can be used to allow polluters to continue to pollute as long as they pay. "Faced with paying for the social cost of their discharges," GWP says, "they have three broad choices: to cease operations, to change their techniques or practices so as to reduce their pollution, or to carry on polluting and pay the charge."

Astonishingly, this organization says if the charge or fee is at an economic level that equals the cost to society of this pollution, "society should be indifferent whether the pollution continues or ceases." As in most market schemes to deal with water protection, pollution is seen in purely economic terms and no mention is made of the damage to ecosystems or habitat.[205]

Selling Water a Bottle at a Time

While water markets and water pollution trading may be water commodification by the back door, extracting spring and groundwater and putting it in plastic bottles for sale is a straightforward commodification. Despite anti bottled-water campaigns, the bottled water industry continues to skyrocket. According to Transparency Market Research, the global annual market for water was valued at almost $160 billion in 2013 and will be worth just under $300 billion by 2020. In volume, annual sales will increase from 268 billion litres to 465 billion in those same years.[206]

Canadians purchase about 2.4 billion litres of bottled water a year — about 68 litres per person, despite having access to clean safe tap or well water. While tap water is subject to multiple tests a day, bottled water is considered a food and falls under the Food and Drugs Act. It is up to the Canadian Food Inspection Agency to enforce the act, but a study by the Ottawa-based research group Polaris Institute found that on average, the agency only tests each bottled water plant every three years.

Numerous studies have found contaminants in bottled water and some raise concerns about chemicals leaching from the plastic. And the waste footprint of this industry is huge. Plastic bottles found in lakes, wetlands and land-fill take hundreds of years to decompose. The California-based Pacific Institute says that bottled water is up to 2,000 times more energy intensive than tap water. This respected water research group also says that if the water used to make the plastic is taken into account, it takes three litres of water to produce one litre of bottled water.

The industry claims that it uses very little raw water compared to food production and mining. This is true but what it does not discuss is that its bottled water plants are located on specific springs or groundwater sources that can be harmed or drained by their operations. Bottled water companies are like gold miners; they come for their "blue gold," and when it is gone, they move on. But while they are extracting, their trucks carrying away the water often operate 24/7, churning up country roads and spewing greenhouse gases.

Bottled water companies in Canada — the majority located in Quebec, Ontario and British Columbia — pay next to nothing for the public water they use. Quebec charges $70 for a million litres. B.C. charged nothing for its raw water to industry until its new water act of 2015. Now it charges $2.25 per million litres.

According to the environmental commissioner of Ontario, the province grants permits for about 500 trillion litres of raw water to industry every year, including bottled water companies, and only charges $3.71 per million litres. The province spends about $16.2 million annually managing the water permits but collects only about a million dollars in water fees, recovering only 1.2% of the cost of operating the program.[207] With the price of many brands of bottled water at $2 per bottle, the profits for these companies are clearly enormous.

Nestlé is the biggest bottled water operator in Canada, with major plants in Ontario and B.C. Since 2008, it has been taking 3.6 million litres of water a day from two wells for its bottled water plant in Aberfoyle, Ontario, making a profit at that location alone of over $2 million a year. In 2013, Nestlé sought and was granted an extension of its Hillsburgh well permit to 1.1 million litres a day for five years, but the province placed a condition that in times of drought, the company would have to reduce its water taking. Nestlé resisted this restriction and appealed to the environment ministry. The non-profit legal team at Ecojustice took the case to court on behalf of the Council of Canadians and Wellington Water Watchers and won, maintaining some key principles affirming that water in Ontario is a public trust.

Nestlé is currently seeking approval to take over another well at Middlebrook, near Elora, and extract 1.6 million litres of groundwater a day to be trucked to its plant, a move fiercely opposed by local residents and a new group called Save Our Water that formed to fight the company. The area has experienced several serious droughts in recent years and the Grand River Watershed, where the wells and plant are located, is a fragile ecosystem that feeds into Lake Erie. Allowing a transnational corporation to continue to mine this water is a travesty, especially given that most local people can get clean, safe and affordable water from their taps.

Hope for Change

Nestlé's other major plant is in Hope, B.C, a small community located in the heart of the Fraser Valley. The company takes about 265 million litres a year from this site and has done so for years, although verifying past takings is difficult because, until 2016, there was not only no charge for groundwater takings, there was no reporting requirement. It was truly a wild west where anyone could dig a well and start pumping water for free. Outrage about the Hope site has been growing for years but exploded during the drought and wildfires of summer 2015.

A community petition deploring Nestlé's special water access gathered over 225,000 signatures that summer. Liz McDowell was the campaign director for the action and voiced her community's anger to the CBC: "It's simply scandalous that a company like Nestlé can take hundreds of millions of litres of groundwater at basically pennies at the same time as other B.C. residents are being asked to conserve water because it's in the middle of a drought."[208] The government was forced to announce a review of the rates the very day the group presented its petition at the legislature.

First Nations of the area are particularly incensed. The Chawathil First Nation is laying claim to the water Nestlé takes from its Hope well, saying the well is situated in its traditional territory. "It's no different than the way business has been done in this province since Europeans first arrived," said Chawathil chief Rhoda Peters. "It's time business as usual practices change, because they're not working for our community and it is fundamentally unlawful." Their claim is backed by the Union of B.C. Chiefs, whose grand chief, Stewart Phillip, reminds us the law dictates that First Nations must be consulted on water takings in their territory. "It's not optional," he said.[209]

The B.C. Water Sustainability Act now requires industry, including bottled water companies, to pay what amounts to $5.63 for an amount of water that would fill an Olympic-sized swimming pool — a totally inadequate amount given the profits these companies make, and there are now calls to charge substantially more for the province's raw water. The publicity generated by the summer of 2015 protests has helped to educate British Columbians on the fact that their groundwater had been totally unregulated and it has created a real debate on the wisdom of allowing certain industries, such as fracking and bottled water, to access groundwater sources at all, no matter what they are charged.

In a February 2016 report called "Water Rush," Council of Canadians water campaigner Emma Lui noted that the District of Hope experienced Level 4 drought conditions (extremely dry) during the summer of 2015.

In the report, she urged governments to establish a process for prioritizing water access, pointing out that many groups who participated in the consultation process for the new act called for a hierarchy of use, giving priority to human consumption, local food production and security and ecosystem protection. From this perspective, Lui says, "Despite the costs, we do not have to — and should not — consent to water being bottled and exported out of a region, nor should we consent to water being used for polluting industries like fracking or tar sands development projects."

Lui praises parts of the new act, including the regulation of groundwater, inclusion of environmental flows to ensure there is enough water in lakes and rivers and a framework for regional water sustainability plans. However, she is critical that the government plans to base the new groundwater regulation system on first in time, first in right, the same system it uses to regulate surface water. This system continues to give preferential treatment to those who used water in a region first, cutting access to new users in times of water scarcity.

Calling this a remnant of the gold rush, Lui explains that there are an estimated 20,000 wells in B.C from which industrial users draw groundwater. Existing groundwater users will get three years to establish their priority access. After that, all new groundwater licences will be issued on a priority basis. Regardless of what the water is to be used for, users with older licences will be given priority and, during times of shortages, they will still be entitled to take their full allocation of water over junior licences. Under this system, Nestlé could get preferential access over expanding or new municipalities, small farmers or other community water users.

Further, some industrial water users can claim priority from the date the well was first used, whether or not they owned it at the time. Nestlé can establish priority access to the oldest of the four wells it operates in Hope, which was built in 1987 and previously owned by Aberfoyle Springs even though their ownership dates just to 2000. And, outrageously, the act does not give priority to indigenous communities, the first "first in time" users of water.[210]

Exports Back on the Table?

Canadians have been debating the issue of bulk water exports for a half-century. The Great Recycling and Northern Development (GRAND) Canal project, first introduced in the 1960s, would have built an aqueduct through the Great Lakes. A western route called the North American Water and Power Alliance (NAWAPA) proposed to dam most rivers in British Columbia and divert the water to the United States. There were at least seven other water-diversion projects floated in the 1960s and '70s.

The issue heated up in the 1980s when then Quebec premier Robert Bourassa, backed by Prime Minister Brian Mulroney, proposed to dam the mouth of James Bay and send water to the U.S. Midwest via a series of pipelines, tunnels and dams. The ensuing cry of opposition from all corners of Canada shelved these plans. Then in 1998, Nova Group of Sault Ste. Marie obtained a licence from former Ontario premier Mike Harris to export 600 million litres of water a year from Lake Superior to Asia by tanker. This led to a firestorm of protest on both sides of the border, including from U.S. secretary of state Madeleine Albright, leading to a revocation of the licence.

The same year, Newfoundland premier Brian Tobin granted the McCurdy Group, a local business consortium, the right to export 52 billion litres of water annually from a glacier watershed called Gisborne Lake without an environmental assessment. Public outcry put the project on hold until 2001 when the new premier, Roger Grimes, announced he saw no reason to ban the sale of Newfoundland water for export and allowed proceedings for a licence application to begin once more. Again, the government was forced to back down in the face of opposition from the public and the Chrétien government, worried the practice would spread to other provinces, and the project was abandoned altogether.

Polls and repeated public reaction to these initiatives over the years clearly show that Canadians oppose the bulk commercial export of Canadian water. They understand instinctively that water is needed in the watersheds where it resides. Removing mass amounts of water from central Asia's Aral Sea — once the fourth largest lake in the world — has all but destroyed it. The same can be said of Africa's Lake Chad, once the sixth largest lake in the world, now shrunk by 90%.

The once-mighty Ogallala Aquifer, located beneath the Great Plains of the United States, is a shadow of its former self, so mercilessly has it been pumped by the 200,000 deep bore wells operating there. The U.S. Department of Agriculture says the Ogallala will run out, probably within our lifetimes. William Ashworth, author of *Ogallala Blue*, says groundwater mining is not an accident in the farming communities depending on that aquifer, but a way of life. It is also, he cautions, a way of death.

Author Julene Bair grew up in a family farm in western Kansas and witnessed a profound culture shift as industrial farming came to her region. In *The Ogallala Road*, her 2014 memoir, Bair recounts a family that ran a modest, water- and land-conscious wheat and sheep operation that gave her a wonderful childhood with roots in the land. But her father and brother sold out to corporate corn investors when deep bore well technology allowed the aquifer to be mercilessly pumped. Farming went from "intense labor that broke men's and women's backs" to "intense pillage and poison that broke the earth's." Family farms, and the small communities that supported them, were replaced by massive, chemical-dependent, water-guzzling corporate operations that changed the landscape of her youth forever. Her book is a true cry from the heart that the "planned depletion" of the Ogallala is a tragedy of epic proportions.[211]

A global study of groundwater pumping by the distinguished team of scientists working with the University of Utrecht's Dr. Marc Bierkens, said that if the groundwater sources of the Great Lakes were to be drawn down at the same rate as in other parts of the world, the Great Lakes could be "bone dry" in 80 years.[212] With these realities, how could Canadians approve mass exports from our watersheds?

Given the corporate interest over the years in the possibility of piping water to the U.S., it is clear this would be no humanitarian effort but an endeavour to profit from something that should belong to the people and to future generations.

Some downplay the concern over exports, citing how expensive it would be to move large amounts of water, which is heavy, long distances by pipeline or aqueduct. But crude oil is heavy too and we pipe it. And there are major water pipelines in other parts of the world. The Goldfields water pipeline in western Australia carries water to towns and homes 530 kilometres away from the source. Libya constructed a 2,800-kilometre-long pipeline to carry desert groundwater to its major cities. As well, there are numerous aqueducts and pipelines carrying water long distances around California.

In any case, the issue will not die. In 2008, the Manitoba-based Frontier Centre for Public Policy estimated that the province could earn $1.33 billion annually by exporting just 1% of the freshwater flowing into Hudson Bay. The same year, the Montreal-based Economic Institute published a report called "Freshwater Exports for the Development of Quebec's Blue Gold," in which it claimed that Quebec could generate income of $6.5 billion a year by exporting 10% of its renewable freshwater resources. It would do that by damming three major rivers in the James Bay area, flooding more than 1,000 square kilometres of northern Quebec each spring and then pumping the water through the Great Lakes Basin.

In 2010, Jeff Rubin, former chief economist with CIBC World Markets, called Canada's water the country's most valuable resource and said Canada has a "lot of room for water exports." Water prices are going up everywhere, he said, and this could be good news for us: "Americans are increasingly paying their northern neighbour to fill their gas tanks. In time, they may pay them even more to fill their taps."[213]

The same year, the Vancouver-based Fraser Institute released a report saying that Canada has an abundance of water and the country needed to "move beyond fear mongering and protectionism" and look instead at the "benefits and opportunities presented by bulk water exports." The report also called on the federal and provincial governments to create institutional mechanisms for assigning and promoting the trade in private water rights.[214] Between 2007 and 2011, the Fraser Institute received half a million dollars from the American oil billionaires and Tea Party funders, the Koch brothers.[215]

In March 2011, former prime minister Jean Chrétien told a Toronto water conference that Canada should not be afraid of opening up the debate on water exports. "We're selling oil," he said. "It's finite. We're selling natural gas. It's finite. Water, it's raining and snowing in Canada every year. Water is something that is not finite."[216]

More recently, with reports of the severity of the drought in the American Southwest, calls for Canada to open up the debate on bulk water exports is back. In February 2014, then Canadian ambassador to the United States Gary Doer predicted that water wars with the U.S. will become a bigger issue than the Keystone pipeline. He quoted that oft-repeated, inaccurate statistic that Canada is blessed with 20% of the world's water and said that means "water flows south to north and north to south." In September 2015, Barrie McKenna of the *Globe and Mail* called for a reassessment of Canada's stance on selling its water, saying global warming will eventually force the debate on Canadians.

Parag Khanna is a bestselling author, international relations expert, CNN global contributor and senior research fellow at the National University in Singapore. In his 2016 book, *Connectography: Mapping the Future of Global Civilization*, Khanna says that Americans should get to know the names of Canadian provinces because that's where their water will likely be coming from in the future. It's time to "dust off" the GRAND and NAWAPA water export plans, he says, and take a page from Chinese and

Dutch experiences using dikes and canals to move water. Arizona, Nevada and California are running out of water, he reminds us: "Without Canadian water, it is hard to imagine the United States continuing to produce one-third of the world's corn and soybean exports — especially as America's own corn subsidies have encouraged the rapid draining of the Ogalalla Aquifer."[217]

Rhett Larson is an associate professor of law at Arizona State University. In his September 2015 report, "The Case for Canadian Bulk Water Exports," he repeated the claim that Canada has over 20% of the world's water and recommended bulk water exports to "help solve the global water crisis." Canada should treat water the same way it treats oil or gold, he argued, a valuable commodity on the international markets with "benefits from exportation outweighing the costs of depletion."

Larson didn't define the world water crisis and did not mention the billions in the global South who are its direct victims. Nor did he explain how bulk exports of Canada's water would help them.[218]

The report was written for and published by the University of Calgary's School of Public Policy, whose advisory council is made up of a who's who of the corporate world. It includes major construction companies such as Aecon Group; oil and pipeline companies such as Total Energy and Precision Drilling; major financiers of the oil and gas industry such as Gardiner Group Capital; the ATCO Group, a "world-wide group of companies with assets of $19 billion" that specializes in utilities such as pipelines; investment bankers such as AltaCorp Capital; U.K.-based Goal Group of Companies, which describes itself as "a global leader in withholding tax reclamation and securities action recovery services" and whose clients include the top ten global fund managers; and the China Investment Corporation, a sovereign wealth fund of the foreign exchange reserve of the People's Republic of China.

Perhaps they all have things in mind for Canada's water other than humanitarian relief.

eight

The Corporate Free Trade Threat to Canada's Water

At one time, trade negotiations between countries were intended to take down tariff barriers to trade. If an industry sector in one country had a complaint with access or treatment in another country, it had to depend on its own government to state its case. But as corporations outgrew their countries of origin and became transnational, they sought a system free of nation-state rules. As a result, free trade today is very different from its original intent. Governments everywhere craft trade agreements under the supervision of their corporate sectors in order to pave the way for companies' easy entrance to markets around the world.

Transnational corporations use the World Trade Organization and bilateral and regional agreements to challenge what they call non-tariff barriers — government regulations in finance, culture, intellectual property rights and public services that hamper their "right to profit." Large corporations and investors use new powers to bypass their own governments and challenge nation states and their laws as equals.

Corporate-driven free trade and investment deals threaten the environment and water in a number of important ways. Their very existence is based on the growth imperative and that in turn leads to more fossil fuels, more logging, more manufacturing, more mining, more meat, more commodity exports, more highways and trucks, more pipelines and more shipping. All of this impacts water.

The world's growing water footprint has been directly linked to free trade. In a 2012 study published by the National Academy of Sciences, world-renowned water scientist Arjen Hoekstra and his team at the University of Twente in the Netherlands, found that more than one-fifth of the world's water supplies go toward crops and commodities produced for export, placing immense pressure on freshwater supplies, often in areas where water governance and conservation policies are lacking.

Their report, based on international trade indicators, shows that patterns in international commerce create disparities in water use and burden water sources. Water supplies follow the flow of goods around the world. "Water consumption and pollution are directly linked to the global economy," said the scientists.[219]

The First Modern Free Trade Deals

From the beginning, free trade has threatened Canada's water in many ways, allowing American corporations to challenge water protection laws, and making federal and provincial governments' attempts to ban bulk exports of water more difficult.

The Canada Water Preservation Act was tabled in August 1988 and was the legislation that would have enacted the Federal Water Policy described in chapter two. This act, among other very good things, called for a ban on large-scale water diversions and national regulation of small-scale diversions through cooperation with the provinces. It never became law. The reason for this, says Ralph Pentland, who was at the time director of water planning and management at Environment Canada, is because former prime minister Brian Mulroney was facing an election that was almost solely to be fought over the contentious Canada-U.S. Free Trade Agreement (CUSFTA), predecessor to the North American Free Trade Agreement (NAFTA).

"I don't think many Canadians realize just how important that failed piece of legislation was in Canadian history," he said in an email. "At the time, public opinion was split about evenly for and against the free-trade deal and public opinion on the water export issue was beginning to work against both the deal and the re-election of the Mulroney government. They made the political gamble of tabling the anti–water export bill as a ploy to defuse the issue, and it worked. The Mulroney government was re-elected, the free trade agreement was signed and the bill was never reintroduced."

The reason for the conflict is that water was defined in CUSFTA (and in NAFTA that followed four years later and superseded CUSFTA) as a tradable "good." Included in the annex that lists all the goods to be covered by the agreements are "waters, including natural or artificial mineral waters, and aerated waters not containing added sugar or other sweetening matter nor flavouring; ice and snow." Since these treaties say, "No party may adopt or maintain any prohibition or restriction on the exportation or sale for export of any good destined for the territory of another party," it became clear that it would be very difficult to impose export controls on water or introduce any true ban on the commercial export of water "goods."

Proponents of these deals accused opponents of fear mongering and said that nothing in NAFTA forced Canada to start exporting its water, as water in its "natural state" — such as rivers and lakes — is not a good. This is true. NAFTA cannot force Canada to start selling its water. But NAFTA did dramatically limit the ability of the federal government to stop the provinces from selling water. It also made it very hard to turn off the tap once any province turns it on.

NAFTA article 315 says that any quantitative restriction on exports as a result of shortage of domestic supplies must be done in a way that does not disrupt normal channels of supply and that both parties must share any reduction in supply "proportionately." This means, if any province was selling water to the U.S. and attempted to restrict those exports due to concerns over depletion of the water source in question, it would have to reduce supplies to its domestic users in the same proportion. Under the Canadian Environmental Protection Act, this is clearly a violation of the right of the Canadian government to conserve and protect the country's water resources.

The Federal Government Abdicates Its Authority — Again

As calls for water exports continued to grow, successive federal governments tried to find ways to ban exports without running afoul of NAFTA. Dr. Frank Quinn, now retired, had a long and distinguished career with the federal government on water policy. In a 2007 report for the University of Toronto Program on Water Issues, he said that when the Chrétien government decided it had to act in the wake of the attempted water exports from Ontario and Newfoundland, it was shocked to learn just how badly its hands were tied by NAFTA in terms of taking action. The government was forced to deal with water exports as an environmental issue rather than one of jurisdictional control and Environment Canada took over the portfolio.

The department chose a watershed approach, attempting to protect Canada's waters along natural rather than political boundaries. In 2002, it amended the International Boundary Waters Treaty Act to prohibit the removal of bulk water transfers of more than 50,000 litres of water a day from shared U.S.-Canada boundary waters. This way, it could not be construed that Canada was trying to impose a ban on water exports but merely controlling water in its "natural state." The problem with this approach is that it only covered the 20% of Canadian waters that are boundary (waters such as the Great Lakes that straddle the international boundary between Canada and the U.S.) and did not apply to the 80% of watersheds that lie within provincial borders or flow north in rivers.

To deal with this gaping omission, the Chrétien government asked the provinces to create their own bans. All but New Brunswick did so, but on an uneven basis. The problem was that the so-called cooperative approach was voluntary and therefore not binding. Any province could change its mind at any time to further its own trade interests. Once again the federal government abdicated its responsibility and left the situation in limbo. Frank Quinn had scathing words to describe this betrayal:

The government of Canada has placed so much emphasis on trying to persuade Canadians that they still have sovereign control over their water resources (regardless of the rules of NAFTA and the World Trade Organization) that it has lost sight of what is now emerging as a more important question: can the government of Canada overrule provincial governments that decide to act independently in their own interests, on a matter of national importance and public will? . . .

After years of deferring to provincial water management and downplaying its own responsibilities with respect to interprovincial and international waters, external trade and commerce, fisheries, navigation, aboriginal peoples and federal lands, the government of Canada seems almost to have drifted into irrelevance on the water field, sitting on the sidelines as each province plays its own cards and the public waits in vain for any sign of leadership at the national level. The continuing failure to resolve the water export issue is attributable, unfortunately, not just to timidity but also to outright deception on the part of successive federal governments.[220]

Quinn said that for the Mulroney and Chrétien governments, the opportunity to increase trade in resources and manufactured goods with the United States was clearly worth putting Canada's water at risk. For Ottawa, he said, it has not been about exchanging water for revenue, but using water as a lever to gain access for Canadian producers to the huge U.S. market. This is why these governments refused to negotiate an exemption for water resources in these trade deals. It was not worth risking the great prize

— increased trade — to keep water off the negotiating table. These governments were also wary of risking their political futures by being open about their real agenda; according to Quinn, "ambiguity became [their] refuge."

After many years of lobbying, water advocates finally had a limited victory. In 2012, the Harper government introduced the Transboundary Waters Protection Act, which came into effect July 1, 2014. It amends the International Boundary Waters Treaty Act with stronger penalties for offenders and amends the International River Improvements Act to prevent water situated inside a province or territory from being diverted to a boundary or transboundary waterway for export. As Ralph Pentland explains, neither the GRAND nor the NAWAPA export projects of decades ago would likely be permitted under this law.

However, there are both constitutional and trade-related flaws with this act. David Johansen, then with the Library of Parliament's law and government division, explained in a report to Parliament in 2001 that because of the constitutional division of powers over water, both levels of government may lay claim to the authority to ban or initiate bulk water sales. A province might question the authority of the federal government in this case if, in the future, it decided to sell its water.[221]

Trade lawyer Steven Shrybman reminds us that under international law, all Canadian law must comply with Canada's international trade obligations, such as NAFTA, not the other way around. If a province were to pass a law opening the door to water exports, thus rendering water a tradable good, the U.S. could challenge the federal ban. As well, because of the "national treatment" clause of NAFTA, one province could not open up exports to another province without opening up water exports to our NAFTA partners. Even in-province private-water trading, such as Alberta's, might be challengeable if a foreign investor from the U.S. wanted to buy in.

Liberal member of Parliament Francis Scarpaleggia said the legislation should have prevented any province from lifting its own voluntary bulk water bans: "This frightening loophole left by Bill C-383 is an oversight that can put the other provinces at risk of a NAFTA challenge as NAFTA provisions will consider any internal prohibition on bulk water exports to be trade limited should a provincial ban be lifted." Scarpaleggia also pointed out that the bill allows for marine and truck transport of water exports from the east and west coasts and Gisborne Lake in Newfoundland, the site of the dispute back in 2001.[222]

Indigenous rights expert Merrell-Ann Phare raises another flag. In an article written before the new act was adopted, she noted that no current legislation or policy in Canada can prohibit indigenous people from engaging in expansive use of their water rights. While the issue has not been adjudicated, current decisions strongly suggest that the use of water by a First Nations community to engage in economic development of any sort, including bulk water exports, would be within the scope of protected treaty rights. Given the "national treatment" provisions of NAFTA, she warns, Canada would have no basis upon which to deny non-Canadian investors these same rights. Would the bulk water ban supersede these established treaty rights? It is unclear and raises a cautionary note.[223]

The only way to truly tradeproof a bulk water ban is to remove the reference to water as a good and an investment in NAFTA. As Canadian governments continue to sign new trade agreements that define water in this way, it seems likely that Canada's water bans — federal and provincial

— will be vulnerable in an increasingly thirsty world.

Governments of All Stripes Blindly Promote New Trade Deals

NAFTA is only one of many free trade agreements already in place or currently being negotiated by the Canadian government. The Canada-EU Comprehensive Economic and Trade Agreement (CETA) is a proposed far-reaching deal between Canada and Europe to open up their markets to one another's corporate sectors such as pharmaceuticals, textiles, energy and agriculture. It is the first regional free trade agreement to apply to subnational governments, which means that it gives European corporations the right to compete for local procurement contracts. Although WTO restrictions already somewhat constrain local governments, under CETA, municipal, state and provincial governments will be further limited in their ability to favour local companies and local economic development, substantially restricting them from using public spending to achieve other goals such as encouraging local employment or addressing climate change.

The Trans-Pacific Partnership (TPP) is a massive proposed trade and investment agreement thousands of pages long, involving 12 countries — Canada, U.S., Australia, Brunei, Chile, Malaysia, New Zealand, Peru, Singapore, Vietnam, Japan and Mexico. As the Canadian Centre for Policy Alternatives explains, TPP is, like CETA and all other current free trade deals, only marginally about trade. A far greater part of the text has to do with harmonizing regulations, including environmental, food and chemical standards; opening up new sectors such as water services to privatization and foreign investment; and putting strict limits on how governments choose to protect the environment and water.

In almost every case, participant countries will be required to adopt the preferences of powerful U.S. corporate lobbies, and these lobbies invariably seek the lowest possible standards in any trade block.

The Trade in Services Agreement (TISA) is a project of the World Trade Organization and includes 23 members with a collective services market of 1.6 billion people and a combined GDP of more than $50 trillion — two-thirds of the world's economy. Its aim is to open up the trade in private service delivery and, if ratified, TISA could undermine public services, locking in privatization of water services.

These Deals Harm the Environment

In a 20-year assessment of NAFTA's environmental impacts, a number of North American organizations, including RMALC, a Mexican network of social and environmental justice groups, the Institute for Policy Studies in the United States and the Sierra Clubs of both Canada and the U.S., sounded the alarm. NAFTA facilitated the expansion of large-scale, export-oriented farming that relies heavily on fossil fuels, pesticides and genetically modified organisms, the groups said. Commodity exports from Canada to the U.S. exploded in those years, fuelling the high degree of consolidation in the water-intensive meat sector.

Canada also gave up control of its energy sector, leading to a dramatic increase in energy exports to the U.S. and a growth in the water-destructive tar sands. The same "proportionality clause" that would impact Canada's water if bulk water exports were ever to commence has facilitated trade in environmentally dangerous fossil fuels by obligating Canada to maintain a fixed share of energy exports to the U.S. The more we export, the more we are obliged to export. This NAFTA rule has not only expanded the trade in fossil fuels, it has compromised Canada's energy security and restricted Canada's legal capacity to regulate the extraction and trade in tar sands oil, and thus to protect water.

"These are not unfortunate side effects, but the inevitable result of a model of trade that is designed to protect the interests of corporations instead of the interests of communities and the environment," said the authors. The evidence documented in this report demonstrates that NAFTA has reduced the ability of governments to respond to environmental issues while it also empowered multinational corporations to challenge environmental policy.[224]

Even without being law yet, CETA has already caused the European Union to lower standards in a way that threatens the environment and water. In 2014, the Harper government used CETA negotiations to get Europe to weaken its Fuel Quality Directive, a key piece of EU legislation allowing it to distinguish between various kinds of fuel imports based on their CO_2 emissions at source. EU officials, speaking on condition of anonymity, told the CBC that CETA was indeed a factor in this decision, which cleared the way for Canada to export oil directly into Europe.[225] Friends of the Earth Europe said this will allow crude from Alberta's water-intensive tar sands unfettered access to Europe.[226]

CETA's EU-U.S. counterpart, the Transatlantic Trade and Investment Partnership (TTIP), has also already caused environmental standards to be lowered, even though it is not scheduled for ratification until 2017 at the earliest. In

May 2015, the EU shelved plans to regulate 31 pesticides containing endocrine-disrupting chemicals after an aggressive lobby by European and American chemical companies. The American Chamber of Commerce and the U.S. Trade Mission to Europe threatened EU officials with a trade backlash if these chemicals were banned.[227]

The Trudeau government, like the Harper government before it, is promoting a free trade agreement with China. But China has said there is a condition. In a January 2016 visit to Ottawa, China's vice-minister of financial and economic affairs said his country is willing to sign such a deal, but only if Canada builds a pipeline to the west coast. Chinese companies are gaining increasing ownership of the tar sands and pipeline companies and want access to tidewater for their bitumen.

"Simply put," said Kai Nagata of the B.C.-based environmental group Dogwood, "if the cost of a trade agreement involves dangerous bitumen-laden supertankers on our coast, then the people of B.C. aren't going to accept the terms."[228]

Corporate Charter of Rights and Freedoms

Another way in which free trade threatens water is the power these deals give to corporations to sue one another's governments if their "right to profit" is interfered with by government policy. Investor-State Dispute Settlements (ISDS) grant private investors from one country the right to sue the government of another country if it introduces new laws, regulations or practices — be they environmental, health or human rights — that cause the foreign investor to lose money. Foreign investors gain a legal process outside of a country's own courts, one closed to its domestic companies. Originally used to protect private companies from wealthy countries against the threat of nationalization in poorer countries, ISDS has dramatically expanded in recent decades.

Some disputes are dealt with under the World Bank's International Centre for the Settlement of Investment Disputes. This process has been used to challenge the right of governments to require that cigarettes be sold in plain packages and to phase out nuclear power, to name just two cases of many. Bilateral or regional agreements such as NAFTA that include ISDS set up a private panel to settle the kind of disputes between a government and a foreign investor that in the past would have come before a country's own domestic courts. ISDS privatizes the dispute settlement system and is profoundly undemocratic.

According to the United Nations Conference on Trade and Development (UNCTAD), there are now over 3,500 ISDS agreements (mostly bilateral) in the world — with one concluded every other week. Corporations have used ISDS to launch challenges against government measures almost 700 times. A record 70 were filed in 2015 alone. Corporations from rich countries have laid the strong majority of ISDS cases against poor countries.

Corporations are winning everywhere. A 2015 report by UNCTAD found that 60% of decided cases favoured the private investor and just 40% favoured governments, showing that corporations are steadily and successfully challenging government regulations and public control.[229] The bigger the corporation, the bigger the settlement it gets, reported Osgoode Hall trade expert Gus Van Harten. In a January 2016 legal brief, Van Harten and private practice lawyer Pavel Malysheuski showed that the main global beneficiaries of ISDS are overwhelmingly companies with more than $1 billion in annual revenue, with biggest wins going to companies with more than $10 billion.[230]

Texas-based Occidental Petroleum is worth $57 billion and was listed as one of *Forbes*'s 2016 World's Largest Companies. In 2012, the World Bank's dispute settlement court awarded $2.3 billion ($1.77 billion with interest) to the company from the government of Ecuador after that country's 2007 seizure of an oil field the company had sold to another oil company — China's Andes Petroleum — without government approval. This award was equivalent to the amount that Ecuador spends every year on health care for its people, and the government fought back against the ruling. In January 2016, Ecuador finally accepted a compromise and paid Occidental $980 million, allowing the company to claim that its rights had been violated. "We're conscious that the award is enforceable," said Attorney General Diego García Carrión. "If Ecuador doesn't honour it, even if we're right, it could be enforced."[231]

The silent rise of a powerful international investment regime has ensnared hundreds of countries and put corporate profits before human rights and the environment. This "investment arbitration boom" is costing taxpayers billions of dollars and preventing legislation in the public interest.

ISDS Targets Laws That Protect Water

In April 2015, the World Bank ordered Argentina to pay the utility giant Suez $405 million after that country took its water back into public hands. Argentina had plenty of evidence that the company had not fulfilled its contract and had dramatically increased water tariffs, leaving millions of its citizens unable to pay their water bills. But the World Bank decided that investor state rights trumped the rights of government to make such decisions.

El Salvador is the most water-scarce county in Latin America. According to Meera Karunananthan, who runs the Ottawa-based Blue Planet Project, 98% of El Salvador's water is contaminated, much of it from metal mining. Australia-based OceanaGold (which purchased Canada's Pacific Rim Mining) is suing El Salvador for over $300 million because the government refused to issue a permit to the company to build a new mine. Concern had been steadily growing about water contamination due to mining, and the government said the company had not followed proper procedures. El Salvador has since placed a moratorium on mining, and no new permits have been issued since 2008.

In January 2016, TransCanada launched a NAFTA ISDS challenge against the American government because President Obama vetoed the Keystone pipeline. Of the many concerns about it, none was stronger or garnered more attention than the fact that the pipeline would endanger the Ogallala Aquifer and carry diluted bitumen over hundreds of waterways it would cross on its way to Texas for refining.

NAFTA Targets Canadian Laws That Protect Water

NAFTA was the first trade agreement among "developed" countries to include ISDS and, as a result, Canada is now one of the most ISDS-sued developed countries in the world. Cases can come before a three-person binding private arbitration panel, usually made up of trade lawyers, instead of a country's own courts. A country's domestic companies do not have access to this special treatment and decisions are binding.

Of the 80 known NAFTA investor state claims, 37 have been against Canada, 22 have targeted Mexico and 21 have targeted the U.S. The U.S. government has won 11 of its cases and never lost a NAFTA investor state case or paid any compensation to Canadian or Mexican companies. This is evidence that even though trade agreements appear to treat all parties equally, the more powerful are usually more immune to trade challenges.[232]

Canada has paid American corporations over $200 million in seven cases it has lost and foreign investors are now seeking over $2.6 billion in new cases from the Canadian government. Even defending cases that governments win is expensive. Canada has spent over $65 million defending itself from NAFTA challenges to date. Importantly, reports the Canadian Centre for Policy Alternatives, almost two-thirds of claims against Canada involved challenges to environmental protection or resource management that allegedly interfered with the profit of American corporations.

A number of cases have targeted water protection laws such as bans on chemicals and water destructive energy operations. Ethyl, a U.S. chemical corporation, successfully challenged a Canadian ban on imports of its gasoline, which contained MMT, an additive that is a suspected neurotoxin. The Canadian government repealed the ban in 1998 and paid the company $13 million for its loss of revenue. SDMyers, a U.S. waste disposal firm, challenged a similar ban on the export of toxic PCB waste. In 2000, Canada paid the company over $8 million.

In 2010, the Canadian government paid American pulp and paper giant AbitibiBowater (now Resolute Forest

Products) $131 million after it successfully used NAFTA to claim compensation for the "water and timber rights" it left behind when it abandoned its 100-year-old operation in Newfoundland, leaving the workers with unpaid pensions. The provincial government reclaimed its assets after the company's departure. This challenge is particularly disturbing because it gives a foreign investor leave to claim compensation for the water it had a right to use while operating in another jurisdiction. Additionally, the case made it clear that it is the federal government that is liable for a province's actions under NAFTA.

In 2006, Quebec banned 2,4-D, a pesticide that harms groundwater and has been shown to be toxic to mammals and aquatic life. In 2011, it was forced to publicly acknowledge that the chemical does not pose an "unacceptable risk" to human health after chemical giant Dow AgroSciences threatened Canada with a $2 million NAFTA challenge.

In 2013, Lone Pine, a Canadian energy company, sued the Canadian government for $250 million through its American affiliate because Quebec introduced a temporary moratorium on all fracking activities under the St. Lawrence River until further studies are completed. This challenge is also disturbing because it involves a domestic company using a foreign subsidiary to sue its own government.

New Jersey–based Bilcon Construction is claiming $300 million in damages from the Canadian government after winning a 2015 NAFTA challenge when its plan to build a quarry and marine terminal to ship basalt aggregate through the Bay of Fundy (site of the highest tides in the world and an environmentally sensitive area) was rejected by an environmental assessment panel.

As Canada moves to deal with climate change and declining water stocks, could NAFTA and the other trade and investment deals be used to challenge new laws? The answer is yes. Foreign mining, fracking and agribusiness investors could sue for compensation if any level of government tries to impose new rules in an attempt to protect its water sources. If Canada and China sign the trade deal the Trudeau government is proposing, Chinese state-owned oil companies could sue Canada if the pipelines they understood would be built are not.

Dr. Howard Mann and Carin Smaller of Canada's International Institute for Sustainable Development wrote that free trade agreements give foreign investors new rights to land and water as they become increasingly commodified and subject to global trade rules. The growth in investments in actual land and water, not just crop purchases, increases the potential to shift rights from domestic to foreign players, providing "hard rights" for foreign investors, including "potentially disastrous" compensation claims.[233]

In a 2007 study, University of Toronto law professors Joseph Cumming and Robert Froehlich argued that U.S.-owned, water-use-intensive oil companies operating in the tar sands could sue Canada under NAFTA for hundreds of millions of dollars in compensation for lost profits should restrictions be placed on their water use. They also warned that the threat of such lawsuits alone could prevent the Alberta government from taking the steps necessary to protect its water.[234]

This warning is not theoretical. Many new laws or changes to laws are not enacted because of the "chill effect" of free trade prior restraint. The Canadian government adopted a new policy soon after NAFTA was ratified whereby all new laws and any changes to existing laws have to be vetted by trade experts to ensure they are not challengeable under ISDS rules.

Public Water at Grave Risk under NAFTA, CETA and TPP

Unlike many parts of the world, Canada has largely maintained water services in the public interest and it is imperative to protect this commitment to water as an essential public service. The privatization of water services has been tried in many countries and discredited. Multiple studies show that private water utilities cut workers and services, skirt pollution rules and raise water rates. After Moncton privatized its water filtration system in 1998, leasing it to a company eventually bought out by French-based transnational Veolia, water rates soared 75% in a year. In 2015, when the city considered a public-private partnership (P3) for an $80-million wastewater treatment upgrade with the same company, local outcry forced it to back down.

A White Rock, B.C., official praised the city's decision in fall 2015 to bring its water back into public hands, saying that high levels of arsenic and manganese in its water would never have been discovered otherwise. Councillor Lynne Sinclair said that the previous operator, EPCOR, an Edmonton-based private utility company, had no plans to treat for arsenic and manganese: "Now that we own the water we are fully in charge of that, and I think that's a huge benefit to our community to be able to address these issues, rather than have them in the hands of a private company."[235]

In a February 2016 U.S. survey of the 500 largest American community water systems, Washington-based Food & Water Watch found that for-profit privately owned systems charge 58% more than large publicly owned systems. The survey also showed that water systems are publicly owned and operated in the ten most affordable cities for water of the 500 systems surveyed.[236]

Around the world, municipalities are rejecting privatization. The Transnational Institute and Public Services International Research Unit have been following water privatizations around the world, as well as the trend to reject this model of water delivery and return to a public system. In their March 2015 book, *Our Public Water Future*, they report that the growing trend of cities returning water services to public control has now spread to 37 countries, affecting 100 million people. The groups document that between March 2000 and March 2015, 235 municipalities have re-municipalized their previously privatized water systems. Ninety-four cities in France alone, including Paris, which saved money for both its ratepayers and sustainable water programs, have re-municipalized their water services.[237]

Had CETA and its American equivalent TTIP been in place when these European re-municipalizations occurred, they would all have been challengeable. The right to public water is a key component of the fight against ratifying these deals in Europe.

Canadian Water Services Vulnerable

While the vast majority of municipalities in Canada deliver water on a not-for-profit basis, a number of cities have entered into P3s for their water treatment systems. The Harper government actively promoted this privatization, setting up a crown corporation called Public-Private Partnership Canada and giving it billions of dollars to promote P3s. Harper also brought in a directive that any municipality seeking federal funding for upgrading or building new water infrastructure projects that cost more than $100 million must adopt a P3 as a condition of receiving federal money. The Trudeau government has rescinded this condition. It remains, however, very supportive of the concept of public-private partnerships.

Normally, a municipal government that privatized its water services can change its mind and return to a public system if it did not work out. But the ISDS provisions of CETA and TPP would give foreign-based utilities, like Paris-based Veolia and Suez Environment, the right to sue for compensation if any Canadian municipality does this. As in NAFTA, water is treated in these other deals as a good once it starts to be used in any but its "natural state." Treated water has been extracted from its natural state and is therefore a commodity. CETA says, "Where a Party permits the commercial use of a specific water source, it shall do so in a manner consistent with the Agreement."

What this means is that while CETA does not give anyone the right to force a water privatization in the first place, it will be nearly impossible to return to a public management of water services once management has been assigned to a private company, said a 2014 report by the European Water Movement, a Europe-wide network of unions, activists and researchers. As well, the regulatory cooperation provisions of CETA — new to trade deals — allow private companies to be consulted on legislative procedures in Europe or Canada if they affect trade or investment and permit companies to interfere with the procedure if it seems detrimental to their interests.

Suppose a provincial or federal government decides to allow only the public management of water. In that case, private companies could challenge this as a barrier to trade. It is important to remember that the world's two biggest water utilities — Suez Environment and Veolia — are headquartered in France and are big supporters of CETA.

A February 2016 paper written by New Zealand law professor Jane Kelsey and others says the binding and enforceable rules of the Trans-Pacific Partnership go further than any previous such agreement and will impose new constraints on local governments' authority and autonomy to regulate and make decisions, including those about water services. The ISDS provisions of TPP will greatly limit the right of local authorities to make key decisions about public management.

If a municipality decides to try a P3, it cannot favour a domestic supplier and once privatized, foreign investors will be able to challenge any attempt to re-municipalize the service and even any attempt by local governments to block water rate hikes. Foreign investors in land and water grabs will also have rights closed to domestic investors, because only foreign investors can use the power of ISDS challenges.[238]

In another report, Simon Terry, executive director for the Sustainability Council of New Zealand, said, "The environment, including water protection, is a significant casualty under the TPP. There is a gross asymmetry in the rights and means accorded organizations that would seek to protect the commons for the public good, and rights and means accorded foreign investors to protect private wealth. Adopting the lens of the foreign investor when making broad governance changes through the TPP has sidelined the opportunity to properly integrate management of the economy with management of other domains — such as the environment."[239]

The Trade in Services Agreement (TISA) would also lock in water privatization, says the Canadian Centre for Policy Alternatives. In a 2014 study, CCPA researchers Scott Sinclair and Hadrian Mertins-Kirkwood, said that TISA would make it difficult or even impossible for future governments at all levels to restore public services, including those instances where private service delivery has failed. While the TISA does not force governments to privatize public services, the TISA's "standstill" and "ratchet" clauses would lock in existing and future privatization of public services, because they would freeze current levels of privatization and commercialization, said the authors.[240]

Three current Canadian examples show how specific communities will be vulnerable to these trade agreements once they are all signed. Regina has entered a P3 for a new wastewater treatment plant. Among the bidders is United Water, which is a North American subsidiary of Suez, making the city vulnerable to both a NAFTA and CETA ISDS challenge should this be the successful bid. Macquarie Capital Group of Australia is also in the competition, making Regina vulnerable to a TPP challenge. In early 2016, Saint John gave its P3 contract to a consortium that includes Spain's giant ACCIONA Agua, making that city vulnerable to a CETA challenge. Moncton has a 20-year contract to French company Veolia, leaving it exposed to a future CETA challenge as well.

Free Trade Threatens the Human Right to Water

In June 2015, ten UN rapporteurs on various aspects of human rights issued a statement drawing attention to "the potential detrimental impact" that free trade agreements, such as CETA and TPP, may have on the enjoyment of human rights as enshrined in legally binding UN instruments. "Our concerns," said the experts "relate to the right to life, food, water and sanitation, health, housing, education, science and culture, improved labour standards, an independent judiciary, a clean environment and the right not to be subjected to forced resettlement."

The experts noted that investor state rules provide protection for investors but not for states or for their populations. In looking at the history of ISDS settlements, the UN human rights experts concluded that "the regulatory function of many States and their ability to legislate in the public interest have been put at risk."[241]

Certainly in Canada free trade has played a part in the way governments have approached the human right to water. If water is a good, how could it also be a human right; how can a right be traded or sold?

"Unfortunately, the most significant developments in international law that bear upon the human right to water are not taking place under the auspices of the United Nations," Canadian trade and public interest lawyer Steven Shrybman explained, "but rather under the World Trade Organization and more importantly, under a myriad of foreign investment treaties. Under these regimes, water is regarded as a good, an investment and a service." As a result, governments are severely constrained from establishing policies and practices needed to protect human rights, the environment and other non-commercial societal goals.[242]

This conflict between water as a good and a human right is the likely explanation for the otherwise inexplicable position taken by the Chrétien, Martin and Harper governments to repeatedly oppose the human right to water at the United Nations. All three of these governments refused to support attempts to have water and sanitation declared basic human rights when they came up for discussion during their tenure.

In fact, the Canadian government was the most vocal opponent of the 2010 human right to water resolution that was overwhelmingly adopted by the General Assembly. Confronted with treaties they had signed that defined water as a tradable good, the Harper government did not want to set up an obvious conflict and expose itself to criticism of the human rights violations taking place in First Nations communities in its own country.

The University of Winnipeg's Merrell-Ann Phare says that NAFTA and other trade agreements the Canadian government has signed may restrict any power the Crown possesses to fulfil its Charter obligations to indigenous peoples. NAFTA's definition of water as a tradable good and the ISDS provisions of the deal are of particular concern to her. She gives the example of a foreign-owned bottled water company operating within First Nations territory. If a government goes to limit the company's access to a local water source in order to protect indigenous water rights, it would likely violate NAFTA's investment provisions.

"Canada has not ensured that Aboriginal water rights are protected from the broad reach of NAFTA provisions. It is very likely that neither the federal nor provincial governments could fulfil fiduciary and other obligations to Aboriginal peoples if those obligations conflicted with the rights and obligations under NAFTA," she wrote.[243]

A Different Trade System Is Possible

The purpose and rules of trade have profoundly changed since the post-war Bretton Woods international institutions were established to rebuild a shattered world economy and promote international economic cooperation. Those of us critical of the way these deals have evolved are criticized as being "anti-trade," which is an easy and unfair way to dismiss our concerns. Over the decades, trade and investment agreements have come to be driven by transnational corporations and industry lobbies whose interests they serve above all.

In the mid 1990s, the Organisation for Economic Co-operation and Development was promoting an international investment deal called the Multilateral Agreement on Investment (MAI) that would have given all the corporations of the member countries the right to sue one another's governments using ISDS. When I learned about it in 1996, I called the Chrétien government's trade department and was told there was no such thing as an MAI. Mere weeks later, the deal — almost completed — was leaked and our worst fears were confirmed. Our movement launched an international campaign that we won a year later when the deal was finally abandoned. But under access to information, we in Canada found out that our government — while it had been denying the very existence of the MAI — had been quietly meeting for three years with the business community in Canada, who helped draft the actual agreement.

Since then, the process has become even more secretive. Canadians didn't learn about the contents of CETA until it was signed in principle by the Harper government in October 2013, and TPP and TISA are still being negotiated in secret. Anything we learn about these deals comes from leaks. If they are so good for us, why are they negotiated behind closed doors?

There is a movement growing around the world to reassess the purpose and goals of trade. Yes, people, industry and governments will continue to trade across borders. Yes, a hungry world needs to trade food. Yes, we want to be able to share our bounty with the world.

But what would trade agreements look like if they promoted a more sustainable model of food production, one based on fewer chemicals, better soil protection, mixed farms that allow the land and water to heal, and respect for farmers' rights? What would trade agreements look like if they promoted alternative, more sustainable sources of energy such as wind, solar, thermal, tidal and energy-efficient retrofitting?

What would trade agreements look like if they had to take into account their water and environment footprints at home and in other countries? What would they look like if, instead of giving preferential treatment to global corporations, they established binding human rights and environmental obligations on corporations and placed capital controls on runaway financial speculation of the kind that caused the 2008 crash?

One thing is certain: the backlash against the ISDS provisions of the new generation of trade and investment agreements is growing. Many countries, including South Africa, Bolivia, Brazil, India and Australia, have either rejected ISDS outright or have expressed serious reservations about it. Anger about the way NAFTA has hollowed out middle America has played a key role in the U.S. 2016 presidential elections. Reactions in the European Parliament against the ISDS provisions of TTIP and CETA are deep and mounting.

The world is ready for a movement to ban all forms of ISDS in trade agreements and re-assess their current structures altogether.

The growth-at-all-cost imperative is not sustainable and neither are the trade and investment agreements fuelling them. We can find a better way to trade.

There are numerous local fights against the commodification of water, either the privatization of water services or bottled water operations. Water Watch is a coalition of community groups and national organizations founded by the Canadian Union of Public Employees, the Council of Canadians and Eau Secours in Quebec to fight water privatization.

In 2001, Vancouver reversed its decision to privatize the operation of its water filtration plant in the face of opposition. The district board had short-listed four transnational corporate utilities, including Bechtel and Vivendi (now Veolia), but public resistance was strong and the city's drinking water operation was kept in public hands.

In 2004, spurred to action by Hamilton Water Watch, the City of Hamilton cancelled a ten-year water privatization contract riddled with environmental problems and mismanagement. Despite the promises of local economic development, new jobs and cost savings, the workforce was cut in half within the first 18 months. Millions of litres of raw sewage spilled into Hamilton Harbour, flooding homes, and many additional costs were incurred. The company that was originally contracted to provide water services changed hands four times. Two of the subsequent companies went bankrupt and one was a subsidiary of the infamous Enron. In the first year following the city's reclaiming of its water services under public management, the in-house operation saved the city at least $1.2 million.[244]

In November 2011, the citizens of Abbotsford, British Columbia, overwhelmingly voted against a public-private partnership for their water infrastructure expansion even though the federal government had promised the town $66 million if it did so. The mayor of Abbotsford and all town councillors but one supported the private proposition and spent $200,000 of taxpayers' money in a marketing campaign to promote a "yes" vote in a referendum that was also an election for city council. Every single councillor who supported the private partnership, including the mayor, was defeated. The only councillor to oppose the project won with an historic number of votes.

Not all pro-public campaigns have won. In March 2013, Regina City Council announced its intention to pursue a 30-year P3 privatization for the city's wastewater system. By June of that year, the Regina Water Watch coalition delivered over 24,000 signatures from residents in a petition calling for a referendum. Through a freedom of information request to the municipality, the Water Watch coalition discovered that the mayor and city council spent well over $400,000 promoting the P3, many times the budget of Regina Water Watch. With the promise of federal funds for choosing a private operator, the city council voted in the P3 option by a narrow margin in the referendum held in September that year.

Wanting to avoid getting stuck in reaction mode, the Council of Canadians and the Canadian Union of Public Employees started a project called Blue Communities so that municipalities could take a proactive position regarding their responsibility to water services. A Blue

Community treats water as a common good to be shared by everyone and as the responsibility of all. Because water is central to life, it must be governed by principles that are based on sustainability and justice in order to preserve water for nature and future generations.

To become a Blue Community, a municipality must recognize water as a human right; promote public, not private, water services; and ban the sale of bottled water in municipal public facilities and at municipal events. Some have amended the third promise to promote public water and set up a timeframe to phase out bottled water. To date, 18 Canadian municipalities, including Victoria and Thunder Bay, have become "Blue," with another dozen or so under consideration. In all cases, it was local action by citizens that was the impetus. The concept has started to go global, with Bern, Switzerland, and Paris, France, leading the way.

In most communities, it is the elected officials who take the decision to become a Blue Community. But in Bayfield, a lovely village located within the town of Bluewater, Ontario, on the eastern shore of Lake Huron, it is the citizens who have decided to go completely bottled-water free and become a Blue Community. Led by retired teacher, passionate environmentalist and winner of the 2015 Earth Day Canada Hometown Heroes Award Ray Letheren, all the local businesses, stores, inns and B&Bs have agreed not to sell or provide bottled water. The Bayfield community is deeply concerned about the prevalence of microplastics in the waters of Lake Huron and the other Great Lakes.

In late 2014, Jennifer Pate, a young environmental activist and co-owner of a local Bayfield eco park, crossed the Atlantic Ocean on a 72-foot sailboat with a crew of female sailors, scientists and artists to test for microplastics. In August 2016, Jennifer organized further expeditions on each of the Great Lakes, as well as Lake St. Clair and the St. Lawrence River to study the amount of microplastics found in the lakes and to raise awareness of this crisis. As Letheren and Pate remind us, 99.99% of all plastic that has ever been produced is still around in one form or another, and in the last decade, humans have produced more plastic than during the entire last century. A great deal of it lands in our freshwater lakes, streams and rivers.

Ray Letheren says the Blue Community project has allowed the people of Bayfield to become "water ambassadors." Jennifer Pate says her work on microplastics in the Great Lakes has led her to believe that the earth has reached a tipping point. Blue Communities is a way to put the power into everyone's hands, a way to "vote with our values, our feet and our voices."

nine

A Blue and Just Canada Is Possible

In the pre-election of summer 2015, over 80 organizations came together in a network called Our Living Waters to help shape water policy in the election and beyond. It is coordinated through the Canadian Freshwater Alliance and its Federal Call to Action on Fresh Water was produced by World Wildlife Fund's Tony Maas, University of Victoria POLIS Project's Oliver Brandes and the University of Winnipeg's Merrell-Ann Phare. The network called on the next government to set a national target of "all waters in Canada in good health by 2025," an exciting, ambitious and doable goal.

The network called on the federal government to build consensus among all levels of government, indigenous people and local communities toward a shared action agenda. High on the list is developing a common national approach to assessing and reporting on the health of

Canada's waters, a goal long called for by water experts and activists. It called for the creation of a Living Waters Canada Fund to provide resources for the restoration of Canada's water and urged the new government to elevate freshwater as a priority of the federal cabinet.[245]

Toward a New Water Ethic

Canada has a water crisis. For most Canadians raised with the myth of water abundance, this is difficult to believe. But it is time to realize that the freshwater issues facing the planet are all at play here in Canada. We need strong federal leadership, a plan of action, a real process of community empowerment and widespread civil society participation if we are to avoid the kind of problems facing many other countries. We need to stop seeing water as a resource for our convenience and profit and start seeing it as the most essential element of a living ecosystem upon which all life depends.

To do this, we need a new water ethic that puts water protection and water justice at the heart of all policy and practice. All policy, from the way we grow our food and produce energy to the way we trade across borders, must ask, What is the impact on water? If the impact is negative, we must go back to the drawing board. Water can no longer take a back seat to other interests and priorities.

The Canadian government, like other governments, makes policy decisions in silos. Agriculture and Agri-Food Canada promotes the growth and export of Canadian agricultural commodities. Newly named Global Affairs aggressively promotes international trade and trade and investment agreements, such as CETA and TPP, that have far-reaching environmental impacts. Natural Resources Canada promotes the development and sale of Canadian natural resources, from metals and minerals to forests and energy. Worrying about water or the environmental impacts of growth is not the core job of these pro-growth departments.

Environmental matters are separated off into other departments whose mandates and concerns are often ignored by the pro-development bureaucracies and the big business interests that drive them. Water scientists have been muzzled and largely ignored. Budgets at the departments tasked with caring for water — Environment Canada, Parks Canada and Fisheries and Oceans — were brutally cut. For a new water ethic to work in practice, these departments have to be restored and renewed, and the expertise of their scientists must be directly integrated into the plans and policies of other departments.

Fundamental Principles

As we develop this water ethic in Canada, we need to establish the underlying principles that will guide us as we move forward. As noted in chapter seven, there are very different views on how to deal with the world's water crisis. There are far too many examples where the governments of water-scarce countries have chosen to use their limited water supplies to promote the elite, or tourism, or free-trade zones, or the production of commodities and goods for export over the urgent needs of local people, communities and the ecosystem. The following are fundamental.

Water Justice ~

This principle recognizes that denying people or communities access to safe drinking water and sanitation is a violation of their human rights. The human right to water places the onus on the federal and provincial governments to provide water and sanitation to all the people in Canada and prevent harm to the source waters that supply it.

This principle is critical in Canada in two areas. Clearly, one is in the many First Nations communities that continue to be denied access to safe drinking water and sanitation. This is the most obvious and the most pressing. But we must also be on guard for a scenario playing out in a number of American cities where those who cannot pay for high water tariffs are having their water shut off. As the income gap grows in Canada and water rates rise, there is likely to come a time when Canadian municipalities will face similar challenges. It is imperative to hold fast to the principle that water is a human right.

Public Trust ~

This principle recognizes that water in Canada is a common heritage of all the people and of future generations. Because it is necessary for life and ecosystem health and because there is no substitute for it, water must be regarded as a public trust and preserved in law and practice. Federal and provincial governments must be required to maintain the water commons in the public's name.

This principle is critical for Canada to preserve water as an essential public service and prevent the privatization of municipal water services. The private sector should never be allowed to determine access to water. It is also essential to use this principle to challenge those who are promoting a market solution to the water crisis, including water trading, water pollution fees and water pollution trading. As the stewards of this public trust, Canadians can challenge the bottled water industry making profit from local public water supplies or the mining and energy industries when they pollute public water sources.

Water Sustainability ~
This principle recognizes that Canada's waterways and watersheds need to be protected, not just because they serve humans, but because they form the basis of all ecosystems and provide life and habitat to other species as well as our own. It forces us to confront our treatment of water as a tool for industrial development and, increasingly, as a form of property, and to create laws based on the conservation, protection and restoration of watersheds and habitat.

This principle is critical in Canada, as we have an urgent need to stop exploiting, polluting, mismanaging and diverting our lakes, rivers and groundwater. It is based on the integrity of watershed ecosystems and habitat and the need to keep them as intact as is possible. As Ralph Pentland and Chris Wood explain, we must view and manage Canada's water resource as one body, above and below ground, and organize the governance of water issues within the hydrologic perimeters of watersheds. Under this principle, we must address the other ways in which we are allowing the destruction of water resources, including wetland and forest loss and climate change.

Trudeau's Promises

When in opposition, Justin Trudeau and his Liberal Party made many promises regarding water. Minister of Foreign Affairs Stéphane Dion pledged that they would create a new water minister portfolio and MP Francis Scarpaleggia served as an effective critic on water issues. Trudeau himself pledged to eliminate boil-water advisories in First Nations within five years, calling it a "top priority." The Liberal platform included a promise to review the changes the Harper government made to the Fisheries Act, the Navigable Waters Protection Act and the Canadian Environmental Assessment Act, changes that "weakened environmental protection." The platform promised to "restore lost protections and incorporate more modern safeguards."[246]

Trudeau's first budget was delivered on March 22, 2016, World Water Day. In some very important ways, his government did deliver on a number of key promises. Budget 2016 allocated $2.24 billion over the next five years for improving on-reserve water and wastewater infrastructure and waste management. Averaged out per year, this comes to $448 million per year, which is very close to the $470 million called for by the Assembly of First Nations and the Canadian Centre for Policy Alternatives' Alternative Federal Budget.

However, the government allocated only $2 billion for the new Clean Water and Wastewater Fund over five years, a greater amount than ever promised by the Harper government but far short of the $6 billion needed annually, according to the Federation of Canadian Municipalities, as discussed in chapter two. But the budget does not require municipalities to enter into a P3 if they want to access these funds, and this is progress.

The budget brought in much-needed relief to the beleaguered programs and scientists hurt by the Harper cuts at Fisheries and Oceans. That department will get almost $200 million over five years to increase ocean and freshwater science, monitoring and research activities and provide support to the Experimental Lakes Area. However, funding was not restored to Environment Canada's Water Resources Program that addresses the risks to and impacts on water resources from industrial activities, agriculture and climate change. Just over $3 million was allocated to the Great Lakes through Environment Canada to continue to improve near-shore water and ecosystem health and reduce phosphorus and nitrates in Lake Erie. While this is welcome, it is not a huge improvement over previous spending on the Great Lakes.[247]

The Professional Institute of the Public Service of Canada (PIPSC), which represents federal government scientists and researchers, said this budget "marked a turning point" after years of deep program cuts and hiring freezes. But the institute was quick to point out that the year-over-year cuts to science and services were so far-reaching that "much remains to be done if the federal public service is not only to gain lost ground but become the agent of real change the government intends it to be."[248]

The budget did not address the gutting of environmental laws. More than $14 million over four years was promised to the Canadian Environmental Assessment Agency to support its responsibilities — a good step — but no promises were made to revisit the changes Harper made to its mandate. Nor were there references to the promises to restore the former power of the Fisheries Act or the Navigable Waters Protection Act. And as of June 2016, no minister for water has been appointed.

In April 2016, then Fisheries minister Hunter Tootoo said that he intended to fully restore the lost protections in the Fisheries Act. However, he added that there would be a "consultative process" to allow "all the stakeholders" to have input into what those changes should be.[249]

Why that would be necessary became clear less than a month later, when *Globe and Mail* reporter Simon Doyle reported that the government was feeling heat from industry over its plans to restore the lost powers to these three laws. The Canadian Construction Association said that it wants to halt reforms to the Navigation Protection Act (its revised name) that "would relist all waterways across Canada." The Mining Association of Canada expressed concerns about certain provisions of the old assessment act it considered onerous. Shell Canada and the Canadian Energy Pipeline Association are among those who have registered to lobby the government when the consultation process commences, and Environment Minister Catherine McKenna has already met with energy companies as Suncor and Cenovus.[250]

On June 20, 2016, the government announced a consultation process for the three gutted water laws, sending fisheries protection and navigable waters to Parliamentary subcommittees and setting up an expert panel to deal with the Canadian Environmental Assessment Act. While outreach to the public is always a good thing, it is imperative that this process not be allowed to be hijacked by the very industry lobby groups that gutted the laws in the first place, resulting in new laws that do not adequately protect Canada's lakes and rivers.

The Need for Strong Federal Leadership and Consultation

While the provinces and municipalities have very important roles and responsibilities with regard to freshwater,
and while local communities are the stewards of local
waterways and must have a meaningful way of partici-
pating in decisions that affect them, it is imperative that
all water in Canada is protected by strong, enforceable
national laws and standards. The Trudeau government
must assert its legitimate authority to safeguard and
govern Canada's water.

As Pentland and Wood write, the Canadian constitution
gives the federal government powers substantially similar
to those of its American counterpart: "But rather than
wield that authority to defend Canadian's environmental
interests, generations of federal leaders have accepted the
shackles of what has been termed 'political constitution' —
a polite term for cowardice in the face of provincial recalci-
trance and rivalry. While successive (and, strikingly, mainly
Republican) presidents instituted and sought to enforce
national standards for safe water and air in the United
States, Canada's leaders performed a dance of promise,
bluster, retreat and betrayal."[251]

The Trudeau government must take leadership in developing a new national water policy and strategy, asserting its
right to do so while recognizing those areas of jurisdiction
that come under provincial and territorial domain. This will
mean working in cooperation with other levels of government and incorporating local community consultation and
input. As well, there are at least 20 federal departments and
agencies with responsibilities for water management that
need better coordination. All policy and strategy should be
based on the fundamental principles of water sustainability,

water justice and public trust while also recognizing the special inherent and treaty rights of First Nations.

Consensus is growing around several priorities.

Reinstate the Navigable Waters Protection Act ~
The Navigable Waters Protection Act must be reinstated to protect the majority of Canada's lakes and rivers now unprotected by federal law. As Mark Mattson of Lake Ontario Waterkeeper explains, "The act was unique in that it protected the right of all Canadians to travel on any of Canada's waters unless exceptions were made . . . The changes to the Act leave a hodgepodge of different rules and processes in each province. This needs to be addressed if we desire national standards."[252]

Ecojustice believes that a strong Navigable Waters Protection Act is required to fulfil Canada's international obligations under the Boundary Waters Treaty and it notes that the federal government holds Canada's water in trust for the benefit of all Canadians. It is the duty of the federal government to protect the public right of all Canadians to navigate waterways in a fair and transparent manner. This duty falls exclusively to the federal government as it is granted sole authority in the constitution over navigation and shipping. As Ecojustice stated, "The government holds Canada's resources in trust for Canadian citizens; as such it has a responsibility to ensure that public resources, including navigable waters, are not disrupted, depleted or destroyed for present and future generations."[253]

Reinstate and Improve the Fisheries Act ~
Environmental and conservation groups are clear on the need for the Trudeau government to undo the damage done by the former government as a baseline in protecting

Canada's water. Two days after the federal budget, West Coast Environmental Law published a report calling for the Fisheries minister to restore the lost protections in the Fisheries Act. Specifically, the group calls for the restoration of the lost protections for fish and their habitat and for all native fish and their habitat that sustain First Nations food, ceremonial and social needs. They urge a return to the prohibition against destroying fish by means other than fishing, such as blasting near water and diversion for irrigation and oil sands operations. It also calls for the restoration of a policy of "no net loss" to ensure the health of entire ecosystems.

But West Coast Environmental Law goes further than simply calling for the old Fisheries Act to be reinstated. They cite the need for a "complete modernization" of the legislation. Its recommendations include:

~ acknowledging indigenous rights and the
  need for reconciliation;
~ strengthening provisions for co-management
  with other levels of government and public
  consultation with local communities;
~ limiting ministerial discretion in the implementation of the act;
~ expanding the guiding principles to include sustainability and the precautionary
  principle;
~ incorporating the goal of rebuilding depleted
  fish stocks;
~ protecting environmental flows;
~ requiring consideration of cumulative effects
  to fish and fish habitat as well as habitat
  monitoring;

~ and increasing enforcement, which has been
ineffective for decades.[254]

The report, "Scaling Up the Fisheries Act," has been
endorsed by leading scientists and dozens of conservation
and environmental groups and First Nations.

To these demands should be added the need to close
the loophole in the Metal Mining Effluent Regulations of
the Fisheries Act, which allows mining companies to have
certain lakes classified as toxic dumpsites.

Reinstate and Improve the
Canadian Environmental Assessment Act ~
The previous powers of the Canadian Environmental
Assessment Act must be reinstated and applied to all major
projects across Canada, providing a clear process for public
consultation and input. Soon after the new government
was elected, Nature Canada published a set of "quick start"
ways in which the government could improve environmental assessments of important projects while preparing to
reinstate the act's former powers.

These include sorting out the "procedural mess" that is
the National Energy Board's hearing process on pipelines
such as TransMountain and Energy East, as well as a series
of regulatory changes to achieve ecological, social and economic sustainability. Nature Canada said it is crucial for
the Trudeau government to

~ rebuild public trust in environmental assessments;
~ demonstrate early commitment to protecting
species at risk;
~ reduce greenhouse gas emissions;

~   and advance sustainability as a key factor in
    federal decision-making.

The group also called on the new government to reduce
political discretion when it comes to overseeing which
projects get assessed and to reassert the rule of law.[255]

Establish National Enforceable Drinking Water Standards ~
As outlined in chapter two, Canada is alone among industrialized countries in not having clear, national and enforceable standards on drinking water. Canada has no standard
for over 100 substances banned in countries comparable
to Canada. This allows provinces and municipalities to
set varied and uneven benchmarks. National enforceable
drinking water standards must replace the current system
of voluntary guidelines and must give the government the
right to go to court when they are violated.

Ecojustice suggests the creation of a Safe Drinking
Water Act and calls on the federal government to:

~   review all problem standards immediately;
~   incorporate health-based objectives into the
    regulatory process;
~   and introduce a review policy for standards
    that would be triggered when countries
    similar to Canada implement or strengthen
    a standard to a level more stringent than
    Canada's.

Enforceable national drinking water standards, says the
group, would mean that, anywhere in the country, people
could be confident that the water coming out of their taps
is safe to drink. Water quality would be well monitored

and municipalities and provinces would apply the highest standards of source water protection.

Establish National Enforceable
Wastewater Disposal Standards ~
As explained in chapter two, the regulations adopted in 2012 to bring national standards to the treatment and discharge of wastewater in Canada are flawed, leaving municipalities to bear the majority of the cost. As well, regulations on discharges from combined storm sewer overflows (CSOs) contain a loophole that will allow many facilities not to comply with the new rules until 2041. The rules also lack a microbiological water treatment standard that provides protection from waterborne pathogens such as *E. coli*.

This act must be amended to address these shortcomings. Compliance with the new regulations must be measured in years, not decades. The loophole regarding CSOs must be closed. Reduction targets, reduction timelines and standards must be established for CSOs. A full environmental-effect monitoring program must be put in place. Federal funding under the Clean Water and Wastewater Fund must be increased and allocated to adequately address this commitment.

Re-tool and Properly Fund the Canadian
Environmental Protection Agency to Do Its Job ~
The Canadian Environmental Protection Agency is not fulfilling its mandate and has not been doing so for decades. Deep funding cuts combined with a political culture rife with fear and paranoia has hamstrung the agency and, in some cases, caused enforcement officers to not pursue infractions. This has to change. The act itself is still powerful and gives the federal government the mandate to:

- prevent harm and protect the environment and public health;
- implement pollution prevention as a national goal;
- eliminate the most persistent and bioaccumulative toxic substances;
- recognize an ecosystem approach;
- establish environmental standards;
- and implement the precautionary principle.

The problem is how this mandate has been carried out, and with the agreement that allowed the federal government to relinquish enforcement of the act to the provinces. The federal government must:

- re-establish its authority in this crucial area;
- re-tool the agency;
- de-politicize the culture at the agency;
- create inspired leadership;
- and properly fund the agency to do its job.

Elizabeth May and the Green Party also say that the agency's mandate should be expanded to include pesticides and radionuclides.

Map and Protect Groundwater with Enforceable National Standards ~

At the current rate of study, Canada's groundwater supplies will not be mapped for decades. Adèle Hurley writes, "At the national level, it is time to close the gaps on basic groundwater science and reset the annual reporting responsibilities of Natural Resources Canada for mapping and monitoring the country's aquifers. Enhanced mapping and monitoring is needed to protect and sustain the resource and understand the cumulative impacts of human use and climate change."[256]

It is urgent that the government speed up this mapping process, set national legislated rules to prevent contamination of groundwater and establish standards for priority access. Currently, access to groundwater and wilderness lakes and rivers is a free-for-all. Strict priorities must be set to ensure that water for human need, ecosystem protection and local sustainable food production have priority rights over those of industry and export-oriented agriculture.

Properly Fund the New Water and Wastewater Fund and Use It to Promote Public Water Services ~
The Trudeau government has created a new fund for infrastructure upgrades and expansion in Canada's cities. While the $2 billion pledged over five years is a good start, it is nowhere near the $6 billion a year needed to bring these facilities up to modern standards. This fund should be used to promote water as a public trust and public service and not to promote the interests of private for-profit water operators.

Fulfil the Promise of Safe Water on First Nations within Five Years and Recognize the Inherent Indigenous Right to Water ~
It appears that the Trudeau government takes its election pledge to end boil-water advisories within five years seriously and recognizes that it is the responsibility of the federal government, working with the provinces and the communities themselves, to honour this commitment. It is very promising that the Trudeau government has adopted the United Nations Declaration on the Rights of Indigenous Peoples and promised to implement it. This

means recognizing the inherent right of indigenous people to water and to free, prior and informed consent regarding any development in their territory.

It would also be a great contribution to the principle of water justice if the Trudeau government were to do what 110 other countries around the world have done and enshrine the right of all the peoples of Canada to clean air, clean water and a healthy environment in the Canadian Constitution as promoted by the Suzuki Foundation's Blue Dot campaign.

Reject the Energy East Pipeline and Plan the Transition Away from the Tar Sands ~

The Energy East pipeline and the proposed western pipelines pose a clear and present threat to waterways and watersheds across the country. It would be irresponsible to expose thousands of lakes and rivers to spills of one of the dirtiest energy sources on earth. The Trudeau government must have the courage to say no to Energy East, which would also dramatically increase production in the tar sands, prolonging its productive life for decades and tying Canada into a fossil fuel energy future.

In his 2015 book, *After the Sands: Energy and Ecological Security for Canadians*, Alberta political economist Gordon Laxer calls for a cap and phase out of the tar sands by 2030, starting with the older projects. He says Canada can meet its target of reducing carbon emissions by 80% if it phases out tar-sands oil and relies on its slowly falling output of conventional oil and natural gas as transition fuels while Canada converts to a low-carbon future run on renewables.[257]

Ban Shipping, Transport and Burial of Extreme Energy
on or Near the Great Lakes and other Waterways in Canada ~
The Great Lakes are becoming a carbon corridor for some
of the most dangerous energy sources on earth. It is time to
recognize the Great Lakes Basin as a public trust and a protected bioregion that must not be endangered. Governments
must ban the shipment of diluted bitumen, fracked oil and
gas and fracked wastewater on ships, tankers and barges on
the Great Lakes and other waterways in Canada. Extreme
energy sources should not be carried by pipeline near or
under the Great Lakes or other waterways. All transport
of nuclear waste on, under and near the St. Lawrence River
should be banned. This includes marine transport of spent
nuclear rods, burial of nuclear waste in deep geologic deposits and truck transport of liquid and solid nuclear waste.

As well, strict regulations are needed for the rail transport
of energy. As the Council of Canadians' Mark Calzavara
notes, rail shipments can be made safer by shipping bitumen in its raw, not diluted, state. All train shipments could
be made safer by forcing companies to use the most modern
braking technology and by bringing in post-Lac-Mégantic
safety regulations sooner than scheduled, as the government gave the industry years to phase out unsafe cars. The
number of dangerous-goods cars allowed to travel together
should be reduced, as should their speeds. No more "bomb
trains," said Calzavara, with 100 loaded tankers going 100
kilometres per hour. All dangerous goods must be rerouted
around population centres.

Ban Fracking ~
In a May 2014 report, the Council of Canadian Academies
raised a host of grave concerns over the safety of fracking, pointing to large gaps in our understanding of well

leaks, chemical migration underground, well deterioration, the cumulative impacts of fracking and the safety of fracking chemicals.[258] A number of provinces have placed bans or moratoriums on fracking, and it is necessary for other provinces to follow suit. In particular, B.C. needs to move away from its aggressive pursuit of fracking and LNGs if it is to protect its freshwater resources.

But the Council of Canadians' Emma Lui says there is a powerful argument for a federal ban as well. She notes that while the provinces are responsible for issuing water and oil and gas drilling permits, the federal government is responsible for oil and gas activities under the Fisheries Act, the Canadian Environmental Protection Act, the Species at Risk Act, the Canadian Environmental Assessment Act and the Indian Oil and Gas Act. Much fracking activity is taking place in indigenous territory and the federal government is responsible for protecting the land and water on these communities from abuse. Canada needs a comprehensive national water policy that addresses the scale and pace of industrial water use, including a ban on fracking.[259]

Bring in Strict Rules on Mining ~

Similar shared responsibilities are at play in the mining sector. Federal and provincial/territorial governments, communities and First Nations must collectively address the damage done by mining and prevent new damage under the ambitious plans to extend mining in many parts of the North. MiningWatch's Jamie Kneen says the frontier mentality of the past has to end. He says we need an end to Free Entry (a law that grants the mineral industry privileged access to Crown land and gives top priority to resource development) and the principle that mining is the highest and best use of the land.

"The principle should be sustainability; mining should be allowed only where it can make a positive contribution to sustainability in a larger context, since mining itself is inherently and inevitably destructive and unsustainable. A strong federal commitment and coordination with the provinces is needed to impose strict requirements on new and existing mines, and to institute rigorous and participatory planning and assessment processes ahead of government decisions. We need to ensure that mines are not being subsidized by the public and are actually contributing more than they will cost us, including social, economic and environmental damage. New mines must not be permitted if they will require perpetual care, or if they cannot be made safe from spills and collapses, or if they will infringe on indigenous land rights and title of areas of special cultural or ecological importance."[260]

Promote Local, Sustainable Food Production ~

The solution to blue-green algae hurting so many Canadian lakes, says David Schindler, is simple: prevent excess nutrients from entering lakes; keep inflows, outflows and wetlands in the catchments of lakes intact; and allow the food chains and fish habitats of lakes to remain in their natural states. For this to happen, local, provincial, federal and, in some cases, American governments have to set rules and standards around how we grow food. Western Europe has brought in strict regulations to protect animals, air and water in large agricultural operations; Canada must follow suit. Factory farms are largely unregulated and are creating huge water-pollution problems.

Government policy must assist local, sustainable family farms growing food for local consumption, rather than ever-bigger corporate agribusiness growing food largely for export. The impact on water of export-oriented food production must become a factor in government policy, and local waters must be protected from the overuse of chemical-based fertilizers and pesticides. Governments must move to put strict controls on land and water grabs, oppose the control of commodities in fewer and fewer corporate hands and support farmer-oriented food policies and farm marketing boards. The Trudeau government should bring back the Prairie Farm Rehabilitation Administration, cut by the Harper government.

Protect and Renew Forests and Wetlands ~
Canada has made strides in the protection of forests since 2007, says the forest conservation group Canadian Boreal Initiative, doubling the amount of its boreal forest protected from industrial development to 12%. Canada has also committed to increasing this amount to 17% by 2020. While this is far less than what is scientifically recognized as necessary to sustain the ecosystem, it is proof that governments, forestry companies, First Nations and environmental and community groups can make progress together. As well, large areas where logging is permitted are now harvested through sustainable practices. The group praises the governments of Ontario and Manitoba for holding on to promises made to protect northern forests but expresses concern over rampant deforestation in Quebec, Alberta and the Yukon.

This group and others have set the ultimate target of protecting half of Canada's forests in large interconnected protected areas.[261] The Boreal Songbird Initiative supports this goal in its Boreal Birds Need Half campaign, as it is the minimum area needed for migratory birds to have a fighting chance of survival.[262]

First Nations and conservation groups are calling on the federal government to support the Northwest Territories Protected Area Strategy, a network of protected areas across each of the 45 ecoregions identified in the NWT. Protecting forests means also protecting wetlands, and all levels of government, First Nations and communities must work together to protect, restore and rejuvenate the damaged forests and wetlands of Canada.

Remove All References to Water from All Trade and Investment Agreements ~

The federal government should remove all references to water in all existing and upcoming trade and investment agreements as a good, a service or an investment, unless to allow for the specific protection or exclusion of water. As well, no trade or investment treaty agreement should contain Investor State Dispute Settlement (ISDS) in any form. Removing all references to water as a good from NAFTA would end the debate on whether the federal and provincial bans on water exports are sufficient, as it would remove any potential for a NAFTA challenge. Removing water as a service would help protect water as an essential public service. Removing it as an investment and excluding ISDS provisions would make it much harder for foreign corporations to use trade treaties to fight domestic or international rules that protect water.

Further, the impact on Canada's water must be taken into account when trade agreements are negotiated. When agreements open the door to more trade in water-intensive operations or commodities, the question of how it will affect local water supplies must be assessed and the findings made public. Conversely, the Canadian government should be asking about the water impact of imported goods and commodities in their countries of origin. Water scientist Arjen Hoekstra says that fair international trade rules must include the right for a country to ban the import of a product that has harmed the water or the communities around that water in another country.

Reject False Market Solutions to the Water Crisis ~
It is imperative that governments at all levels reject market solutions to water issues in Canada. Those countries that have not done so have experienced a loss of democratic control as private water brokers and investors have taken over the management of their water resources. Experiments with water trading, water pollution fees and water pollution trading should end. Sound regulations based on good law will protect freshwater better than any market mechanism and maintain control of water in the hands of the people and their elected representatives. Antiquated laws such as First in Time, First in Right (FITFER) that favour prior ownership and big users must be phased out, and water allocated through a licencing scheme based on the principles of community need, ecosystem sustainability, justice and indigenous title.

Above all, Canada's waters must be protected as a public trust and a common heritage of all who live here and of future generations. Several years ago, a group of legal experts on the idea of the commons gathered to examine how to protect the Great Lakes. "In theory," they said, "a commons approach is simple — it requires only that we envisage water as a shared resource and so recognize our shared responsibility to carefully steward our water resources. The goal of a commons approach to water is to ensure that there is sufficient water to meet human, ecological and community needs for many generations to come."

This means that lakes, rivers and groundwater belong to every living being that lives around them and that private interests of those with claims to these waters are subordinate to public rights.[263]

Paying for "All Water in Good Health by 2025"

Many of the same interests that call for market solutions to water also promote water pricing. How shall we pay for water protection and restoration and continue to provide municipal water services without large increases in water tariffs or allowing private investments to enter the sector? they ask. Some are environmentalists hoping pricing will promote conservation. But many promote "full-cost recovery" — market-based water pricing — as a way to eventually remove government from the equation and turn the payment for water entirely over to water "consumers." They view water as a good like any other and would see the end of government subsidies for the provision of water services.

(Market-based water pricing is different from service charges for public water services, which help governments provide water treatment, source protection and water provision for all.)

There are many problems with a market-based approach to water pricing. The most obvious, of course, is that as governments remove themselves from the equation and water rates rise, the poor and even middle class find it hard to pay their water bills. We are seeing this all over the U.S. But the biggest problem is that water pricing targets a small portion of the population and lets the big users off the hook. In Canada, municipal water use — including residential, commercial and public uses such as firefighting, as well as the water lost from reservoirs and pipes — accounts for just 9% of all water withdrawals. And most municipal water use is not consumptive; that is, it is returned to the watershed.

Most reports, academic papers and environmental studies ignore the elephant in the room: the 90% of water used by what are referred to as "water-reliant natural resource industries" — industrial agriculture, manufacturing, mining, oil and gas, pulp and paper and electricity generation. The reason that most governments avoid these players is that they are a large and powerful lobby. However, we need to begin to charge these users for the water they use. Having them pay, through licenses and permits, would take enormous pressure off families, public institutions and municipalities for the cost of water protection and water services.

Charging these industries could also serve as a conservation incentive. Before it was disbanded, the National Round Table on the Environment and the Economy said that raising the price of water for natural resource industries in Canada by just $0.05 per cubic metre would reduce their water intake by 20%. A lower block rate could be offered to those who convert to solar or other sustainable energy use. It is imperative that big industry not see these charges as a way to pay for polluting or getting around strict environmental laws. It is time for this debate in Canada.[264]

The other place to find money for "all waters in good health by 2025" as well as all the funds we need for infrastructure upgrades and water services is through more inclusive taxation. One of the Harper government's first acts upon taking office was to lower corporate tax rates, saving big business over $60 billion since 2006. Canadian corporate tax rates are among the lowest in the industrialized world. The Parliamentary budget officer says that even a modest 1% increase in corporate tax would put an extra $1.3 billion annually into federal coffers.

Further, reports Canadians for Tax Fairness, there is at least $199 billion in offshore tax havens, money that could pay for public services and environmental protection for years. The Panama Papers revealed that Canadian corporations and wealthy individuals transferred a record $40 billion to tax havens in 2015 alone, more than four times greater than the $9 billion sent offshore in 2014. The group praises the 2016 budget for earmarking nearly $90 million a year to fight tax evasion and hopes this is a signal that the Trudeau government realizes just how much it is losing as wealthy Canadians shift their money offshore to avoid paying taxes at home.[265]

The above recommendations are ambitious — far-reaching and perhaps daunting. But we must consider the ramifications of not addressing the issues before they get worse and we must try to imagine the task (and the cost — human, ecological and financial) we will face in mere decades if we do not tackle this now.

Last Thoughts

Two decades ago I asked Oscar Olivera, the leader of the first "water war," what it was about water that inspired the kind of courage he and others had displayed in standing up to the army in his country. At the direction of the World Bank, Cochabamba, Bolivia, allowed Bechtel to privatize and run its water services. The company tripled the price of water, making it too expensive for the majority of this largely indigenous, poor population. It even started fining people for capturing rainwater. The people rose up against terrible odds; many were hurt, some were killed. But they did not back down and Bechtel was forced to abandon Bolivia.

Oscar was a shoemaker by trade and had never done anything like this before. But his anger at the injustice of this situation gave him courage he didn't know he had. "Why water?" he said, knowing I meant that there were many other terrible injustices his people, the Aymara, had endured over time. "Because water is life. Local water is personal. Mine, ours. How dare they claim it for their faraway investors? And because I would rather die of a bullet than of thirst."

I remembered that conversation a decade later, on that 2008 tour of the tar sands. Accompanying our group were some activists from the Athabasca Chipewyan First Nation, which lives downstream from the site. Among them was a young leader named Mike Mercredi. At a press conference we held in Edmonton to describe what we saw and experienced on the tour, Mercredi tried to explain what life was like for his people: "Sometimes you just look around and say, 'Where did all of this come from?' Some nights when you are out there, out on the lake, or when you are out in the bush, when you look toward the south you can actually see the lights glowing from industry, which tells us this is coming, it's coming toward us. The trees are gone and being cut, the land is upside down and the water is being poisoned. It's like a moonscape out there." Mercredi said that his people could no longer drink the water and were covered with sores and cysts when they swam in it. He said that people were dying, including members of his family, and that it would be kinder to come in with guns and kill them quickly than to do it this way.

The water crisis is at our door here in Canada. All the issues we thought so far away are upon us now. A greater challenge has never faced the people of Canada. Each and every one of us has a personal responsibility to take action, to collectively confront the very power structures that have prevented the change needed to protect and honour the great water heritage of this land. Future generations have the same right to breathe clean air and drink clean water. Much rests with what we do now.

Acknowledgements

I am grateful to so many people for this book. Once again, Susan Renouf has served as friend and editor and made it eminently more readable. I thank Susan, Jen Knoch and all the team at ECW Press for your faith in me.

Colleagues at the Council of Canadians have been awesome. National water campaigner Emma Lui and political director Brent Patterson have been with me step by step through the writing of this book. Their research and support were key. Campaigners and organizers Meera Karunananthan, Mark Calzavara, Andrea Harden-Donahue, Angela Giles, Harjap Grewal and Brigette DePape and board members Leo Broderick, Lois Frank and Steven Shrybman have all shared information, checked facts, read parts of the book or given quotes. My assistant, Kathie Cloutier, has been a steady support and my rock.

There are so many groups and individuals to recognize in this work, but I am especially grateful to David Schindler, Ralph Pentland and Robert Sandford whose lives have all been dedicated to fighting for water. Mark Mattson of Lake Ontario Waterkeeper, Jamie Kneen of MiningWatch and Scott Sinclair and others with the Canadian Centre for Policy Alternatives have all provided essential background information, as have the National Farmers Union and the Canadian Union of Public Employees. Former CUPE president Paul Moist read the whole manuscript and gave me great feedback. I am very grateful, as all Canadians should be, for the incredible work of Ecojustice. I especially thank Randy Christensen, Elaine MacDonald and Margot Venton for their kind help on specific laws and cases. I also thank Tony Clarke for allowing me to use "Boiling Point," the title of the 2008 Polaris report on the water crisis on six First Nations communities.

Then there is the incredible grassroots water justice movement to thank. Right across the country, tireless environmentalists, public sector workers and First Nations and community activists work day after day to protect water and local community rights. They often do the work of absent governments and we owe them a great debt. A special shout-out to the Council of Canadians chapters right across Canada, whose members give so freely of their time and talent.

Finally, I want to thank my wonderful family for their support and love. Our grandkids are the love of my life. My husband, Andrew, turned his lawyer's eye to an early manuscript and gave terrific advice. He has been my best friend and partner for almost four decades, and I am blessed to have him in my life.

Endnotes

One: A History of Neglect and Abuse

1   Statistics Canada, "Freshwater Supply and Demands in Canada," 1971 to 2004, September 2010.

2   C.M. O'Reilly et al., "Rapid and Highly Variable Warming of Lake Surface Waters around the Globe," *Geophysical Research Letters Journal* 42, no. 24 (December 16, 2015): 10,773–10,781.

3   Reuven Shlozbery, Rob Dorling and Peter Spiro, "Low Water Blues: An Economic Impact Assessment of Future Low Water Levels in the Great Lakes and St. Lawrence River," Mowat Centre, June 26, 2014.

4   Union of Concerned Scientists, "Confronting Climate Change in the U.S. Midwest," September 2009.

5   World Wildlife Fund — Canada, "Canada's Rivers at Risk," October 2009.

6   Ed Struzik, "Canada's Great Inland Delta: A Precarious Future Looms," *Yale Environment 360*, November 12, 2013, http://e360 .yale.edu/feature/canadas_great_inland_delta_precarious_future_ looms/2709/.

7   Brent Patterson, "Land Defenders Maintain Camp to Stop Site C Dam Construction, Allies Arrested at Peaceful Protest," *Brent Patterson's Blog, Council of Canadians*, January 7, 2016, http://

canadians.org/blog/land-defenders-maintain-camp-stop-site-c-dam-construction-allies-arrested-peaceful-protest.

8   Mark Hume, "Signs of Drought Appear to Be in Western Canada for the Long Term," *Globe and Mail*, June 14, 2015.

9   "Arctic Lakes Shrink, Disappear," radio script, *Arctic Science Journeys*, 2005, https://seagrant.uaf.edu/news/05ASJ/06.10.05 arctic-lakes.html.

10   "N.W.T. Scientists Predict 'Catastrophic Lake Drainage' Due to Thawing Permafrost," *CBC News*, July 17, 2015, http://www .cbc.ca/news/canada/north/n-w-t-scientists-predict-catastrophic-lake-drainage-due-to-thawing-permafrost-1.3158206.

11   "Canada's Subarctic Lakes Drying up Due to Less-Than-Snowy Winters," *HNGN*, November, 30 2013, http://www.hngn.com/ articles/18459/20131130/canadas-subarctic-lakes-drying-up-due-to-less-than-snowy-winters.htm.

12   "David Schindler: Canada Spending Its Way into Dangerous Water Debt," *Desmog Canada*, September 27, 2015, http://www.desmog.ca/2015/09/27/david-schindler-canada-spending-its-way-dangerous-water-debt.

13   "St. Lawrence Not Only Canadian Waterway Sullied by Sewage," *CBC News*, October 6, 2015, http://www.cbc.ca/news/canada/ montreal/raw-sewage-common-problem-examples-1.3258594.

14   Commission for Environmental Cooperation, "Taking Stock: North American Pollutant Releases and Transfers, vol. 14," 2011.

15   Kelly Crowe, "Drinking Water Contaminated by Excreted Drugs a Growing Concern," *CBC News*, September 22, 2014, http:// www.cbc.ca/news/health/drinking-water-contaminated-by-excreted-drugs-a-growing-concern-1.2772289.

16   Ralph Pentland and Chris Wood, *Down the Drain: How We Are Failing to Protect Our Water Resources* (Vancouver: Greystone, 2013).

17   Lake Ontario Waterkeeper, "Toronto Sewage," http://www .waterkeeper.ca/toronto-sewage/?rq=toronto%20sewage.

18   Council of Canadian Academies, "Water and Agriculture in Canada: Towards Sustainable Management of Water Resources," 2013.

19   Daniel Cressey, "Widely Used Herbicide Linked to Cancer," *Scientific American*, March 25, 2015, http://www

.scientificamerican.com/article/widely-used-herbicide-linked-to-cancer/.

20 Ecojustice, "Environmental Groups Force Ottawa to Review Approval of Hundreds of Pesticide Products," press release, February 5, 2014.

21 Center for Biological Diversity, "EPA Finds Atrazine Likely Harming Most Species of Plants, Animals in U.S.," press release, May 3, 2016.

22 Ecojustice, "Exposing the Toxic Legacy of Canada's Mining and Tar Sands Projects," 2010.

23 Micki Cowan, "Microplastics at 'Alarming Levels' in Canadian Lakes and Rivers," *CBC News*, July 17, 2015, http://www.cbc .ca/news/technology/microplastics-at-alarming-levels-in-canadian-lakes-and-rivers-1.3157701.

24 Canadian Science Publishing, "Potent Human Toxins Prevalent in Canada's Freshwater," press release, August 14, 2012.

25 Dirk Meissner, "First Nations Bring Contaminated Fish to Legislature to Protest Site C Dam," Canadian Press, May 11, 2015.

26 Leah Burrows, "Poison in the Arctic and the Human Cost of 'Clean' Energy," *Harvard Gazette*, September 7, 2015.

27 Amina T. Scartup et. al. "Freshwater Discharges Drive High Levels of Methylmercury in Arctic Marine Biota," *Proceedings of the National Academy of Sciences of the United States of America* 112, no. 38 (September 22, 2015): 11789–11794.

28 Ducks Unlimited, "Southern Ontario Wetland Conversion Analysis," March 2010.

29 Canadian Press, "Climate Change Could Threaten Alberta's Wetlands, Study Suggests," *CBC News*, January 27, 2015, http:// www.cbc.ca/news/canada/edmonton/climate-change-could-threaten-alberta-s-wetlands-study-suggests-1.2933709.

30 Jim Robbins, "Deforestation and Drought," *New York Times*, October 9, 2015.

31 Roxanne Palmer, "Cutting Down Tropical Forests Means Less Rain, Study Says," *International Business Times*, September 5, 2012, http://www.ibtimes.com/cutting-down-tropical-forests-means-less-rain-study-says-761521.

32 William Marsden, "Canada Leads the World in Forest Decline, Report Says," Postmedia News, September 4, 2014.

33 Emily Chung, "Most Groundwater Is Effectively a Non-Renewable Resource, Study Finds," *CBC News*, November 18, 2015, http://www.cbc.ca/news/technology/groundwater-study-1.3318137.

34 Abrahm Lustgarten, "Injection Wells: The Poison Beneath Us," *ProPublica*, June 12, 2012, https://www.propublica.org/article/injection-wells-the-poison-beneath-us.

35 Stephen Hume, "Private Sampling by MLA Finds Contamination from Vancouver Island Soil Dump," *Vancouver Sun*, July 18, 2015.

36 Paul Watson, "Once Again, Dreams of Gold Spark a Rush to the Yukon," *Toronto Star*, May 14, 2011.

37 Tom Clynes, "Yukon Government Opens Vast Wilderness to Mining," *National Geographic*, January 25, 2014.

38 Ontario Nature, "Ring of Fire Background."

Two: A Federal Government Missing in Action

39 "Shared Responsibility," *Environment and Climate Change Canada*, accessed June 8, 2016, https://www.ec.gc.ca/eau-water/default.asp?lang=En&n=035F6173-1.

40 Hanneke Brooymans, *Water in Canada: A Resource in Crisis*, (Vancouver: Lone Pine Publishing, 2011).

41 Pentland and Wood, *Down the Drain*.

42 Susan Rowntree, "Water Safety, on Tap," letter to the editor, *Globe and Mail*, December 8, 2015.

43 Todd Scarth, "Hell and High Water: An Assessment of Paul Martin's Record and Implications for the Future," Canadian Centre for Policy Alternatives, 2004.

44 Linda Nowlan and Anna Johnston, "Scaling Up the Fisheries Act: Restoring Lost Protections and Incorporating Modern Safeguards," West Coast Environmental Law, March 24, 2016.

45 Glen McGregor, "Conservatives Defend New Waterways Rules against Opposition Accusations of Favouritism," *Ottawa Citizen*, October 30, 2012.

46 "Rivers and Lakes Be Damned," *New Brunswick Media Co-Op*, January 29, 2013, http://nbmediacoop.org/2013/01/29/rivers-and-lakes-be-damned-why-bill-c-45-concerns-us-all/.

47 Thomas Duck "Will Harper Gut the Species at Risk Act Next?"

Thomas J. Duck (blog), October 15, 2015, http://tomduck.ca/posts/2015-10-15_species-at-risk.html.

48   Tim Harper, "Environment Commissioner's Farewell Audit Screams the Obvious," *Toronto Star*, February 5, 2015.

49   Will Amos et al., "Getting Tough on Environmental Crime?" Ecojustice, 2011.

50   Mike De Souza, "Environment Canada Hits Alleged Polluters with Warnings Instead of Prosecutions," *Ottawa Citizen*, January 22, 2013.

51   Bob Weber, "Fish Habitat Protection Waning under Harper Government, Analysis Finds," Canadian Press, September 2, 2015.

52   Professional Institute of the Public Service of Canada, "Vanishing Science: The Disappearance of Canadian Public Interest Science," 2014.

53   Mark Hume, "Environment Canada Officers Failed to Uphold the Law: Report," *Globe and Mail*, January 29, 2016.

54   Warren Wishart, "2014 Canadian Municipal Water Priorities Report," Presentation to the Canadian Water and Wastewater Association, October 28, 2014.

55   Hugh Mackenzie, "Canada's Infrastructure Gap: Where It Came From and Why It Will Cost So Much to Close," Canadian Centre for Policy Alternatives, January 2013.

56   Council of Canadian Academies, *The Sustainable Management of Groundwater in Canada* (Ottawa: 2009).

57   Alfonso Rivera, ed., *Canada's Groundwater Resources* (Markham, ON: Fitzhenry and Whiteside, 2013).

58   Adèle Hurley, "Let's Make Groundwater an Issue of National Security," *Globe and Mail*, December 4, 2015.

59   "New Wastewater Systems Effluent Regulations," *Willms & Shier*, July 23, 2012, http://www.willmsshier.com/resources/news/2012/07/23/new-wastewater-systems-effluent-regulations.

60   Elaine MacDonald, "New Sewage Treatment Rules Fall Short," *Ecojustice*, February 17, 2015, http://www.ecojustice.ca/new-sewage-treatment-rules-fall-short/.

61   Mark Mattson, "Why I Think Montreal's Sewage Dump May Be Illegal," *Lake Ontario Waterkeeper*, October 6, 2015, http://www.waterkeeper.ca/blog/2015/10/6/why-i-think-montreals-sewage-dump-may-be-illegal.

62 Ecojustice, "Waterproof: Standards," 2014.

63 Holly Moore, "Drinking Water in Canadian Cities Not Always
    Tested for All Contaminants," *CBC News*, June 19, 2015, http://
    www.cbc.ca/news/canada/manitoba/drinking-water-in-canadian-
    cities-not-always-tested-for-all-contaminants-1.3111908.

64 Hannah Hoag, "Canada's Renowned Freshwater Research Site
    to Close," *Nature*, May 21, 2012, http://www.nature.com/news/
    canada-s-renowned-freshwater-research-site-to-close-1.10683.

Three: First Nations on the Front Line

65 Andrea Harden-Donahue, "Visiting Shoal Lake 40," Council
    of Canadians, blog, April 13, 2015, http://canadians.org/blog/
    visiting-shoal-lake-40-i-don%E2%80%99t-look-sympathy-i-
    look-knowledge-justice.

66 Emma Lui, "On Notice for a Drinking Water Crisis in Canada,"
    Council of Canadians, 2014.

67 Joanne Levasseur and Jacques Marcoux, "Bad Water: Third
    World Conditions on First Nations in Canada," *CBC News*,
    October 14, 2015, http://www.cbc.ca/news/canada/manitoba/
    bad-water-third-world-conditions-on-first-nations-in-
    canada-1.3269500.

68 Neegan Burnside Ltd., "National Assessment of First Nations
    Water and Wastewater Systems — National Roll-Up Report,"
    Indigenous and Northern Affairs Canada, April 2011.

69 Jody Porter, "Mercury Levels Still Rising Near Grassy Narrows
    First Nation," *CBC News*, June 15, 2015, http://www.cbc.ca/
    news/canada/thunder-bay/mercury-levels-still-rising-near-grassy-
    narrows-first-nation-report-says-1.3109261.

70 André Picard, "Harper's Disregard for Aboriginal Health," *Globe
    and Mail*, April 9, 2012.

71 Pamela Palmater, "Canada Was Killing Indians, Not Cultures,"
    telesur, June 8, 2015, http://www.telesurtv.net/english/opinion/
    Canada-Was-Killing-Indians-Not-Cultures-20150608-0018.html.

72 Canadian Press, "Justin Trudeau Vows to End First Nations
    Reserve Boil-Water Advisories within 5 Years," *CBC News*,
    October 7, 2015, http://www.cbc.ca/news/politics/canada-election-
    2015-justin-trudeau-first-nations-boil-water-advisories-1.3258058.

73 Cathy Gulli, "Why Can't We Get Clean Water to First Nations

Reserves?" *Maclean's*, October 7, 2015.

74   "Statement: CHRC Applauds Historic Decision in the First
     Nations Child Welfare Case," press release, Canadian Human
     Rights Commission, January 26, 2015.

75   Russell Diabo, "Harper Launches Major First Nations Termina-
     tion Plan," *Idle No More*, June 16, 2013, http://www.idlenomore
     .ca/harper_launches_major_first_nations_termination_plan_as_
     negotiating_tables_legitimize_canada_s_colonialism.

76   Karen Busby, "First Nations Water Act Doomed?" *Winnipeg Free
     Press*, June 26, 2013.

77   David Boyd, "No Taps, No Toilets, First Nations and the Con-
     stitutional Right to Water in Canada," *McGill Law Journal* 75,
     no. 1 (2011): 83–134.

78   Amanda Klasing, "Make It Safe: Canada's Obligation to End the
     First Nations Water Crisis," Human Rights Watch, March 2016.

79   Gordon Hoekstra, "Nadleh Whut'en and Stellat'en and
     Hereditary Leaders Proclaim B.C.'s First Aboriginal Water Laws,"
     Vancouver Sun, March 30, 2016.

80   Merrell-Ann Phare, "Aboriginal Water Rights Primer," Assembly
     of First Nations of Quebec, Labrador, Assembly of Manitoba
     Chiefs and Chiefs of Ontario, April 2009.

81   "Canada's Statement on the World Conference on Indigenous
     Peoples Outcome Document," *Permanent Mission of Canada
     to the United Nations*, September 22, 2014, http://www
     .canadainternational.gc.ca/prmny-mponu/canada_un-canada_onu/
     statements-declarations/other-autres/2014-09-22_wcipd-padd.
     aspx?lang=eng.

82   "Canada Officially Adopts UN Declaration on the Rights of
     Indigenous Peoples," *CBC News*, May 10, 2016, http://www.cbc
     .ca/news/aboriginal/canada-adopting-implementing-un-rights-
     declaration-1.3575272.

83   Canadian Press, "Alberta First Nations Sue Ottawa Over Safety
     of Drinking Water," *CBC News*, June 16, 2014, http://www.cbc
     .ca/news/canada/calgary/alberta-first-nations-sue-ottawa-over-
     safety-of-drinking-water-1.2677316.

84   Brent Patterson, "Council Thanks Mikisew Cree on Their Court
     Win against the Omnibus Bills," *Brent Patterson's Blog*, Council
     of Canadians, December 23, 2014, http://canadians.org/blog/

council-thanks-mikisew-cree-their-court-win-against-omnibus-bills.

85 Crystal Lameman, "Life above the Alberta Tar Sands — Why We're Taking the Government to Court," *The Guardian*, April 8, 2015.

Four: Where Oil Meets Water

86 Kyla Mandel, "Canada's Oil Exports Up 65 Per Cent over Last Decade," *Desmog Canada*, February 22, 2016, http://www.desmog.ca/2016/02/22/canada-s-oil-exports-65-over-last-decade.

87 "What Is Extreme Energy?" Extreme Energy Initiative, accessed June 29, 2016, http://extremeenergy.org/about/what-is-extreme-energy-2/.

88 Andrew Nikiforuk, "Two More Ethical Challenges to Canada's Oil Sands," *The Tyee*, October 28, 2011, http://thetyee.ca/Opinion/2011/10/26/Oil-Sands-Challenges/.

89 Tim Gray, "The Tar Sands Don't Have to Pollute the Water. So Why Do They?" *Globe and Mail*, September 27, 2013.

90 Environmental Defence, "Reality Check: Water and the Tar Sands," September 2013.

91 Environmental Defence, Keepers of the Athabasca, National Resources Defense Council, "Alberta Government Chooses Oil over Water: New Rules Bow to Corporate Interests," press release, March 13, 2015.

92 Meagan Wohlberg, "Low Levels on Athabasca River Prompt Requests for Limited Water Withdrawals by Industry," *Northern Journal*, June 1, 2015.

93 Margo McDiarmid, "NAFTA Probe of Alberta's Tailings Ponds Blocked by Canada," *CBC News*, January 28, 2015, http://www.cbc.ca/news/politics/nafta-probe-of-alberta-s-tailings-ponds-blocked-by-canada-1.2935004.

94 Claudia Cattaneo, "Get Used to It, the Oilsands Are Unstoppable," *National Post*, February 25, 2016.

95 "Alberta Pipelines: 5 Major Oil Spills in Recent History," *CBC News*, July 17, 2015, http://www.cbc.ca/news/canada/alberta-pipelines-5-major-oil-spills-in-recent-history-1.3156604.

96 Leslie Young, "Crude Awakening: 37 Years of Oil Spills in Alberta," *Global News*, May 22, 2013, http://globalnews.ca/

news/571494/introduction-37-years-of-oil-spills-in-alberta/.

97 "Kalamazoo River Spill Yields Record Fine," *Living on Earth*, radio broadcast, July 6, 2012.

98 Canadian Press, "Bitumen Spill Effects Unknown: Report," *Global News*, February 2, 2015, http://globalnews.ca/news/1808029/bitumen-spill-effects-unknown-report/.

99 National Academy of Sciences, Engineering and Medicine, *Spills of Diluted Bitumen from Pipelines: A Comparative Study of Environmental Fate, Effects, and Response* (Washington, DC: The National Academies Press, 2016).

100 Council of Canadians, "Energy East: Where Oil Meets Water," August 2014.

101 Amber Hildebrandt, "Pipeline Rupture Report Raises Questions about TransCanada Inspections," *CBC News*, February 4, 2014, http://www.cbc.ca/news/canada/pipeline-rupture-report-raises-questions-about-transcanada-inspections-1.2521959.

102 Mike De Souza, "TransCanada Dismissed Whistleblower. Then Their Pipeline Blew Up," *National Observer*, February 5, 2016, http://www.nationalobserver.com/2016/02/05/news/transcanada-dismissed-whistleblower-then-their-pipeline-blew.

103 Mark Calzavara, "Quantifying Risk: Calculating the Probability of an Energy East Pipeline Rupture," Council of Canadians, September 2, 2015.

104 Mike De Souza, "Harper Government Scraps 3,000 Environmental Reviews on Pipelines and Other Projects," Canada.com, August 23, 2012, http://o.canada.com/news/harper-government-kills-3000-environmental-reviews-on-pipelines-and-other-projects.

105 Environmental Defence, et al., "Energy East: A Risk to Our Drinking Water," Spring 2016.

106 Erin Flanagan and Clare Demerse, "Climate Implications of the Proposed Energy East Pipeline," Pembina Institute, February 6, 2014.

107 Andrew Topf, "Why Canada Would Rather Export Oil than Refine It," *Oil Price*, July 21, 2014, http://oilprice.com/Energy/Energy-General/Why-Canada-Would-Rather-Export-Oil-Than-Refine-It.html.

108 Council of Canadians et al., "TransCanada's Energy East: An Export Pipeline, Not for Domestic Gain," March 2014.

109 Lorne Stockman, "Refinery Report: New Online Tool Tracks Tar Sands Flows through North America," PriceofOil.org, December 13, 2013, http://priceofoil.org/2013/12/13/refinery-report-new-online-tool-tracks-tar-sands-flows-north-america/.

110 Lisa Song, "Another Major Tar Sands Pipeline Seeking U.S. Permit," *Inside Climate News*, June 3, 2013, http://insideclimatenews.org/news/20130603/map-another-major-tar-sands-pipeline-seeking-us-permit.

111 Canadian Press, "Study: Straits Oil Spill Could Affect Vast Shoreline Areas in the U.S., Canada," *Vancouver Sun*, March 31, 2016.

112 Jeff Alexander and Beth Wallace, "Sunken Hazard: Aging Oil Pipelines beneath the Straits of Mackinac an Ever-Present Threat to the Great Lakes," National Wildlife Federation, 2012.

113 FLOW, "Straits Oil Pipelines Not Needed to Meet Michigan, Midwest Demand: Report," press release, December 14, 2015.

114 Nick Cunningham, "Indiana Regulators Let BP Pollute Lake Michigan," *Bulldog Blog, DC Bureau*, July 10, 2013, https://dcbureau.org/201307108833/bulldog-blog/indiana-regulators-let-bp-pollute-lake-michigan.html.

115 Lyman C. Welch et al., "Oil and Water: Tar Sands Crude Shipping Meets the Great Lakes?" Alliance for the Great Lakes, November 2013.

116 Statistics Canada, "Shipping in Canada, 2011," November 27, 2015, http://www.statcan.gc.ca/pub/54-205-x/2011000/part-partie1-eng.htm.

117 "Calumet to Build Terminal in Superior to Ship Oil," *Superior Telegram*, February 13, 2013.

118 Welch et al., "Oil and Water."

119 "Oil Shipments by Rail, Truck and Barge up Substantially," *Institute for Energy Research*, September 9, 2013, http://instituteforenergyresearch.org/analysis/oil-shipments-by-rail-truck-and-barge-up-substantially/.

120 Dan Murtaugh, "Marathon Bare Damage Halts Loading of Crude at Wood River Dock," *Bloomberg*, May 3, 2013, http://www.bloomberg.com/news/articles/2013-05-03/marathon-barge-damage-halts-loading-of-crude-at-wood-river-dock.

121 IHS Global Inc. for the American Petroleum Institute, "Oil & Natural Gas Transportation & Storage Infrastructure: Status,

Trends & Economic Benefits," December 2013.

122 Harry Valentine, "Prospects for Oil Transportation on North American Inland Waterways," *Maritime Executive*, July 26, 2013, http://www.maritime-executive.com/features/ Prospects-for-Oil-Transportation-on-North-American-Inland-Waterways-2013-07-26.

123 "Canada Not Prepared for Major Oil Spill," *CTV News*, December 7, 2010, http://www.ctvnews.ca/canada-not-prepared-for-major-oil-spill-report-1.583453.

124 Peter O'Neil and Gordon Hoekstra, "Canada's Tanker Spill Response System Needs Upgrading," *Vancouver Sun*, December 3, 2013.

125 Council of Canadian and Équiterre, "Doubling Down on Disaster: Transporting Tar Sands Bitumen Threatens Lac Saint-Pierre and the St. Lawrence River," January 2015.

126 Brent Patterson, "Oil Shipments on the Great Lakes, Now and to Come," *Brent Patterson's Blog, Council of Canadians*, November 3, 2013, http://canadians.org/blog/oil-shipments-great-lakes-now-and-come.

127 Andrew Slade, "Oil Shipping Plan for Great Lakes Raises Big Concerns," *Duluth News Tribune*, November 24, 2013.

128 Canadian Press, "Beluga Whale Population in St. Lawrence on 'Catastrophic' Path," CBC News, September 29, 2014, http://www.cbc.ca/news/canada/montreal/beluga-whale-population-in-st-lawrence-on-catastrophic-path-1.2781318.

129 Derek Leahy, "TransCanada Confirms No Energy East Tanker Terminal in Cacouna, Quebec, Near Beluga Breeding Grounds," *Desmog Canada*, April 2, 2015, http://www.desmog.ca/2015/04/02/transcanada-confirms-no-energy-east-tanker-terminal-cacouna-quebec-beluga-breeding-grounds.

Five: Hewers of Wood, Drawers of Water

130 Wenonah Hauter, *Frackopoly: The Battle for the Future of Energy and the Environment* (New York: New Press, 2016).

131 Andrew Nikiforuk, "Shale Gas: How Hard on the Landscape?" *The Tyee*, January 8, 2013, http://thetyee.ca/News/2013/01/08/Shale-Gas-Hard-On-Landscape/.

132 Hauter, *Frackopoly*.

133 Theo Colborn et al., "Natural Gas Operations from a Public Health Perspective," *Human and Ecological Risk Assessment: An International Journal* 17, no. 5 (2011): 1039–1056.

134 Food & Water Watch, "The Case for a Ban on Gas Fracking," June 2011.

135 Paul Boothe, "Regulation and Environmental Impacts of Shale Gas in Canada," Environment Canada memorandum to minister, MIN-144492, March 8, 2011.

136 Elizabeth Ridlington and John Rumpler, "Fracking by the Numbers: Key Impacts of Dirty Drilling at the State and National Level," Environment Canada, October 3, 2013.

137 Aaron Cantú, "Radioactive Wastewater Dumped by Oil Companies Is Seeping out of the Ground in North Dakota," *AlterNet*, January 24, 2014, http://www.alternet.org/radioactive-waste-dumped-oil-companies-seeping-out-ground-north-dakota.

138 Andrew Nikiforuk, "Safety Alert Issued over Dangers of Fracked Oil," *The Tyee*, January 6, 2014, http://thetyee.ca/Blogs/The-Hook/2014/01/06/Fracked-Oil-Alert/.

139 Steve Horn, "Permit Shows Bakken Shale Oil in Casselton Train Explosion Contained High Levels of Volatile Chemicals," *Desmogblog*, January 5, 2014, http://www.desmogblog.com/2014/01/05/exclusive-permit-shows-bakken-oil-casselton-train-contained-high-levels-volatile-chemicals.

140 Christopher Bateman, "A Colossal Fracking Mess," *Vanity Fair*, June 21, 2010.

141 Fracking and Health Awareness Project, frackingandhealth.ca (site discontinued).

142 Rivka Galchen, "Weather Underground: The Arrival of Man-Made Earthquakes," *The New Yorker*, April 13, 2015.

143 Andrew Nikiforuk, "Did Alberta Just Break a Fracking Earthquake Record?" *The Tyee*, January 29, 2015, http://thetyee.ca/News/2015/01/29/Alberta-Fracking-Earthquake/.

144 Dean Bennett, "Alberta Fracking an Unregulated Free-For-All, Licence Data Shows," *Huffpost Alberta*, April 2, 2014, http://www.huffingtonpost.ca/2014/02/04/alberta-fracking-_n_4724808.html.

145 David Hughes, "A Clear Look at BC LNG," Canadian Center for Policy Alternatives, B.C., May 2015.

146 NoMorePipelines.ca, accessed June 10, 2016.

147 Cheryl Martens, "Fort Nelson First Nation Chief Liz Logan Wins Court Battle to Save Water from Fracking," Treaty 8 Tribal Association, September 15, 2015, http://treaty8.bc.ca/fort-nelson-first-nation-chief-liz-logan-wins-court-battle-to-save-water-from-fracking/.

148 Ed Struzik, "A New Frontier for Fracking: Drilling Near the Arctic Circle," *Yale Environment 360*, August 18, 2014, http://e360.yale.edu/feature/a_new_frontier_for_fracking_drilling_near_the_arctic_circle/2794/.

149 "Pennsylvania and Fracking," *Earthjustice*, accessed June 10, 2016, http://earthjustice.org/features/pennsylvania-and-fracking.

150 Council of Canadians, "A Fractivist's Toolkit," 2014.

151 Sara Gosman et al., "Hydraulic Fracturing in the Great Lakes Basin: The State of Play in Michigan and Ohio," National Wildlife Federation, June 21, 2012.

152 Food & Water Watch, "Trouble Brewing in the Great Lakes," 2014.

153 Maureen Googoo, "Sipekne'katik to Decide Next Steps in Alton Gas Storage Opposition," Kukukwes.com, February 3, 2016, http://kukukwes.com/2016/02/03/sipeknekatik-to-decide-next-steps-in-alton-gas-storage-opposition/.

154 Earthworks and MiningWatch Canada, "Troubled Water, How Mine Waste Dumping Is Poisoning Our Oceans, Rivers and Lakes," February 2012.

155 Ian Bickis, "Environment Canada Accuses Vale of Decades of Water Pollution," *Globe and Mail*, October 23, 2015.

156 MiningWatch Canada, "Wake-Up Call: Ontario Ranks Worst in Canada for Environmental Liability of Mine Sites," press release, December 9, 2015.

157 MiningWatch Canada, "Ontarians on the Hook for Water & Mine Site Clean-Up Costs — Alarming Report from Eco-Commissioner," press release, November 10, 2015.

158 Saskatchewan Environmental Society, "The Legacy of Uranium Mining in Saskatchewan: The Unacceptable Environmental Impacts of Uranium Mining," March 2015.

159 Carolyn Jarvis, Brennan Leffler and Francesca Fionda, "Toxic Dust Buried under Yellowknife's 'Giant Mine' to Cost Taxpayers

$900M," *Global News*, November 18, 2014, http://globalnews.
ca/news/1678141/toxic-dust-buried-under-yellowknifes-giant-
mine-to-cost-taxpayers-900-million/.

160 Kelly Sinoski, "Major Imperial Metals Shareholder Held Private
Fundraiser for Clark's Re-Election Bid," *Vancouver Sun*, May 8,
2014.

161 Canadian Press, "B.C. Mining Giant Admits Polluting U.S.
Waters," *CBC News*, September 10, 2012, http://www.cbc.ca/
news/canada/british-columbia/b-c-mining-giant-admits-polluting-
u-s-waters-1.1177305.

162 Peter O'Neil, "Southeast B.C. Coal Mines Draw the Ire of U.S.
Environmental Agency," *Vancouver Sun*, February 8, 2013.

163 Wilderness Committee, "Cleaning Up B.C.'s Dirty Mining Industry," January 2016.

164 MiningWatch Canada and Clayoquot Action, "The Big Hole:
Environmental Assessment and Mining in Ontario," December
2014.

165 Larry Pynn, "Feds Drop Environmental Assessment of 492 Projects," *Vancouver Sun*, August 22, 2012.

166 "Anti-Shale Gas Protest Resumes in Kent County," *CBC News*,
June 6, 2013, http://www.cbc.ca/news/canada/new-brunswick/
anti-shale-gas-protest-resumes-in-kent-county-1.1318114.

167 Julie Gordon, "Police Arrest 40 as Canada Shale Gas Protest Turns Violent," *Reuters*, October 17, 2013, http://
www.reuters.com/article/us-newbrunswick-protests-
idUSBRE99G1DF20131017.

Six: Agribusiness Imperils Water

168 Jessica Pressler, "Michael Burry, Real-Life Market Genius from
The Big Short, Thinks Another Financial Crisis Is Looming,"
New York Magazine's Daily Intelligencer, December 28, 2015,
http://nymag.com/daily/intelligencer/2015/12/big-short-genius-
says-another-crisis-is-coming.html#.

169 Stephanie Brown, "The EU vs. Canada: Fixing Factory Farms by
Granting 'The 5 Freedoms,'" *Diplomat & International Canada*,
September 30, 2013, http://diplomatonline.com/mag/2013/09/the-
eu-vs-canada-fixing-factory-farms-by-granting-the-5-freedoms/.3

170 "Spallumcheen's Drinking Water Polluted by Liquid Manure Says

UVic Law Center," *CBC News*, February 4, 2016, http://www
.cbc.ca/news/canada/british-columbia/spallumcheen-s-drinking-
water-polluted-by-liquid-manure-says-uvic-law-centre-1.3434372.

171 Scott Sutherland, "Lake Erie's Toxic Algae Bloom Is Back and
It's Spreading," *The Weather Network*, August 6, 2015, https://
www.theweathernetwork.com/news/articles/lake-eries-toxic-algae-
bloom-is-back-and-its-spreading/55354.

172 David W. Schindler and John R. Vallentyne, *The Algal Bowl:
Overfertilization of the World's Freshwaters and Estuaries*
(Edmonton: University of Alberta Press, 2008).

173 Robert William Sandford, *Saving Lake Winnipeg* (Victoria, B.C.:
Rocky Mountain Books, 2013).

174 Raveena Aulakh "Toxic Algae Is Likely to Get Worse in Lake
Erie," *Toronto Star*, February 27, 2014, https://www.thestar.com/
news/world/2014/02/27/toxic_algae_is_likely_to_get_worse_in_
lake_erie_heres_how_to_fix_it.html.

175 Alissa Figueroa, "In a Fertile Valley, Toxic Drinking Water,"
Fusion, September 12, 2013, http://fusion.net/story/4370/in-a-
fertile-valley-toxic-drinking-water/.

176 Sharon Labchuk, "PEI: Pesticide Exposure Island," *Prevent
Cancer Now*, May 12, 2012, http://www.preventcancernow.ca/
pei-pesticide-exposure-island.

177 Kate Prengaman, "Groundwater War Pits Wisconsin Farms
Against Fish," WisconsinWatch.org, July 21, 2013, http://
wisconsinwatch.org/2013/07/groundwater-war-pits-wisconsin-
farms-against-fish-2/.

178 Kate Golden, "Nitrate in Water Widespread, Current Rules No
Match for It," WisconsinWatch.org, November 15, 2015, http://
wisconsinwatch.org/2015/11/nitrate-in-water-widespread-current-
rules-no-match-for-it/.

179 "International Trade," Canadian Meat Council, accessed June 30,
2016, http://www.cmc-cvc.com/en/international-trade.

180 Council of Canadians, "Leaky Exports: A Portrait of the Virtual
Water Trade in Canada," May 27, 2011.

181 Alicja Siekierska, Randy Shore, Will Chabun, and Alex
MacPherson, "Hot, Dry and Disastrous: Western Canada's
Drought Is Taking a Toll," *Edmonton Journal*, July 23, 2015,
http://www.edmontonjournal.com/disastrous+Western+Canada+

drought+taking+toll/11240817/story.html.

182 Stephen Leahy, "In a Warmer World, There Will Be More Fire. That's a Virtual Certainty," StephenLeahy.net, May 4, 2016, https://stephenleahy.net/2016/05/04/in-a-warmer-world-there-will-be-more-fire-thats-a-virtual-certainty/.

183 Junchang Ju and Jeffrey G. Masek, "The Vegetation Trend in Canada and U.S. Alaska from 1984–2012: Landsat Data," *Remote Sensing of Environment* 176 (April 2016): 1–16.

184 Trevor Herriot, "Why Is Ottawa Abandoning Swaths of Prairie Grassland?" *Globe and Mail*, April 8, 2013, http://www.theglobeandmail.com/news/national/why-is-ottawa-abandoning-swaths-of-prairie-grassland/article10823827/?page=all.

185 "The Death of the PFRA," *Canadian Cowboy Country Magazine*, October 1, 2012.

186 Paul Waldie, "Family Farms Are Fewer and Larger, StatsCan Says," *Globe and Mail*, May 10, 2012, http://www.theglobeandmail.com/news/national/family-farms-are-fewer-and-larger-statscan-says/article4106102/.

187 Cathy Holtslander, "Losing Our Grip: 2015 Update," National Farmers Union, March 2015.

188 Eric Atkins, "Water-Poor Saudi Arabia Invests in Canadian Wheat Board's Grain," *Globe and Mail*, April 16, 2015, http://www.theglobeandmail.com/report-on-business/international-business/water-poor-saudi-arabia-invests-in-canadian-wheat-boards-grain/article23997819/.

189 Paul Waldie and Jessica Leeder, "Do Corporate Buyouts Signal the End of the Family Farm?" *Globe and Mail*, November 24, 2010, http://www.theglobeandmail.com/news/national/time-to-lead/do-corporate-buyouts-signal-the-end-of-the-family-farm/article1316189/.

190 Gerald Pilger, "Who's Buying Up Canadian Farmland?" *Country Guide*, February 10, 2015, http://www.country-guide.ca/2015/02/10/whos-buying-up-canadian-farmland/45783/.

191 Worldwatch Institute, "Despite Drop from 2009 Peak, Agricultural Land Grabs Still Remain Above Pre-2005 Levels," June 21, 2012, http://www.worldwatch.org/despite-drop-2009-peak-agricultural-land-grabs-still-remain-above-pre-2005-levels-0.

192 Oakland Institute, "Understanding Land Investment Deals

in Africa: Land Grabs Leave Africa Thirsty, Land Deal Brief," December 2011.

193 Transnational Institute, "The Global Land Grab: A Primer," October 11, 2012.

194 Stop Dump Site 41, "Farmer, 82, and wife, 76, to be charged on Site 41 protest," press release, August 4, 2009.

195 Joe Friesen, "How the Little People Stopped the Tiny Township Dump," *Globe and Mail*, August 28, 2009.

Seven: Water for Sale

196 Lucy Ren, "Sandor Predicts a U.S. Water Futures Market," Medill News Service, June 3, 2015, http://news.medill .northwestern.edu/chicago/sandor-predicts-a-u-s-water-futures-market/.

197 Brian M. Carney, "Can the World Still Feed Itself?" *Wall Street Journal*, September 23, 2011.

198 Wally Braul and Harry Dahme, "Sustainability Shift: The Evolution of Canadian Water Policy," Gowling WLG, September 1, 2015.

199 Kevin Welch, "Group Buys Mesa Water Rights," *Amarillo Globe-News*, June 24, 2011.

200 Elisabeth Rosenthal, "In Spain, Water Is a New Battleground," *New York Times*, June 3, 2008.

201 Gloria Galloway, "Canada Could Benefit from Bigger 'Environmental Markets': Study," *Globe and Mail*, November 17, 2012.

202 Mercedes Marcano, "Ontario's Environmental Markets: Creating Price Signals to Protect Our Natural Environment," Sustainable Prosperity, November 11, 2015.

203 Nancy Goucher and Tony Maas, "Clean, Not Green: Tackling Algal Blooms in the Great Lakes," Environmental Defence and Freshwater Future Canada, August 2014.

204 Food & Water Watch, "Water Quality Trading: Polluting Public Waterways for Private Gain," November 2015.

205 "Pollution Charges," Global Water Partnership, http://www.gwp .org/en/ToolBox/TOOLS/Management-Instruments/Economic-Instruments/Pollution-charges/.

206 Transparency Market Research, "Bottled Water (Still, Carbonated, Flavored and Functional Bottled Water) Market: Global In-

dustry Perspective, Comprehensive Analysis, Size, Share, Growth, Segment, Trends and Forecast, 2014–2020," December 2015.

207 John Lancaster and Jennifer Fowler. "Ontario Mismanaging Its Water, Environmental Commissioner Says," *CBC News*, November 3, 2015, http://www.cbc.ca/news/canada/toronto/ontario-environmental-commissioner-water-1.3302836.

208 "Nestlé Faces Renewed Criticism as B.C. Drought Continues," *CBC News*, July 10, 2015, http://www.cbc.ca/news/canada/british-columbia/nestl%C3%A9-faces-renewed-criticism-as-b-c-drought-continues-1.3145929.

209 Kelly Sinoski, "Nestlé's Extraction of Groundwater Near Hope Riles First Nations," *Vancouver Sun*, August 20, 2013, http://www.vancouversun.com/life/nestl%C3%A9+extraction+ground-water+near+hope+riles+first+nations/8817969/story.html.

210 The Council of Canadians, "Water Rush: Why B.C.'s Water Sustainability Act Fails to Protect Water," February 10, 2016.

211 Julene Bair, *The Ogallala Road: A Story of Love, Family, and the Fight to Keep the Great Plains from Running Dry* (New York: Penguin Books, 2014).

212 Utrecht University, "Groundwater Depletion Rate Accelerating Worldwide," press release, September 23, 2010.

213 Jeff Rubin, "Water: Canada's Most Valuable Resource," *Globe and Mail*, September, 8, 2010, http://www.theglobeandmail.com/report-on-business/rob-commentary/water-canadas-most-valuable-resource/article1391659/.

214 Diane Katz, "Making Waves: Examining the Case for Sustainable Water Exports from Canada," Fraser Institute, June 2010.

215 Alexis Stoymenoff, "'Charitable' Fraser Institute Accepted $500k in Foreign funding from Koch Oil Billionaires," *Vancouver Observer*, April 26, 2012, http://www.vancouverobserver.com/politics/2012/04/25/charitable-fraser-institute-accepted-500k-foreign-funding-oil-billionaires.

216 Renata D'Aliesio, "Chrétien's Call to Canada: Don't Be Afraid of Water-Exporting Debate," *Globe and Mail*, March 22, 2011, http://www.theglobeandmail.com/news/politics/chretiens-call-to-canada-dont-be-afraid-of-water-exporting-debate/article578411/.

217 Parag Khanna, *Connectography: Mapping the Future of Global Civilization* (New York: Penguin Random House, 2016).

218 Rhett Larson, "The Case of Canadian Bulk Water Exports," School of Public Policy, University of Calgary and Canadian Global Affairs Institute, August 2015.

Eight: The Corporate Free Trade Threat to Canada's Water

219 Brian Owens, "World's Water Footprint Linked to Free Trade," *Nature Online*, February 13, 2012, http://blogs.nature.com/news/2012/02/world%E2%80%99s-water-footprint-linked-to-free-trade.html.

220 Frank Quinn, "Water Diversion, Export and Canada-US Relations: A Brief History," Program on Water Issues, Munk Centre for International Studies, August 2007.

221 David Johansen, "Bulk Water Removals, Water Exports and the NAFTA," Parliamentary Research Branch, Library of Parliament, February 20, 2001.

222 Matt Armstrong, "NAFTA and Water," WaterToday.ca, February 12, 2013, http://www.watertoday.ca/nafta-water.asp.

223 Merrell-Ann Phare, "Whose Water Is It? Aboriginal Water Rights and International Trade Agreements," Policy Horizons Canada, May 2006.

224 Quentin Karpilow, Ilana Solomon, Alejandro Villamar Calderón, Manuel Pérez-Rocha and Stuart Trew, "NAFTA: 20 Years of Costs to Communities and the Environment," RMALC, The Council of Canadians, Sierra Club, and Institute for Policy Studies, March 2014.

225 "European Union Drops Plan to Label Oilsands Crude 'Dirty,'" *CBC News*, October 7, 2014, http://www.cbc.ca/news/business/european-union-drops-plan-to-label-oilsands-crude-dirty-1.2789868.

226 Friends of the Earth Europe, "Dirty Deals: How Trade Talks Threaten to Undermine EU Climate Policies and Bring Tar Sand to Europe," July 17, 2014.

227 Arthur Neslen, "EU Dropped Pesticide Laws Due to US Pressure Over TTIP, Documents Reveal," *The Guardian*, May 22, 2015, https://www.theguardian.com/environment/2015/may/22/eu-dropped-pesticide-laws-due-to-us-pressure-over-ttip-documents-reveal.

228 Kai Nagata, "Want Free Trade? Build a West Coast Pipeline, Says

China," Dogwood Initiative, blog, January 20, 2016, https://
dogwoodinitiative.org/blog/want-free-trade-build-a-west-coast-
pipeline-says-china.

229 Howard Mann, "ISDS: Who Wins More, Investors or States?"
Investment Treaty News, International Institute for Sustainable
Development, June 24, 2015.

230 Gus Van Harten and Pavel Malysheuski, "Who Has Benefited
Financially from Investment Treaty Arbitration? An Evaluation
of the Size and Wealth of Claimants," Osgoode Legal Studies
Research Paper, January 11, 2016.

231 Reuters, "Ecuador to Pay $980 Million to Occidental for Asset
Seizure," January 13, 2016.

232 Scott Sinclair, "NAFTA Chapter 11 Investor-State Disputes
to January 1, 2015," Canadian Centre for Policy Alternatives,
January 14, 2015.

233 Carin Smaller and Howard Mann, "A Thirst for Distant Lands:
Foreign Investment in Agricultural Land and Water," International Institute for Sustainable Development, May 2009.

234 Joseph Cumming and Robert Froehlich, "NAFTA Chapter XI and
Canada's Environmental Sovereignty: Investment Flows, Article
1110 and Alberta's Water Act," University of Toronto Faculty of
Law Review, March 22, 2007.

235 Melissa Smalley, "Coun. Sinclair Praises City's Arsenic Response, Saying Former Water Utility Had 'No Plan,'" *Peace
Arch News*, February 18, 2016, http://www.peacearchnews.com/
news/369333701.html.

236 "New Rate Survey of 500 U.S. Water Systems Finds Private Water
Providers Charge 58% More," *Food & Water Watch*, February
16, 2016.

237 Satoko Kishimoto, Emanuele Lobina, and Olivier Petitjean, *Our
Public Water Future: The Global Experience with Remunicipal-
isation* (Amsterdam, London, Paris, Cape Town and Brussels:
Transnational Institute, Public Services International Research
Unit, Multinationals Observatory, Municipal Services Project, and
the European Federation of Public Service Unions, April 2015).

238 Tony Holman, Richard Northey, and Jane Kelsey, "Expert Paper
#6: Implications of TPPA for Local Government," The Law Foun-
dation New Zealand, February 2016.

239 Simon Terry, "Expert Paper #4: The Environment Under TPPA Governance," The Law Foundation New Zealand, January 2016.

240 Canadian Centre for Policy Alternatives, "Secret Trade Negotiations Undermine Public Services: Study," press release, April 28, 2014.

241 United Nations Human Rights Office of the High Commissioner, "UN Experts Voice Concern Over Adverse Impact of Free Trade and Investment Agreements on Human Rights," press release, June 2, 2015.

242 Steven Shrybman, "In the Matter of the United Nations Human Rights Council Decision 2/104: Human Rights and Access to Water: Preliminary Submissions of the Council of Canadians," Blue Water Project, April 15, 2007.

243 Phare, "Whose Water Is It? Aboriginal Water Rights and International Trade Agreements."

244 Water Watch, "Water and Sewer Public-Private Partnerships (P3s)," press release, October 12, 2006.

Nine: A Blue and Just Canada Is Possible

245 Our Living Waters, "Federal Leadership for Our Living Waters: A Call to Action for the Next Government of Canada," August 2015.

246 Brent Patterson, "Council of Canadians Calls on Liberal to Make Good on Their Promises in World Water Day Budget," Brent Patterson's Blog, Council of Canadians, January 7, 2016, http:// canadians.org/blog/council-canadians-calls-liberals-make-good-their-promises-world-water-day-budget.

247 Emma Lui, "Council of Canadians Lukewarm on Water Funding in Federal Budget," Emma Lui's Blog, Council of Canadians, March 23, 2016, http://canadians.org/blog/council-canadians-lukewarm-water-funding-federal-budget.

248 The Professional Institute of the Public Service of Canada, "2016 Federal Budget an Important Step Forward for Public Services, Says Professional Institute," press release, March 22, 2016.

249 "Restore Fisheries Act 'to the T,'" Blacklocks.ca, April 15, 2016 (subscription required).

250 Simon Doyle, "Ottawa Feels Heat over Move to Undo Conservative Changes to Environmental Laws," Globe and Mail, May 6, 2016.

251 Pentland and Wood, *Down the Drain.*

252 Mark Mattson, email to the author.

253 Ecojustice, "Bill C-45 and the Navigable Waters Protection Act," October 2012.

254 West Coast Environmental Law, "Scaling Up the Fisheries Act: Restoring Lost Protections and Incorporating Modern Safeguards," March 2016.

255 Stephen Hazell, "A Quick Start for Federal Environmental Assessment," Nature Canada, November 15, 2015.

256 Hurley, "Let's Make Groundwater."

257 Gordon Laxer, *After the Sands: Energy and Ecological Security for Canadians* (Vancouver: Douglas & McIntyre, 2015).

258 Council of Canadian Academies, "Environmental Impacts of Shale Gas Extraction in Canada," May 2014.

259 Emma Lui, "Why We Need a Federal Ban on Fracking," *Emma Lui's Blog, Council of Canadians*, October 3, 2014, http://canadians.org/blog/why-we-need-federal-ban-fracking.

260 Jamie Kneen, personal email to author, April 1, 2016.

261 Canadian Press, "Canada Boreal Forest Protection Expanded in 2013 but Concerns Remain," *CBC News*, January 5, 2014, http://www.cbc.ca/news/canada/canada-boreal-forest-protection-expanded-in-2013-but-concerns-remain-1.2484843.

262 Scott Weidensaul and Jeffrey V. Wells, "Saving Canada's Boreal Forest," *New York Times*, May 29, 2015.

263 "Water Commons Legal Framework," working document from a 2009 Wingspread meeting of legal and policy experts.

264 Maude Barlow, "Paying for Water in Canada in a Time of Austerity and Privatization: A Discussion Paper," Council of Canadians, 2012.

265 Canadians for Tax Fairness, "Budget 2016: Targeting Tax Evasion," press release, March 23, 2016.

Index

Amazon River, 18
American Chamber of Commerce, 197
American Petroleum Institute, 98
Andes Petroleum, 199
Andrew, William, 71
animal waste, 135, 137
anti–water export bill, 188
Apache, 110
Aquavist, 139
aqueducts, 17, 53, 91, 179, 181–182
aquifers
    contamination of, 20, 135
    mapping of, 43
    monitoring of, 43
    overpumping of, 116
Aral Sea, 180
Arctic lakes, 7–8
Argentina, 199–200
Ashworth, William, 180
Assembly of First Nations (AFN), 60–63,
    102–103, 223
Assiniboia, 153
ATCO Group, 184
Athabasca Chipewyan First Nation, 245
Athabasca River, 6, 78–79, 81–84
Athabasca Sandstone, 121
atrazine, 12–13
Aundeck Omni Kaning First Nation, 70
Australia, 145, 167–168, 181–182, 194
Aware Simcoe, 159, 161

Bair, Julene, 180–181
Bakken fields, 93, 108, 114
Bakken shale gas, 88–89
Baltgailis, Karen, 23
Ban, Ki-moon, xiv
Barlee, Gwen, 127
Bayfield, Ontario, 216–217
Beaton, Danny, 159
Beausoleil First Nation, 159
Beaver Lake Cree First Nation, 73
Bechtel, 214, 244
beef industry, 146, 150
Bellegarde, Perry, 63
Bellringer, Carol, 123
beluga whales, 103
Bennett, Carolyn, 54, 67
benzene, 86, 107, 109
Beyond Factory Farming, 134–135

Bharadwaj, Lalita, 59–60
Bierkens, Mark, 181
Bilcon Construction, 202
Bill C-38 (2012), 33–34
Bill C-45 (2013), 33
Bill C-383, 193
biodiversity, 33, 163–164
biofuels, 79–80
biotic pumps, 18
Bison pipeline, 89–90
bitumen. see tar sands oil/bitumen
bitumen spills, 86–87, 89, 100
    see also oil spills
bitumen wastewater, 84
Blake, Melissa, 77
Blood First Nation, 70
Blue Baby Syndrome, 143
Blue Communities, 215–217
Blue Dot campaign, 234
blue gold, 174, 182
Blue Planet Project, 200
blue-green algae, 14, 136, 237
Boehm, Terry, 154
boil-water advisories, 55, 58, 223, 233
    see also Drinking Water Advisories
    (DWAs); water quality advisories
Bonnefield, 153
Boreal Action, 50
Boreal Birds Need Half campaign, 238
boreal forest, 19, 24, 81, 148, 238
Boreal Songbird Initiative, 238
bottled water, 173–176
    ban of in Blue Communities, 216
    contaminants in, 174
    as energy intensive, 174
    lack of testing of, 174
bottled water industry
    cost of water to, 175
    drought and, 175–178
    lack of oversight in, 176–177
boundary waters, 28, 126, 190, 192
Boundary Waters Treaty, 227
Bourassa, Robert, 179
Bow glacier, 7
Bow River, 7
Bowman, Brian, 54
Boyd, David, 64–65
BP refinery, 97
Brabeck-Letmathe, Peter, 163, 166

Doyle, Simon, 225
drinking water
    court cases over right to, 70–73
    danger from pipelines, 91–92
    as endangered, 9–11
    on First Nations, 52–76
    global problem of, 67
    monitoring of, 230–231
    Safe Drinking Water Act, 230
    UN resolutions on human rights to,
        67–68
Drinking Water Advisories (DWAs), 52,
55, 59
    see also boil-water advisories; water
        quality advisories
drinking water standards, 45–46,
    230–231
drought
    in Australia, 167–168
    in Brazil, 18
    in Canada, 8, 146–149, 177–178
    loss of glaciers and, 7
    rainforest destruction and, 19
    in United States, xiv, 183
    water as commodity and, 162,
        166–167
    water bottling and, 175–178
Ducks Unlimited, 16–17
Dunnottar, 138
Dust Bowl, xiv, 137, 149
Duvernay Shale, 111

E. coli outbreak, 31, 46
Earth Day Canada, 216
earthquakes, 109–111, 113
Earthworks, 119
Eau Secours, 214
Ecojustice
    on Canadian Environmental Protec-
        tion Act (CEPA), 37
    on drinking water safety, 46
    and Experimental Lakes Area (ELA),
        50
    on industrial pollution, 71–72
    on mining waste, 13
    on pesticides, 12
    on public resources, 227
    on raw sewage in waterways, 45
    on Safe Drinking Water Act, 230

on water limits, 175
economic development, 2–3, 23–24, 145,
    149, 194
Economic Institute, 182
ecosystem services, 163–164
ecosystems
    degradation of, 16–19
    Lake Erie Ecosystem Priority (IJC), 140
    protection of, 125, 149–150, 168,
        178, 228, 233, 238
    protection of source waters by, 16–18
    studying, 49–51
    water as part of, 219–222
Ecuador, 199
Edwards, N. Murray, 123
Edwards, Scott, 170
El Niño, xiv, 18
El Salvador, 200
Elk River Valley mine, 124
Ellsworth, William, 110
Elser, Jim, 49
Elson, Elizabeth, 159
Enbridge, 97, 108
Enbridge pipelines, 86, 95–96
Encana, 106, 110, 112
endangered species, 39
Energy East pipeline
    call to reject, 234
    community resistance to, 93–94,
        102–104
    danger to drinking water, 91–92
    hearing process for, 229
    route of, 88–89, 91–92
energy extraction, 34, 79–80, 196
Energy Framework Initiative, 35
energy industry
    Canadian loss of control of, 195–196
    growth in, 75, 105
    see also oil and gas industry
enforcement/lack of
    of Canadian Environmental Protec-
        tion Act (CEPA), 29, 31, 37, 40
    of Fisheries Act, 30, 38, 83, 228–229
    of Food and Drugs Act, 174
    in mining sector, 123, 126–127
    of pollution regulations, 29–30
    of tailings regulations, 82
    of wastewater disposal standards,
        231–232

groundwater standards, 232–233
Group for Research and Education on
   Marine Mammals (Quebec), 103–104
growth imperative, 22–25, 187, 213
Guergis Tony, 160

Halalt First Nation, 71
Halifax, N.S., 9, 46
Hamilton, Ontario, 89, 214
Hamilton Water Watch, 214
Harden-Donahue, Andrea, 54, 89
Harper government
   and Agriculture Growth Act, 152
   anti-terrorism laws, 76
   and CETA, 196, 211–212
   cuts to budgets for agriculture,
     149–151
   cuts to funding for indigenous orga-
     nizations, 60–61
   gutting of regulatory framework by,
     32–35, 223
   gutting of water protection by, 40
   lowering of corporate taxes by,
     242–243
   mining deal, 121
   oil exports during, 79
   position on water as human right,
     209–210
   promotion of P3s by, 205–206
   refusal to recognize UN declaration,
     66, 68
   resource development plan of, 61
   Transboundary Waters Protection
     Act, 192
   war on science, 35–36, 50
Harries, Kate, 159
Harris, Mike, 179
Hauter, Wenonah, 106
Health Canada
   on atrazine, 13
   Drinking Water Advisories (DWAs)
     and, 55
   on glyphosate, 12
   water quality guidelines, 46
   water quality monitoring on First
     Nations, 59–60
healthy environment, 72
heavy metals
   in contaminated soil, 21–22

contamination of water by, 22
   mining and, 118
   in tailings ponds, 82, 118–119
herbicides, 12–13
Herriot, Trevor, 150
Hoekstra, Arjen, 187, 240
Hometown Heroes Award (2015), 216
Hope, B.C., 176–177, 179
Horn River Basin, 113
Howe, Miles, 131
Hughes, David, 113
human rights
   Investor-State Dispute Settlements
     (ISDS) and, 197–199
   obligations of government, 68–69
   right to water, 64–69, 72–73, 163,
     216, 221
   trade agreements and, 212
Human Rights Watch, 65
Hurley, Adèle, 43, 232–233
hydraulic fracturing (fracking). see
   fracking
hydrocarbon drilling, 43, 80
hydroelectric projects, 15–16, 48
hydrogen sulphide, 108
hydrologic cycles, 18, 20

Idle No More, 72–73, 131
Imperial Metals, 122–123
Indian Act, 61
Indian Oil and Gas Act, 236
Indigenous and Northern Affairs Canada, 59, 75
Indigenous Environmental Network, 131
indigenous rights, 65–66, 73, 193, 228,
   233–234
indigenous water laws, 65
industrial agriculture. see agribusiness
industrial fluids, 21
industrial pollution, 13, 71–72
industrial waste, 20, 158
infrastructure
   Canadian Infrastructure Report Card
     (2016), 40–41
   oil and gas, 106
   underinvestment in, 41
   for water, 40–42, 64, 206, 233
infrastructure gap, 41
injection wells, 21

loss of federal protections for, 34
polluting of, 113–114, 123–124
reduced volumes in, 148
as threatened, 5–6
RMALC (Red Mexicana de Acción
Frente al Libre Comercio), 195
Rocky View (Alberta), 165–166
Rosebud Aquifer, 111–112
Rowntree, Susan, 31
Royal Society of Canada, 33
Rubin, Jeff, 182
runoff
of contaminants, 20, 57, 119,
136–137, 140
glacial, 7
reducing, 170
wetlands as filter for, 138

Safe Drinking Water Act, 230
Safe Drinking Water for First Nations
Act (2013), 61–63, 70
Saint John, N.B., 88, 92, 208
Salazar, Mario, 21
SALIC (Saudi Agricultural and Livestock
Investment Company), 152
Sanborn, Calvin, 135
Sandford, Robert, 137–138
Sandor, Richard, 162–163
Sandy Pond, 32, 119
Saskatchewan, 121, 146–147, 151, 153,
155
Saskatchewan Environmental Society,
121
Saudi Arabia, 152, 156
Sautner, Craig and Julie, 109
Save ELA, 50–51
Save Our Water, 176
Saving Lake Winnipeg, 137
"Scaling Up the Fisheries Act," 229
Scarpaleggia, Francis, 193, 223
Schindler, David
on Alberta water supply, 146
on blue-green algae, 237
on drought, 8, 148
and Experimental Lakes Area (ELA),
48–50
on nitrates, 136–137
on tar sands, 13
on toxic waste, 82

School of Public Policy (University of
Calgary), 184
science
budgets for, 39, 224
ignoring of, 220
war on, 35–36, 50
Science and Technology Canada, 31
SDMyers, 201
seed companies, 152
seismic testing, 129–130
Selinger, Greg, 54
Sellers, Patricia, 56
sewage
in streets, 53
in waterways, 9, 45
Shale Gale, 113–114
shale gas, 106, 111–112, 114–115, 129
shale oil, 114
Shawinigan Lake, 21–22
Shell Canada, 113, 225
Shoal Cove Pond, 119
Shoal Lake 39 First Nation, 53
Shoal Lake 40 First Nation, 52–53, 55
Shotyk, William, 158
Shrybman, Steven, 160, 192–193, 209
Sierra Clubs, 101, 195
silica sand, 115
Simon, Serge, 102–103
Sinclair, Lynne, 204
Sinclair, Scott, 208
Sipekne'katik First Nation, 118
Site 41 (Ontario), 158–161
Site C dam, 6
Site C power, 88
Six Nations of the Grand River, 57
Skeena River, 6
Slade, Andrew, 101
Smaller, Carin, 203
Smith, Lawrence, 7–8
Smith, Scott, 108–109
snow
lack of, 8, 147–148
and renewable water, 3
Sock, Aaron, 129–130
source waters
contamination of, 12–13, 22, 118
as endangered, 11–16
fracking and, 116
management of, 59–60

protection of, 9, 11–12, 16, 116, 221

South Saskatchewan River, 5–6, 165

Southwest Energy, 129–130

Spallumcheen, 135

Sparling, David, 153

Species at Risk Act, 34–35, 103, 126, 236

St. John's, Newfoundland, 9, 46

St. Lawrence River
    and Carbon Corridor, 94
    pipeline threat, 92
    transport of nuclear waste and, 235
    water levels in, 5

St. Lawrence River Lowlands, 116

St. Lawrence Seaway, 1–2, 98

State of the Environment Report, 32

Stellat'en First Nation, 65

Stewart, Keith, 104

Stop Oléoduc (No Oil Spills in the St. Lawrence), 104

Strathcona mill, 119

Street, Gary, 97

Struzik, Ed, 6, 114

Suez Environment, 199–200, 206–208

Suko, Lonny, 123

Suncor, 72, 83, 99, 225

surface water
    contamination of, 20, 107
    demands on, 4
    see also renewable water

Surface Water Management Strategy (Manitoba), 139

Surface Water Quality Framework (Alberta), 82

sustainability, 134, 149, 177–178, 212, 222, 237

Sustainability Council of New Zealand, 207

Sustainable Prosperity, 168–170

Suzuki, David, 104, 158

Syncrude, 78, 83

Tabuns, Peter, 116

Tailfeathers, Elle-Máijá, 74, 76

tailings impoundment areas, 32, 122–123

tailings lakes/ponds
    blocking of investigation into, 83
    call for ban on, 125
    extent of, 13, 124

heavy metals in, 82, 118–119

Tailings Management Framework (Alberta), 82

Talisman, 110

tanker farms, 94

tankers, 87, 92, 103–104, 112, 197, 235

tar sands
    call to transition away from, 234
    extent of, 78–79
    growth in, 83–84, 92, 195–196
    return on investment, 80
    water consumption in, 81–83
    water pollution and, 13, 80–81

tar sands oil/bitumen
    described, 81, 86
    exporting of, 94
    pipelines for, 88–89, 95
    refining of, 92–95, 97
    shipping of, 97–101
    see also diluted bitumen (dilbit)

Taseko Mines, 124

tax evasion, 243

Teck Resources, 119, 123–124

Terry, Simon, 207

Thomas-Muller, Clayton, 131

threatened species, 39

Thunder Bay, Ontario, 216

Tillerson, Rex, 109

timber rights, 201–202

Tiny Township, Ontario, 158–161

Tobin, Brian, 180

Tootoo, Hunter, 225

Total Energy, 166, 184

toxic bloom, 140

toxic waste dumps, 32, 97

toxins
    in blue-green algae, 14–15, 136
    in water sources, 12–13

Trade in Services Agreement (TISA)
    described, 195
    "ratchet" clause, 208
    secretive process around, 211–212
    "standstill" clause, 208
    water privatization and, 208

Transatlantic Trade and Investment Partnership (TTIP), 196–197, 205–206, 212–213

Transboundary Waters Protection Act, 192

Western Partnership for Wildland Fire
  Science (University of Alberta), 148
Wetland Policy (Alberta), 164–165
wetlands
    flooding of, 48
    Lac Saint-Pierre, 100
    loss of, 16–17, 138, 141
    protection of, 139, 222, 238–239
    protection of source waters by, 16
    "relative value" of, 164–165
White Rock, B.C., 204
Whitedog First Nation, 56
Wilderness Committee (B.C.), 122, 125,
  127
Winnipeg, 46, 53, 89, 91, 99
Wisconsin Groundwater Coordinating
  Council, 144
Wood, Alex, 169

Wood, Chris
    on the Canada Water Act, 28
    on chemical use, 10–11
    on constitutional powers, 226
    on water management, 30, 222
Wood, Ina and Keith, 159
World Bank, 163, 173, 199–200, 244
World Health Organization, 12, 46
World Resources Institute, 19
World Trade Organization, 145,
  186–187, 194–195, 209
World Water Day, xiii, 223
World Wildlife Fund Canada, 5–6, 218
WorldWatch Institute, 157
Wye River, 158
Wynne, Kathleen, 116

Yukon, 22–23, 27, 114, 238

Maude Barlow is the author of 17 books, including the best-selling Blue Water trilogy. She is the chair of the Council of Canadians and of the Washington-based Food & Water Watch. She is also a board member of the International Forum on Globalization and a councillor with the World Future Council. From 2008 to 2009, she served as the first senior advisor on water to the 63rd President of the United Nations General Assembly and was a leader in the campaign to have water recognized as a human right by the UN.

Copyright © Maude Barlow, 2016

Published by ECW Press
665 Gerrard Street East
Toronto, ON M4M 1Y2
416-694-3348 / info@ecwpress.com

All rights reserved. No part of this publication may be reproduced, stored in a retrieval system, or transmitted in any form by any process — electronic, mechanical, photocopying, recording, or otherwise — without the prior written permission of the copyright owners and ECW Press. The scanning, uploading, and distribution of this book via the Internet or via any other means without the permission of the publisher is illegal and punishable by law. Please purchase only authorized electronic editions, and do not participate in or encourage electronic piracy of copyrighted materials. Your support of the author's rights is appreciated.

Library and Archives Canada Cataloguing in Publication

Barlow, Maude, author
Boiling point : government neglect, corporate abuse, and Canada's water crisis / Maude Barlow.

Includes index.
Issued in print and electronic formats.
ISBN 978-1-77041-355-9 (paperback)
ISBN 978-1-77090-948-9 (pdf)
ISBN 978-1-77090-947-2 (epub)

1. Water security—Canada. 2. Water-supply—Canada. 3. Water—Canada. 4. Water security—Government policy—Canada. 5. Water-supply—Government policy—Canada. 6. Water—Government policy—Canada. 7. Water—Law and legislation—Canada. I. Title.

HD1696.C2B37 2016   333.9100971   C2016-902372-9
C2016-902373-7

Editor for the press: Susan Renouf
Cover design: David Gee
Cover images: steam © Vika Valter/iStock; Earth © NASA. Use of this image does not constitute endorsement by NASA of this work.
Author photo: © Michelle Valberg
Type: Rachel Ironstone

The publication of *Boiling Point* has been generously supported by the Canada Council for the Arts, which last year invested $153 million to bring the arts to Canadians throughout the country, and by the Government of Canada through the Canada Book Fund. *Nous remercions le Conseil des arts du Canada de son soutien. L'an dernier, le Conseil a investi 153 millions de dollars pour mettre de l'art dans la vie des Canadiennes et des Canadiens de tout le pays. Ce livre est financé en partie par le gouvernement du Canada.* We also acknowledge the support of the Ontario Arts Council (OAC), an agency of the Government of Ontario, which last year funded 1,737 individual artists and 1,095 organizations in 223 communities across Ontario for a total of $52.1 million, and the contribution of the Government of Ontario through the Ontario Book Publishing Tax Credit and the Ontario Media Development Corporation.

Canada Council   Conseil des Arts   Canada
for the Arts   du Canada

Ontario
Ontario Media Development
Corporation

ONTARIO ARTS COUNCIL
CONSEIL DES ARTS DE L'ONTARIO
an Ontario government agency
un organisme du gouvernement de l'Ontario

Printed and Bound in Canada   Printing: Marquis   2   3   4   5

RECYCLED
Paper made from
recycled material
FSC® C103567
www.fsc.org

Get the eBook FREE!

At ECW Press, we want you to enjoy this book in whatever format you like, whenever you like. Leave your print book at home and take the eBook to go! Purchase the print edition and receive the eBook free. Just send an e-mail to ebook@ecwpress.com and include:

- the book title
- the name of the store where you purchased it
- your receipt number
- your preference of file type: PDF or ePub?

A real person will respond to your e-mail with your eBook attached. Thank you for supporting an independently owned Canadian publisher with your purchase!